THE

LABRADOR RETRIEVER

The History . . . The People . . .
Revisited

THE
LABRADOR
RETRIEVER

The History . . . The People . . .
Revisited

Second Edition,
Expanded and Updated

RICHARD A. WOLTERS

Foreword by GENE HILL

A DUTTON BOOK

DUTTON
Published by the Penguin Group
Penguin Books USA Inc., 375 Hudson Street,
New York, New York 10014, U.S.A.
Penguin Books Ltd, 27 Wrights Lane,
London W8 5TZ, England
Penguin Books Australia Ltd, Ringwood,
Victoria, Australia
Penguin Books Canada Ltd, 10 Alcorn Avenue,
Toronto, Ontario, Canada M4V 3B2
Penguin Books (N.Z.) Ltd, 182–190 Wairau Road,
Auckland 10, New Zealand

Penguin Books Ltd, Registered Offices:
Harmondsworth, Middlesex, England

Second Edition published by Dutton,
an imprint of New American Library,
a division of Penguin Books USA Inc.
Distributed in Canada by McClelland & Stewart Inc.

Dutton Printing, Second Edition, April, 1992
10 9 8 7 6 5 4 3 2 1

 REGISTERED TRADEMARK—MARCA REGISTRADA

LIBRARY OF CONGRESS CATALOGING-IN-PUBLICATION DATA
Wolters, Richard A.
    The Labrador retriever : the history—the people, revisited /
Richard A. Wolters ; foreword by Gene Hill.—New ed., enl. and
updated.
        p.   cm.
    ISBN 0-525-93360-3
    1. Labrador retriever.   I. Title.
  SF429.L3W64   1991
636.7′52—dc20   91-18177
                                                     CIP

Printed in the United States of America

OTHER BOOKS BY THE AUTHOR
*Gun Dog, Water Dog, Family Dog, Home Dog, Kid's Dog, Game Dog,
Duck Dogs, City Dog, Instant Dog* (with Roy Doty), *Beau, Living on Wheels,
The Art and Technique of Soaring, The World of Silent Flight,
Once Upon a Thermal*

Frontispiece
LABRADOR WITH GROUSE *Francis Golden*

Contents

Color Illustrations

Black and White Illustrations

Author's Notes

No book can be produced in a vacuum. The list of those that gave their time with interviews is a long one and my file of correspondence is in the hundreds. My apology is extended to those who are not named in the book, as space alone became a factor. Many great dogs are not mentioned either, because although they were in the mainstream of the Lab's accomplishments, they were not, in my opinion, evident during the pivotal points of the dog's history. A listing of those dogs is readily available elsewhere.

I would like to give special thanks to the people who were behind the scenes. The idea for this project started while sitting in the gallery at Crossroads of Sport in New York. Owner Drew Holl said, "No one has ever done a book on the history of the Labrador. It's surely needed." That rang the bell. I immediately thought of it in terms of words . . . Drew thought of it in terms of art. My thanks to Drew for masterminding the artistic collection we've put together. And a most special thanks to the artists, for here is an offering of the best sporting art ever assembled on the Labrador.

This book could not have been produced without the use and help of the American Kennel Club library. It is surely one of the most complete dog libraries in the world. A bouquet of roses to Roberta Vesely, the chief librarian, because no matter how obscure my requests, she and her staff never failed to fill them.

My most sincere thanks to Her Majesty the Queen and the cooperation of her good offices in allowing me access to her private records, the kennel at her home in Sandringham and allowing me free discussions with those who know this dog so well. You too would have liked Bill Meldrum, the Queen's dog trainer, and his wife, who is surely one of the best cooks in England. There were many others in England and Scotland who were very kind. This book is the only way I can reciprocate the extremely useful information and the gracious hospitality of Lord Malmesbury, The Duke of Buccleuch and Queensberry, Sir Alec Douglas-Home, Lady Hill-Wood and Sir John Scott. A special thanks to the Duke of Buccleuch and Queensberry for the drawings from his family game book.

One last thought. This book is not a breed book in the usual sense. Although the subjects are predominantly Labradors, we have their breeding and training from an historical point of view by starting in the 18th century and tracing them through the literature until today.

It took two years, 20,000 miles of travel, and exciting detective work to research and write this book. This, my twelfth book, has been the most rewarding to produce.

Richard A. Wolters
July 4, 1981

Foreword

Every so often a book comes along that is truly definitive; a study that is so persuasive that we can write *finis* to the topic. No doubt there are many who think that they knew the subject matter of the history of the Labrador, but they will be surprised—and I think pleased—to discover that the real history is *here,* and nowhere else.

For the first time we have an authority who refused to accept what we felt was fact and undertook years of research through North America and Great Britain to modify, prove and disprove. To question the old sources, discover new ones, to fit the pieces of the puzzle that we had together and to find and put in place the ones that were glaringly missing.

One of the delights of the historical search is the ever fascinating ancillary material and all of that that is pertinent you'll find here too: the most outstanding art of two continents; the people from the humble Maritime fishermen to the peers of the British realm, the American bluestockings who nurtured the Labrador as "their dog"; and how he was trained, and why, from the earliest 18th century records to the methods used today—that will be used tomorrow.

I think this work can best be described as a "celebration" of the Labrador Retriever. This book not only captivates us as a serious work of research, but introduces us to the people and their times and customs, right up to today, that saw and understood and cultivated the unique qualities that make the Labrador, most deservedly, one of the most popular breeds of dogs in the world today.

As long as we have the Labrador, we should be thankful for this book. Few animals on earth have had this much interest to man, this much work applied to their life and history, and in my humble opinion, have deserved it more.

May the future of the Labrador rest in hands as careful and caring as have its past.

Gene Hill
ROBINWOOD FARM
June 1981

THE LABRADOR RETRIEVER *Edwin Margargee*

The Labrador Retriever... Who is He?

The Labrador is the king of retrievers. He may not be the handsomest or the strongest but he is the king. He is intelligent but not cunning; he's lovable but not soft. The Labrador Retriever is loyal but not a one-man dog. He's gentle but not a dog to be backed against the wall. He's a romping fun fellow but won his crown as an honest worker.

The Lab is as much at home on your bed as he is calmly sitting next to an Illinois pit blind undaunted by a cutting wind. He's the waterfowler's first choice, but he is also a fine upland hunter. He'll give you the sportiest woodcock hunting possible in Maine, and he'll unravel the tricks of Iowa's pheasants. He may not be the fastest swimmer, but if you send him for a crippled goose on the Eastern shore he won't quit. He's truly the hunter's dog, yet when he comes into this world he doesn't have a hateful gene in his body.

Versatility is the hallmark of the Lab. Police work? No problem. The London Bobbies use Labs all the time. Leading the blind? He outperforms the breed that started the business. Helping conservationists? He works side by side with game wardens in every state and with scientists in Canada. But the Lab's real conservation efforts are with Harry, Bill, and Joe, the duck hunters, who need his help to protect the bag by making every downed duck count. Ask any waterfowler about Labs, and you will hear stories of courage, persistence, loyalty, and just plain smarts. He can also tell you how the Lab compares with other retrievers: "When a game warden comes around to your blind, the Chesapeake will try to tear his arm off, a Golden will lick his face, but a Lab will show him where you hid the extra ducks or where the bag of corn is kept."

Mallard, Canvasback, Wood Duck, Blue Winged Teal, or even Merganser — the kind of duck makes no difference, nor does it make any difference what fly-way he's on. The Lab is as good a worker in Oregon as he is in Louisiana. He can learn the ways of the oak swamp hunters in the Ozarks, run the shore line and toll the ducks in Nova Scotia, sit quietly in a punt off Chicoteague, scan the skies from the rocks on Long Island Sound, work from a stilt blind on California lakes, or walk at heel in Central Park. And that is really the point with this dog: He can be taught anything that is possible for a dog to learn. He takes to training as easily as any breed and he laps it up. Both in America and in England, he has proven to be such a good worker, so biddable and with such a dependably docile temperament, generation after generation, that it is no wonder the Lab has become the fifth most popular dog in the United States and the third in England.

Contrary to popular belief, the Labrador Retriever did not see the shores of Labrador until modern times; in fact, his name is a fluke, a misnomer derived from the nineteenth century British concept of geography that lumped Labrador and Newfoundland together in the same land mass. In the same century, the Lab almost became extinct in England because of complex business and political situations, and the same thing almost happened in America during the Great Depression.

In the early 1930s, when the Lab outperformed the Chesapeake Bay Retriever in field trials, the American waterfowler took him into the marshes and he has been there ever since. In the field the true test is the field trial, and the record book shows overwhelmingly that if you want to win consistently you might as well start with Labradors. Other breeds sneak in and win once in a while, but not very often. Hunters call the Lab an "honest" dog; he lives to work. He'll break the Minnesota ice to retrieve a downed bird and shake the crystals off his back after he delivers the bird to hand. Then he's raring to go again when the next flight drops into the decoys. He'll work in the heat of the Texas desert all day gathering doves and his pay is the retrieve and a pat.

During most of the nineteenth century the Lab was owned only by a few aristocratic British sportsmen. Although he was introduced to England in the beginning of that century, he was not available to the average British sportsman until the twentieth century. When he was first brought to the United States in the late 1920s, he had much the same history — used by only a very few wealthy sportsmen and then only in the traditional British hunting manner.

Credit must be given to two sources for keeping the Labrador breed alive: (1) the aristocratic families and their gamekeepers in

The Unique Lab Temperament

both England and America, and (2) the American sportsmen who gradually "adopted," developed, and trained the dog for their hunting needs. Though American waterfowlers had a good hunting dog, the Chesapeake Retriever, the Lab proved to be a better dog for them — and their families.

The Labrador has proven to be a strong breed, passing down his attractive qualities through hundreds of years. From his days in Newfoundland he has passed on his traits as a "workaholic" and from his earliest days in England, his wonderful temperament.

The temperament of the Labrador Retriever is an enigma. A dog tends to assume his temperament from the nature of his environment or the characteristics of his people. For example, the Eskimo dog is a tough dog in his native habitat and illustrates the principle of the survival of the fittest; he will kill for food. His temperament comes from his environment; he is not a house pet. The Doberman Pinscher, on the other hand, adopted the character of his masters — Prussian military officers who commanded strong one-man loyalty. Neither dog could be considered for baby-sitting duties.

The Labrador's ancestors were developed in Newfoundland, which has the harshest environment settled by any Europeans in North America. The conditions under which they lived made the lives of the Pilgrims seem rich by comparison. The dog's heritage began in sub-survival living conditions, which should produce a rough temperament. The dog's first job in Newfoundland was working with the fishermen from Devon, England, who were considered the roughest, toughest men of Britain. The first settlers on the island were ship-jumpers and deserters from the British fishing fleet and the navy, a lawless society that defied any authority. Yet from this raw society the even-tempered St. John's dog, the direct ancestor of the Labrador, was developed.

To solve the mystery of the Labrador's ancestry, we must thoroughly investigate not only the history of the dog but the history of his owners and the times in which they lived. This is no easy task, for there were no men of letters to record the dog's earliest days in Newfoundland. In fact, the dog was not mentioned in the English sporting literature until the early nineteenth century.

Puzzling history or no, we are lucky. We have the dog today, almost 500 years from his modern beginnings. Documenting his past, loving his presence, and looking toward his future is an exciting, challenging, intellectual gambit — and a celebration of the Labrador Retriever.

Whence He Came

In tracing the history of the Labrador Retriever, we encounter a great deal of confusion and misinformation. One of the most confusing facts is that there were *two* famous breeds developed in the 300 years in Newfoundland prior to the Lab's introduction to England: the big dog that carries the name of the island, and the smaller one called the "St. John's dog" in England ("water dog" in Newfoundland), which was finally renamed *Labrador Retriever*.

Most modern chroniclers believe that the big Newfoundland dog was the original breed and give it credit for being the stock from which the Chesapeake, Labrador, and Golden were created. However, we will show this to be untrue. We will demonstrate why the Newfoundland dog could not have been the original dog, and then we will show where the original stock of today's Labrador came from.

To understand the origins and background of the dog, it is necessary to understand the history of Newfoundland itself. The first people to settle in Newfoundland were the Dorset Eskimos. Three thousand years ago, they journeyed from Labrador by crossing the frozen Strait of Belle Isle. The Eskimos lived on the northern part of the island, with no boats or dogs; they pulled their own sleds. The Dorsets died out 200 years before the island was discovered by European explorers. Archaeologists have uncovered Viking settlements on the northern tip of Newfoundland that date back to 1000 A.D. Despite our schoolbook teachings, there was no "discovery"

The Labrador retriever sheds water like a duck, and the Newfoundland is twice its weight. Both are strong swimmers.

of North America by Europeans after the Norse. The New World was known by whalers and fishermen well before John Cabot's "discovery" of Newfoundland in 1497. Even the Basques were hunting whales off the Labrador coast and set up a whaling factory in Labrador in 1450.

Although historians generally give Cabot the credit for discovering Newfoundland, he was actually a latecomer. Rather, the honor belongs to Robert Thorne and Hughe Elliot from Bristol, England. In 1527, Thorne's son tried to establish that his father was the true discoverer, and sixteenth century chronicles specifically state that the discovery was made by Bristol traders in 1494. The proof came when a letter in the Spanish archives turned up in 1956 (misfiled under the South American country, Brazil) establishing the real discoverers. Cabot's voyage was the official follow-up of the earlier discoveries by the Bristol merchants. Now it is believed that Cabot never even set foot on Newfoundland but instead landed in New England. His course had him sailing 900 miles and passing two islands before he turned east for home. One of those two islands was indeed Newfoundland. Moreover, one of the artifacts that Cabot brought back from the New World was a carved net needle that he picked up on the shore. For centuries historians thought it Indian-made, but no such tool was ever used by the Indians; it had to be a relic of an earlier fishing voyage.

After Cabot's "discovery" of Newfoundland, the colonists arrived, but no one knows just when or where. The Bristol Company tried a settlement in 1504, but by 1506 there were no indications that the venture survived. It would be 100 years before it was tried again (by John Guy from Bristol), and once again without success, which should indicate how difficult the living conditions were on the island — for man and dog.

Although Newfoundland was not established as a colony in the same way as the American colony of Virginia, for example, it did become a summer fishing station. Cabot reported that "The sea was swimming with fish which can be taken in a bucket let down with a stone." Within a year of his report the English fishing fleets were already at work. From the very beginning of the fishing industry, however, the British business interests were tyrant masters. The fishermen were forbidden to remain as settlers for fear that settlements would start their own industry and compete with the London and Bristol merchants. Ship masters were fined for each seaman they failed to bring back to England in the fall.

Needless to say, the industry attracted very unsavory individuals. Each spring, as the fishing season started, a makeshift "government" was improvised: The captain of the first boat to arrive from England became the fishing admiral and ruled the fleet and any people who lived on shore. These people became little more than serfs to the merchants.

"Discovery" of Newfoundland

The Dorset Indians were the first people on Newfoundland. They had no boat or dog, they died out before the white man arrived.

STARTLED BLACKS *Chet Reneson*

During the rule of Charles I, a law was passed prohibiting any settlement within six miles of the Newfoundland coast, and the English navy enforced the law. Another law established that no building could have a stone chimney, a means of preventing would-be settlers from staying over the winter. (Eventually these laws were ignored; the settlers moved into remote areas where even today Elizabethan English dialect is still spoken.)

The fishing ships carried women crew members as well as men. Most of them lived lives of semi-slavery under indenture to the fishing masters and were glad to escape if they could. Gradually, the island was populated with families of deserters. By 1650, half the Newfoundland population were crews that jumped ship. As late as 1800, the British navy was sent to capture them and hang them from the yard-arm of a man-o'-war. For centuries the island had no law whatsoever . . . no courts, no police, no schools, no churches. It became an outlaw society. British marines were the law, and the law of the land was as harsh as the law at sea.

By the end of the 1700s, hordes of men, calling themselves the "Masterless Men," organized into bands and declared their independence from the rest of the world. They fled inland and lived for 150 years in the interior. They defended themselves by building roads that only led into swamps the British marines could not penetrate.

Hanging, flogging, and murder was the way of life. The Newfoundland Indians, the Beothucks, did not survive the chaos. They became scapegoats and were murdered for sport. There are documented stories of women bearing their breasts as a sign of submission and then being shot with their children. One man boasted of killing sixty in one year.

Is it any wonder that Newfoundland became the haven for the most notorious pirates in history? Henry Mainwarring, feared throughout the Spanish world, described Newfoundland as the best of all places to recruit a fighting crew. His bitter enemy, Peter Easton, who became one of the richest men in the world, built a fortress at Harbour Grace near Conception Bay and made it his headquarters. His Newfoundland men were trained cutthroats.

It was a harsh life in a harsh land. Through it all, the fishing industry never faltered. Each year the English merchants sent their fleets in the spring with thousands of men to fish the waters of the Avalon peninsula but always feared that they would become too independent. The plan was the same for decades: send the fleet off in the spring and have them return in the fall. The dried salted fish was shipped south to the Catholic countries. It was all done with an iron hand. Individuals fled, but in more than 200 years there was never a general revolt.

A stage was used in the 18th century for throwing fish ashore before they were prepared for curing.

This brief background of Newfoundland life in the sixteenth and seventeenth centuries provides us with our first baffling questions in unraveling the ancestry of the Labrador Retriever: If there

St. John's during the fishing season in 1831.

were dogs native to the island, how did they work and survive in this ruthless, coarse, almost barbaric society? And if the dogs were the ancestors of today's Lab, as is commonly believed, how did the Lab survive this era with such an easy, lovable temperament? To answer these questions we must dig into the history of the period.

The needs of the Newfoundland settlers offer the first clues to unscrambling the background of the Labrador Retriever. In this time and place in history dogs had to be workers. From the sixteenth to the nineteenth centuries only the aristocrats could afford the luxury of a pet. For the common man, an extra mouth had to earn its own keep. Yet there was no aristocracy in Newfoundland. Rather, early Newfoundland settlements consisted of only the British peasant working class, laborers, fishermen, sailors, and woodsmen. So we must examine the kind of life the earliest settlers led, what their needs would have been for a dog, and then seek a course of logic that shows why a particular kind of animal would have developed to meet a particular kind of need.

Popular Theories of Origin

As a means to accomplishing this, let's explore the popular theories of the Labrador ancestry and see how they evolved. The history of the Lab can be divided into two distinct periods, and the dividing point is the first decade or so of the nineteenth century. During this decade, authors on both sides of the Atlantic first recorded observations about a dog that for almost 300 years had been developed and gone almost unnoticed as a yeoman worker. Post-1815 history can be documented chronologically, but it is much more difficult to explore the Lab's history before 1800. However, the facts, although scant, are accessible, and if we apply the right questions to the old facts we may find some startling new answers.

The first question, of course, is: Where did the Labrador Retriever come from? The most popular theory is that the Lab is an offshoot of the Newfoundland dog, referred to by the early dog writers as a "lesser Newfoundland." They believed that if you found the origin of the Newfoundland dog you automatically found the origin of the Lab. For example, in 1936 Sir John Middleton wrote in *The Labrador Dog — Its Home and History,* "It is generally accepted that the 'Labrador' dog is a variety of the Newfoundland dog."

Most books treat the Lab's early history the same way. As late as 1971 Migliorini wrote in his book, *Labrador Retrievers*: "The origin of the Labrador Retriever has generally been linked with the Newfoundland dog, an unusually hardy specimen that was frequently found accompanying the Newfoundland fishermen. . . . Where space was a factor, a smaller but equally hardy variety of 'Newfoundland dog,' probably resulting from Flatcoated Retriever or Water Spaniel crosses, became popular."

Helen Warwick, in her 1964 book *The Complete Labrador Retriever*, begins her chapter on origins by quoting from the 1814 classic, *Instructions to Young Sportsmen in All That Relates to Guns and Shooting*, by Colonel P. Hawker. However, for the most part she ignores the years before 1800. Only one paragraph is devoted to the origins of the Newfoundland. The assumption is made that the Newfoundland came first, and that the Lab is a development of the bigger dog.

The popular dog writers of the early twentieth century were not any more reliable than their nineteenth-century predecessors when discussing the Lab's origins; too often they accepted written material as fact without thoroughly checking it. The truth is that the nineteenth-century writers tried to explain the origins of a dog they rarely saw as a purebred; they seemed to know more about hunting than they did about history.

The following story, by the top dog writer of his era, demonstrates the confusion that has existed about the history of the Lab breed right up to modern times.

In 1945, *Field and Stream* magazine published a brochure to honor the famous wildlife and dog artist Edwin Megargee. Freeman Lloyd, the magazine's veteran dog writer, produced the text for each of the sporting dogs represented. Under the drawing of the Labrador Retriever, Lloyd relates a charming story of the Lab's introduction into England: A British seaman fancied a dog he came upon while ashore in Labrador. His fishing boat had set out from Poole, a

The Myth of Newfoundland Ancestry

Edwin Megargee's rendering of the Labrador.

small town in the south of England, where the sailor had a sweet-heart whose father was the gamekeeper to the third Earl of Malmes-bury (1807–1889). (Note: Although Lloyd does not say so, the date of this story should fall after 1841 because that was the date the third Earl took his title.) The dog, purchased for a trifle, was taken to England as a present for the mariner's prospective father-in-law, who found the dog to be an excellent retriever of game. Subse-quently, more dogs of this kind arrived at Poole and those too be-came the property of Malmesbury.

A sailor wins the heart of his true love with the gift of a dog to her father and so the Lab is introduced to England. What a roman-tic way for the dog to come to British shores! If only it were true . . . On close reading, however, parts of the story are clearly historically inaccurate. First, fishing boats from Poole did not sail to Labrador, unless the legend-tellers said Labrador instead of Newfoundland be-cause many, in the early twentieth century, assumed the name of the dog indicated the dog's place of origin.

Second, even if he did get to that coast, it is very questionable, according to some, that the dog was there at that time. Even if we give our young lover every benefit of the doubt and assume that he found a stray dog to buy in Labrador, or even in Newfoundland, the story doesn't survive historical scrutiny because we know from the gamebook of the third Earl's father that he already had the black retrieving dogs from Newfoundland on his estate at Heron Court in 1809. This first documentation of the use of the dog from New-foundland as a retriever was written when the third Earl of Mal-mesbury was only two years old.

It would be fun to believe Freeman Lloyd's story, but when the dog was first introduced into England the third Earl was not an earl at all and most likely hadn't even been born.

The New Complete Newfoundland, published in 1955 by Mar-garet Booth Chern, is an excellent starting point for examining in-depth today's popular — but inaccurate — theory on the origins of the Labrador Retriever. Chern's book, like many others, assumes that the great Newfoundland dog is a native of North America. Chern states: "The Newfoundland, the great dog of the Algonquin and Sioux Indians, takes its name from the island of Newfoundland where the breed first became known to the British settlers. The giant black dog once roamed the central plains in great numbers and was found among the Indian tribes from the Eastern seaboard to Montana, from the headwaters of Saskatchewan to the Gulf of Mexico." The author goes on to say that in pre-Columbian times the big dog was just as important to the Indians of North America as the llama was to those in western South America. But because the dog was no match for the horse in speed and carrying power, the dog began to disappear.

Chern's analysis seems logical at first reading, but her conclu-

SENTINELS AT SUN-UP *Tom Hennessey*

sion deserves questioning: "Thus, when the British came to the New World they only found the Newfoundland dog on the island of that name and the nearby continent." We already know that the Norsemen discovered Newfoundland about 1000 AD but left no record. When John Cabot "rediscovered" it in 1497, he left no written record about a dog on his trip. The following year, the British started fishing off the coast of Newfoundland using the island for a work base. Although they did not establish a settlement, they left work crews of skilled woodsmen and woodworkers each winter to prepare things for the next fishing season. The Portuguese appeared in 1501 and the French in 1504. Despite all this activity it was more than 200 years before anyone reported sighting a dog — *any* dog. Nothing in the literature sustains the claim that the British or anyone else found a dog on arrival. As Chern should have known and as we will later see, the original Newfoundland dog, unlike the Indian dog, was not black.

Archaeological findings establish without a doubt that a large dog indigenous to North America was used by the Indians before the horse replaced it. However, none of the early settlers who came to North America ever found the dog, nor was it found as the settlers moved west. Yet, Chern claims it was this dog that became known to the British who settled in Newfoundland and the "continent," which we must assume means the Labrador area since the dog was never observed any other place by the later settlers. Why would the Indian dog only have survived *there?* If the dog was found only on the island of Newfoundland, then one could make the argument that it was trapped on the island; but this theory does not work either because, as the author states, the dog was seen on the continent, too.

Perhaps the more important question is, what aborigines would have taken the dog to the island? The Dorset Eskimos had no dog. Certainly the Algonquin and Sioux were never in this part of North America. To the contrary, the records show conclusively that the aboriginal inhabitants of Newfoundland had no dog. The Beothucks or Red Indians, according to authority J. P. Howley, were a sad unfortunate people. The last member of the tribe died in 1829. Their origins were a mystery, but it is generally agreed that they were refugees in Newfoundland, and had come from the mainland. They were an isolated people, having no relationship with other Indians or Eskimos. From 1500 until they became extinct, they continued to live in primitive ignorance, sustaining themselves by fishing and hunting.

In the mid-1700s, Lieutenant John Cartwright made an inland journey with his brother, Captain George, to try to establish friendly relations with the Beothucks, but to no avail. John's journal gives a good picture of the people and even describes in detail how they hunted deer without dogs: "The Red Indians have no intercourse with Europeans except a hostile one. These Indians are not only secluded thus from any communications with Europeans, but they are effectually cut off from society of every other Indian people. To complete their wretched condition Providence has even denied them the pleasing services and companionship of a faithful dog."

George Cartwright wrote in his journal: "In my opinion they are the most forlorn of any of the human species which have yet come to my knowledge, for they are not only excluded from intercourse with the rest of mankind, but are surrounded by inveterate enemies and not even possessed of the useful services of the dog."

The Cartwright journals, written in 1768, establish that there was no indigenous dog in Newfoundland and also tend to discount the existence of the Esquimaux or Greenland dog there because of the natives' isolation from both the Eskimos and other Indians on the mainland.

Chern assumes that the indigenous dog of North America was the dog the British called the Newfoundland, based only on the fact that they were both big dogs. Although archaeological tracings show that the great Indian dog existed 1000 to 2000 years before the Vikings visited the Western World, no findings were ever made in Newfoundland or Labrador.

The author cites "supporting evidence of early authorities and explorers" to show that the Beothuck Indians had a dog that strongly resembled the Newfoundland and mentions two sources: W. C. Cormack and George Cartwright. However, Cormack's exploration in 1822, just seven years before the Beothuck tribe became extinct, reveals no evidence of the Indians having a dog. (Even if the explorer's journals *had* mentioned it, his observation could not be considered conclusive because his 1822 inland expedition came 322 years after the English arrived to fish Newfoundland and more than 100 years after the big Newfoundland dog had been introduced into England. Because of the late date, this source would have been of little value in establishing that the dog was indigenous to Newfoundland or the New World.) As for the diary of George Cartwright, the author quotes Cartwright's account of *his* Newfoundland bitch but ignores his already-quoted report, which states that the Beothuck Indians had no dogs.

It is clear, then, that according to historical and scientific evidence, dogs did not exist in Newfoundland before the fishermen arrived. Although this provides us with some good clues about where *not* to look for the Lab's origin, we still need a starting point for further investigation.

After 1800, writers on both sides of the Atlantic began to record their observations of the Newfoundland and the Labrador. Though their writings form valuable tools for the modern researcher, they are clouded by the fact that different writers used different names for the dogs. The researcher today has the difficult

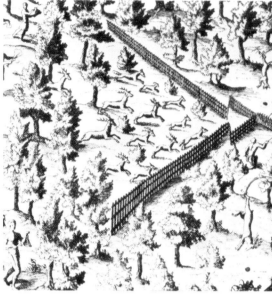

Drawing from the book *Chaplin's Voyages*, showing how the Beothucks hunted deer without dogs.

Unlike the Indian dog that was in North America before the horse arrived, the original big Newfoundland dog was not black.

A Problem of Semantics

Major John Cartwright
Colonial Peter Hawker

task of determining which dog the writers were discussing — after all, we are working with a time span of almost 500 years, from the first fishing fleets to the present day. It is easy to see how some popular stories came to be accepted as fact. The following examples illustrate the point.

Almost every 19th century book on the Labrador Retriever mentions what is considered the first written reference to the Labrador, *Instructions to Young Sportsmen,* by Colonel P. Hawker. This book, first published in 1814, had remarkable success. By 1844, it had gone through nine editions and an American edition was published in 1846. Two more editions, edited by Hawker's son, were printed after his death in 1859, another printing was made in 1921, and the last was made in 1971. This record bears testimony to the success and importance of this book — but could it also have been misleading?

Below is the relevant text from the original edition.

NEWFOUNDLAND DOGS

Here we are a little in the dark. Every canine brute, that is nearly as big as a jackass, and as hairy as a bear, is denominated a *fine Newfoundland dog.* Very different, however, is both the proper Labrador and St. John's breed of these animals; at least, many characteristic points are required, in order to distinguish them.

The one is very large; strong in the limbs; rough haired; small in the head; and carries his tail very high. He is kept in that country for drawing sledges full of wood, from inland to the sea shore, where he is also very useful, by his immense strength and sagacity, among wrecks, and other disasters in boisterous weather.

The other, *by far the best for every kind of shooting,* is oftener *black* than of another colour, and scarcely bigger than a pointer. He is made rather long in the head and nose; pretty deep in the chest; very fine in the legs; has short or smooth hair; does not carry his tail so much curled as the other; and is extremely quick and active in running, swimming, or fighting.

Newfoundland dogs are so expert and savage, when fighting, that they generally contrive to seize some vital part, and often do a serious injury to their antagonist. I should, therefore, mention, that the *only way* to get them immediately off is to put a rope, or handkerchief, round their necks, and keep tightening it, by which means their breath will be gone, and they will be instantly choked from their hold.

The St. John's breed of these dogs is chiefly used on their native coast by fishermen. Their sense of smelling is scarcely to be credited. Their discrimination of scent, in following a wounded pheasant through a whole covert full of game, or a pinioned wild fowl through a furze brake, or warren of rabbits, appears almost impossible. (It may, perhaps, be unnecessary to observe, that rabbits are generally very plentiful, and thrive exceedingly, near the sea shore. It, therefore, often happens, that wigeon, as they fly, and are shot, by night, fall among furzebrakes, which are full of rabbits.)

The real Newfoundland dog may be broken in to any kind of shooting; and, without additional instruction, is generally under such command, that he may be safely kept in, if required to be taken out with pointers. For finding wounded game, of every description, there is not his equal in the canine race; and he is a *sine quâ non* in the general pursuit of wildfowl.

Poole was, till of late years, the best place to buy Newfoundland dogs; either just imported, or broken in: but now they are become much more scarce, owing (the sailors observe) to the strictness of "those —— the tax gatherers." I should always recommend buying these dogs ready broken; as, by the cruel process of half starving them, the fowlers teach them almost every thing; and, by the time they are well trained, chances are, they have got over the distemper, with which this species, in particular, is sometimes carried beyond recovery.

If you want to make a Newfoundland dog do what you wish, you must encourage him, and use gentle means, or he will turn sulky; but to *deter* him *from* any *fault,* you may rate or beat him.

I have tried poodles, but always found them inferior in strength, scent, and courage. They are also very apt to be seasick. The *Portland dogs* are superior to *them.*

A water dog should not be allowed to jump out of a boat, unless ordered so to do, as it is not always required; and, therefore, needless that he should wet himself, and every thing about him, without necessity.

For a punt, or canoe, always make choice of the *smallest* Newfoundland dog that you can procure; as the smaller he is, the less water he brings into your boat after being sent out; the less cumbersome he is when afloat; and the quicker he can pursue crippled birds upon the mud. A bitch is always to be preferred to a dog in frosty weather, from being, by nature, less obstructed in landing on the ice.

If, on the other hand, you want a Newfoundland dog only as a retriever for covert shooting; then the case becomes different; as here you require a strong animal, that will easily trot through the young wood and high grass with a large hare or pheasant in his mouth.

As the reader can see, Hawker seems to give the name *proper Labrador* and *St. John's* to what we call the Labrador today, but he

INSTRUCTIONS

TO

Young Sportsmen

IN

ALL THAT RELATES TO

GUNS AND SHOOTING.

BY

L⸆ COL. P. HAWKER.

———— ————

CONSIDERABLY ENLARGED AND IMPROVED; WITH TEN EXPLANATORY PLATES.

————————

2050

LONDON:

PRINTED FOR

LONGMAN, HURST, REES, ORME, BROWN, AND GREEN.

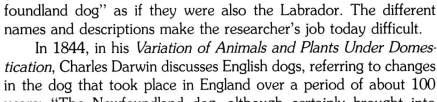

goes on to write about the "Newfoundland dog" and the "real Newfoundland dog" as if they were also the Labrador. The different names and descriptions make the researcher's job today difficult.

In 1844, in his *Variation of Animals and Plants Under Domestication*, Charles Darwin discusses English dogs, referring to changes in the dog that took place in England over a period of about 100 years: "The Newfoundland dog, although certainly brought into England from that country, has since been so much modified that it does not now closely resemble any existing native dog in Newfoundland."

Nineteenth Century Confusion

Thomas Bell, a professor of zoology at London University, was born in 1792 in Poole, the main port of importation of the dogs from Newfoundland. In his *History of British Quadrupeds* of 1837, he writes:

> There are several varieties of the Newfoundland Dog which differ in size, character of the fur, and marking. The old smooth breed, with a rather small head, white, with small black spots scattered over the body, appears now to be extinct. The largest dogs now met with are of the breed which I have figured. The muzzle is broad; the head raised; the expression noble and majestic; the hair waved or curly; the tail very thick and bushy . . . The colour is black and white; the latter equalling, if not predominating over the former. But the most common breed at present is comparatively dwarf, not exceeding in height a large water spaniel, almost wholly black, and deficient in the fine expression which may be considered characteristic of the older races.

In 1847, in his book *Dogs: The Origin and Varieties*, H.D. Richardson goes even further than Bell in discussing the varieties. He describes four kinds of Newfoundland dog, dividing them into two varieties of Newfoundlands and two varieties of Labradors.

According to J.H. Walsh, pseudonym Stonehenge, in his book *British Rural Sports* (1867), the names *St. John's, Smaller Labrador,* and *Newfoundland* were all used for the small dog which is "seldom more than twenty-five inches high and often much less."

It was not until 1870 that the name *Labrador Retriever* became common; before then, the name *English Retriever* was also used, in some circles well into the twentieth century.

The date when the first big Newfoundland dog was introduced into England cannot be exactly determined. In 1732, an unknown author wrote, "The Bear dog is of a very large size, commonly sluggish in his looks, but he is very watchful, he comes from Newfoundland, his business is to guard a Court or House, and he has a thunderous voice when strangers come near him, and does well to turn a water wheel." The term *Bear dog* was used in literature as far back as 1560, apparently to describe an animal that was half dog and half bear. Later it was applied to a Norwegian dog that was claimed to be the ancestor of the Newfoundland. The Norwegian-origin theory was suggested because of the early Norsemen expeditions and the Greenlanders' visits to Newfoundland. However, so little trace of their visits exist that there can be no grounds for supposing that they left behind any domesticated animal that could have survived.

All sorts of theories have been advanced. As late as 1820, in *The Sportsman's Repository,* Scott suggests that it was even possible for the wolf and bear to have joined in contributing to the ancestry of the Newfoundland.

No matter which origin theory is proposed, it is certain that the giant Newfoundland was an instant success throughout the British Isles. Every interested writer tried to make a guess as to the dog's origin. Every big dog of Europe and America was suggested.

Researching the literature becomes a puzzle, and past efforts to solve it have all had the same results: No one has come up with a logical explanation of the Lab that uses all the puzzle pieces. Sir John Middleton came the closest when he included the history of Newfoundland in his thesis. But even he, like almost every other writer on the subject, arrived at the generally accepted position that the Labrador dog is a variety of the Newfoundland dog.

Many of the writers of the early nineteenth century referred to what we consider the Labrador today as the "lesser Newfoundland." If necessity is the mother of invention, we will show logically that the Labrador came first because it was needed first and the Newfoundland dog was bred up from it.

Landseer paints the lifesaving dog

Psychologically, every British writer on this subject has been at a disadvantage. Remember, the literature on this subject started in the early 1800s. At that time the big Newfoundland dog had for almost a century become the darling of the aristocrats. He watched over their families and estates. He was their hero and he saved their children from drowning; they painted his portrait and even Lord Byron sang his praise in poetry. At the turn of the century, another dog from Newfoundland made his appearance. He was also black, but not as elegant or stately in manner. They were both exceedingly strong swimmers and had a lot in common. It was natural that this new fellow, who was imported because he was an outstanding hunter and retriever, would be considered a "lesser," a sub-variety. Colonel Hawker, the most quoted source and the first, set the stage for all writers who followed when he implied that the Lab was a breed of the Newfoundland. It was an innocent slip of the pen and a very logical one for him in his times. However, that assumption survives today and must be investigated more thoroughly.

After exploring how writers of a later period were led astray by semantics and understandable popular misconceptions of the time,

Boatswain, Lord Byron's dog

A Fresh Look at the Facts

let's now return to the issue of the origins of the Lab and the early Newfoundland settlers. By taking a "functionalist" approach, i.e., by examining the needs of the first Newfoundland settlers and the probable functions of a dog within the context of those needs, we will be able to formulate a viable, logical, new theory on the Lab's ancestry that is consistent with the documented evidence.

Specifically, using the historical material, we will show that the St. John's dog is the original Newfoundland dog, and the St. John's "big" brother, the Newfoundland, is *his* offshoot — just the reverse of the general belief.

As we have already described, Newfoundland was different from other settlements in the New World; this rugged island did not attract men of commerce or letters but rather fishermen who were there only during the fishing season (from spring to late fall), and who went home each winter. The fishermen kept no records; there was nothing to keep them *about*. During the fishing season most men lived on board ship, but some were housed in the work sheds on shore. The beaches were used for drying fish, storing it, and preparing it for the market.

We know from British records that the fishing interests did not want settlements because the success of their business depended upon the use of the beaches. Without the beaches they could not process their catch. The absentee owners recognized that if settlements were allowed, it would only be a matter of time before the settlers owned the best beaches and charged rent and land fees. The settlers would gain control of the best facilities, build their own ships, and drive the absentee owners out of business. The British navy saw to it that settlements did not spring up.

Of the other three nations who fished, neither the Portuguese nor the Spanish settled in Newfoundland, and up to 1662 no Frenchman had ever lived a winter on the island. As far as the fishing was concerned, all four countries' boats kept at a respectable distance from one another. There was enough fish for all.

The British area was called Avalon on the southeastern peninsula of Newfoundland. (See accompanying map.) With an area of 3,500 square miles, a little less than ten percent of the whole island, it was almost totally isolated from the main section of Newfoundland, connected only by a narrow isthmus, three or four miles wide. (The French settled for a short period in the second half of the seventeenth century near the western barrier of Placentia Bay. Trinity Bay isolated the English from the area where the Portuguese fished.) As far as we know, no inhabitants ever lived on Avalon before then, not even the Beothuck Indians. The British first used the beaches around St. John's and gradually spread south and southwestward along the coast.

We know one important fact about the British from D.W. Prowse's *History of Newfoundland*: They fished in a different man-

A shore curing station on Avalon drawn in the early 18th century.

LABRADOR

STRAIT of BELLE ISLE

DORSET INDIANS
WILDERNESS AREA

WHITE BAY

NEWFOUNDLAND

BOETHUCK INDIANS
WILDERNESS INTERIOR

GRAND BRUIT

JACK STANLEY

PORTUGESE FISHING AREA
NO LAND SETTLEMENT

TRINITY BAY

CONCEPTION BAY

HARBOR GRACE · TORBAY

ST. JOHN'S
ENGLISH FISHING AREA

AVALON WILDERNESS AREA

FERRYLAND

PLACENTIA BAY

FRENCH FISHING AREA

ner than the other nationals, engaging almost entirely in shore fishing, while the others carried on deep sea fishing on the outer bank. This means that the English, in contrast to the other nationalities, were not confined to their boats. Although they were not allowed to form settlements, they were allowed to work on the mainland to perform fishing-related work.

It soon became evident that the shore fishery could not be carried on successfully in the spring without winter crews remaining to perform certain necessary work. Timbers had to be cut; ship and house carpenters were needed to repair wharves, build sheds and repair or build boats. The winter crews became the first "temporary" settlers; they were rotated. Other settlement was discouraged and, if possible, prevented. The coast line was so rugged, however, that some winter crews made their homes in isolated coves where they would not be harassed by the navy. By 1522, it was believed that there were forty or fifty such houses in Avalon. The English records show that there were 250 British ships and 10,000 English fishermen engaged in the work.

Although the winter crews were supposed to be temporary, they evolved into the first settlements and named them after the places they came from. These Devon crews gave their settlements names like Torbay, after the names of towns on the Devon coast.

From the beginning of the shore fishing, squabbles broke out among ship captains over the beaches they would use from season to season. In the spring it would become a race across the Atlantic to get the best land areas. In 1582, Queen Elizabeth ruled that a captain could retain any shore space he selected for future seasons, as long as he kept up the buildings and shore installations and they were employed for fishing. The Queen sent Sir Thomas Hampshire to Newfoundland to execute her policy, which of course led to an increase in the number of winter crews.

The men of Devon had a reputation throughout England for their hunting and outdoor skills. Their need for a dog would have been quite natural. As we have shown, the evidence overwhelmingly suggests that there were no dogs indigenous to the island. So did the Devon men bring their own? Professor W. Gordon Handcock of Memorial University of Newfoundland says yes. "There is little doubt that dogs were brought to Newfoundland at an early stage, but there are remarkably few references to dogs in any surviving documents. One rare reference dated about 1608 involves an order by King James, who sent a small expedition of men to Devon with orders to find men to go to Newfoundland on a fishing ship in order to capture some hawks. The commission commanded the captain of the ship to carry some dogs to feed the hawks on the return journey" A grisly story, but it demonstrates the reputation of the Devon men as hunters and supports the theory that they took dogs by ship to Newfoundland.

D.W. Prowse, himself a Devonian, left this account of these hardy illegal settlers from the West Country: "Newfoundlanders have been conspicuous from the earliest times "for their skills in woodcraft ... These colonial hunters were the lineal descendants of the old Devonian hunter and poacher ... born hunters, restless roaming spirits, they produced a race still famous for their woodcraft, their sporting skill and their daring courage ... Alone and unaided they maintained the English sovereignity in Newfoundland

The Men of Devon

Queen Elizabeth I

and North America against all-comers a century before the *May-flower,* though they remain still unhonoured and unsung and really unknown."

It was bleak living for the Devon winter crews. Besides the work of repairing and constructing facilities for the spring return of the fishermen, they had to provide shelter and food for themselves. For the Devon man, a dog became as much of a tool as a boat. Game was abundant in Avalon and a good hunting dog was necessary for survival. The dog they brought from their home hunting stock had to be a good hunter. He also had to have a good disposition because he would be a companion as well as a worker during the long, lonely winters. The dog would have to be a good strong swimmer and small enough for the fisherman to take in his dory.

The exclusively British "shore fishing" was done from small dories. This fact is documented at Poole, England, the town that Colonel Hawker's book states was the best place to buy Newfoundland dogs. Poole was the main trading center and the link with Newfoundland for more than three centuries. On the southwest coast of England, it is one of the world's largest natural harbors. The development of the Atlantic fishing trade transformed Poole from a small West Country port to one of the most prosperous trading centers in England; the whole town became involved in the business of supplying the fishing fleets.

Even a visit to Poole harbor today provides a picture of what the town must have been like in Elizabethan days. Its winding streets and waterfront have been restored, reflecting the opulence of the Newfoundland trade. This wealth left a rich legacy in Poole's architecture, and the stories of the merchants and their mansions are still being told. A sailing vessel of that ancient day floats in the quay as if ready to take on supplies of food, salt for preserving the catch, and its human cargo. Walking the quay in the evening you can almost hear the weighman calling out "yaffle to hand," a measure of 100 pounds of fish to the "quitals" (stacks). Stepping into the pub and meeting hall (now the maritime museum), you can envision the scores of men milling around as they did each February, seeking work and signing on with the fleet. The competition for the men was keen and skulduggery rampant, but the fear of merchants and crews alike was the hated Press gangs — the method of compelling trained mariners to serve the Royal Navy. The Newfoundland fishing fleet was considered the "nursery" of the navy and the backbone of the fleet from the days of Elizabeth to Victoria's reign.

After searching Poole records, Mr. G. M. Smith, the curator of Poole's three museums, found this reference to the dogs from Newfoundland. According to Poole's Guildhall Museum, both Newfoundland and St. John's dogs were used in the early 1800s in Poole for local cart-hauling work; the dogs were also trained to guard their load. A relay of the carts, pulled by dogs, delivered fish to London.

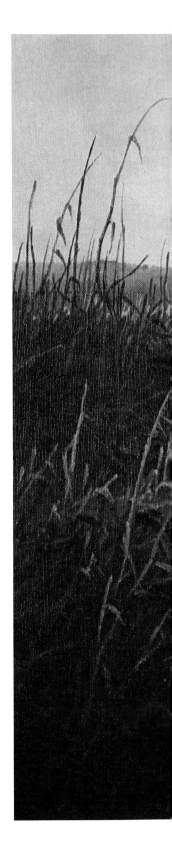

HASTY RETREAT *Richard Amundsen*

POOLE HARBOR about 1833. Poole became one of the wealthiest ports in England.

Upton House is one of the many examples that still stands resulting from the fortunes amassed during the fishing trade with Newfoundland.

Poole Harbor British hub of the Newfoundland fishing trade

The Poole Historical Society has three museums which preserve its four hundred year history.

The waterfront has been restored as it appeared at the height of its commerce.

A replica of an old sailing vessel sits in the harbor.

About 1850, it became illegal to use dogs to pull carts.

The Poole museum contains only one short — but important — statement about the Newfoundland shore fishing. "The trade with Newfoundland falls into two separate periods. At first, the small ships that sailed from the West of England carried their own fishermen. On arrival at the Grand Banks, they would go out fishing in small boats which had been left over there during the winter."

This statement establishes two facts: (1) work crews were left in Newfoundland to do repairs on the boats over the winter season, and (2) small dories were indeed used for the actual fishing. The men worked in teams of four — two on the boats and two helpers on shore to prepare and cure the fish. It is said that when the run was heavy they'd work for as many as twenty straight hours. Therefore, it is highly unlikely that a dog working in such a small boat with two fishermen could have been the massive Newfoundland. Because the dog's job of retrieving fish and swimming lines had him in and out of the water, it follows that a smaller dog with an oily short coat (retaining less water) would serve best. Hauling a wet Newfoundland dog back into a dory would take some doing, and a few such retrievers could swamp a small boat.

It would not have been logical for the fishermen to have bred the Newfoundland dog first, there would have been no need for such a large dog. Most writers on the Newfoundland tell of its great strength and how it was used to pull the sleds of firewood during the winter. However, this did not occur until about 1750, when the Newfoundland settlements developed. The early winter crews and the first settlers built their homes in little wooded coves out of sight of the British Navy, where there was plenty of firewood. So the early crews needed a dog that was a strong swimmer, did not get coated with ice, and could be handled in their dories to retrieve fish. A dog that could also find and retrieve the abundant waterfowl and upland game would be worth its weight in gold to the Devon men.

A letter from the writings of Lord George Scott in the 1930s relates how the dog was used in actual fishing:

> I had a conversation to-day with my friend Captain — late Master of a coastal steamer, on this subject, and he states that men fishing from Pass islands to Cape la Hune fish in very deep water . . . and when hauling fish from such a depth it is not unusual for the fish to escape from the hook when at or near the surface of the water. A dog is kept on board for the purpose of retrieving the fish that break from the hook, and sometimes going under water to do so.

The value of a good retriever becomes even more understandable when we realize that barbed hooks were not in common use at that time. A big Newfoundland dog doing this job would fill a small boat with water in no time.

Though written more than 200 years after the period we are discussing, a letter to the British publication *Field*, dated November 18, 1865, illustrates the importance of the dogs to the fishermen who were the descendants of the original Devon men. "I have always thought," the letter reads, "that this smooth breed of Labrador dog cannot be surpassed for sagacity by any of the canine race. I offered as high as ten sovereigns to very poor men for their dogs, which has been refused, having been told several times that no sum of money would tempt them to part with their chief support, their faithful ally."

New Evidence

The earliest writings on the work of the dogs in Newfoundland is contained in a journal written by able seaman Aaron Thomas on H.M.S. Boston called "A Journal Written During From England To Newfoundland And From Newfoundland to England In the Years 1794 and 1795, Addressed To A Friend." Although the journal generally supports our contention that very large dogs were not required to haul wood over long distances until much later in Newfoundland's history, we must be careful to reserve judgment on what is essentially a subjective and perhaps exaggerated personal correspondence.

In the journal, Thomas lists the "State of population (of St. John's) as taken in 1787":

Masters of Familys	2232
Men Servants	7718
Women Servants	1563
(Not named)	877
Children	5338
Dieters (boarders)	1378
	19106

From these figures we gather that St. John's was already a thriving community by 1790. The reasons for this growth are discussed later, but it indicates that the absentee business interests in London were losing their tight grip on the fishing industry, and that the settlers no longer had to hide their living quarters in remote coves. The letter states that wood had to be carried as far as seven to ten miles, supporting the contention that a big dog would have been needed.

Sunday 25th May. I was ashore at St. John's, and being some part of the day alone I could not resist reflection. Here I am, in full possession of all the little wants that could make some men happy . . . To you, my good friend, I confess this fault for the last time. I shall no longer continue in this strain. From the human specie I shall proceed to treat on a different kind, I mean Dogs — in this Country a useful animal indeed.

The celebrity of Newfoundland Dogs in England is so notorious that the value of them there needs no comment, but their usefulness in Britain cannot be put in competition with the great utility they are to the people of this cold Country. In this Empire of Frost and Snow great quantitys of wood must be used by the Inhabitants whose winter here is from October to April! — or May! In this Country as soon as the Snow falls it freezes. The people then cut their wood for firing, for Fish Flakes and for Building etc., etc. This wood is sometimes cut seven or ten miles in the woods and is drawn home by Dogs. They have gearing the same as Horses; the wood is put into Sledges which they draw, and sometimes they drag a single stick only, attended by one man who wears frost shoes. This labour of Dogs is daily thro the winter and a hard service it is.

These Animals here bear a more hardier aspect in general to what their same specie do in England, so much so that on a superficial view their kind does not appear the same. Their difference ariseth thus — in Newfoundland the Dogs commonly are their own caterers. They chiefly live on Fish and many of these sturdy race fish for themselves. It is no very uncommon thing to see one of these Dogs catch a Fish. Bitter hunger is their monitor and as it presses upon them they go to the waterside and set on a Rock, keeping as good a lookout as ever Cat did for a Mouse. The instant a Fish appears they plunge into the water and seldom come up without their prey. This is a wonderful property in these Animals, but it is as true as it is singular . . .

One of these Newfoundland Dogs, after he had been constantly worked in the woods during the winter, then slain, is not bad eating. The Hams are a new article in the Epicure's Catalogues. Had you sent to the Cock, in Cornhill for a Ham, and had they sent you this specie, you and your friend would of put it down as fine Westphalia as ever was eat.

Thus far, my good Fellow, I have got to the 25th of May. I have wrote 194 Pages filled with something, whether entertaining or informing you will judge. This I know, I have had some trouble in putting my Ideas on paper.

A 16th century woodcut showing that dogs were used to retrieve downed waterfowl in France.

Thomas was most likely pulling his friend's leg about eating the dogs and sending to their favorite eating house, the Cock in Cornhill for a "ham." The last line — "I have wrote 194 Pages filled with something, whether entertaining or informing you will judge" — is perhaps indicative of how seriously we can accept the letter as fact.

In his other reference to the dog, Thomas writes of its fishing ability. (*Note:* A banker was a boat that fished on the Grand Bank and the word was also applied to the fisherman.)

Dogs were hauled aboard large boats by either putting their heads through a noose or, by using their paw and biting the line. In dorys they were hauled aboard by the scruff of their necks.

St. Hubert's Hound . . . The Lab's Ancestor?

A Banker is not a little proud of his Dog at Sea. This Creature exhibited his dexterity and usefullness to a surprizing degree. I shall mention the following trait as a good quality in their composition. The Fishermen, when they hooked a Fish, in drawing the line up [*find*] the Fish sometimes disentangled themselves. The Fish may sometimes float on the Water. The Dog, observing this, dasheth into the Sea and brings the Fish alongside. They then throw a Rope out and the Dog, with the Fish in his mouth, puts Head into the Noose of the Rope and Fish and Dog are hauled into the Vessel together. At Sea those Dogs often pursue and kill Water Fowl. I have heard of a Dog who was absent from a Ship on the Grand Bank for Two days, on the Third he return'd with a Hegdown in his mouth. These Dogs have also been seen to dive after Porpoises but without success.

Thomas's description becomes a very important "first" in the literature on the dogs of Newfoundland. However, the letter still comes late in our story. By this time (almost 300 years after the first Devon fishermen arrived) the original Newfoundland dog would have been developed and well established and the larger dray animal would have already emerged. To get to the origins of these dogs we must plunge still further into the past . . .

What can we ascertain from the British records about the dogs the Devon men owned in their native country? We do know that they had the choice of many different breeds to take with them to the New World. A book written in 1576, *Booke of Hunting*, by George Turbervile, discusses various hunting dogs used by the West Country hunters. One of the available dogs was a black dog called a "Saint Huberts hound" in honor of the patron saint of the hunter. It might be unfair to do any more than speculate that the St. Huberts dog was the one the Devon men took to Newfoundland, but the evidence is strong. In the book's hunting section, the drawing of the dog (see illustration) has such a striking resemblance to the Labrador that we can leave it to the reader to make his own determination. The dog had its origin in France, but the cultural interaction between the French and English nobility was considerable. *Booke of Hunting* establishes that the dog—at least during the latter part of the sixteenth century—was prevalent in England.

Turbervile's accompanying text is just as provocative as the drawing. For reading convenience, the Elizabethan wording has been translated into modern English:

> The dogs are commonly all black, yet nevertheless, their race is so mingled at these days, that we find them of all colors. This kind of dog is mighty of body, nevertheless, their legs are low and short, likewise they are not swift, although they be very good of scent, hunting chases that are farre straggled.

Of blacke hounds aunciently come from Sainct Huberts abbay in Ardene.   Chap. 5

This 16th century woodcut is an artistic presentation of the conformation of the Saint Huberts hound.

The words "farre straggled" have been interpreted as "tracking wounded game" because the text goes on to state:

The dog fearing neither water or cold and do more covet the chase that smells, they find themselves neither of swiftness nor courage to hunt and kill. The dogs of this color prove good, especially those that are coal black. Yet I once found a book which a hunter dedicated to a Prince of Lorayne, wherein was a rhyme about a dog called Soygllard who was white.

My name came first from holy Huberts Race
Soygllard my sir, a dog of singular grace

Whereupon we may presume that some of the kind prove white, whereupon but they are not the kind we have at these days.

YELLOW LABRADOR *Bob Abbett*

Could this be the ancestor of today's Labrador? He was black, but some were known to be other colors. He had short legs and a heavy body. He was not swift but had a good nose. He liked to hunt and track but not to kill, and he had no fear of water or the cold. He was known in the home country of Devon hunters. Because no other definitive documentation exists, we can only suggest, on the basis of this evidence, that the black St. Huberts dog was the ancestor of the Lab.*

It has been often suggested that the Portuguese Water Dog might be the Lab's ancestor, but every approach to this theory has proved fruitless. There are no records that the early men of Devon had any contact with the Portuguese fishermen or that the dog had been introduced into England. As stated, the Portuguese never attempted a settlement in Newfoundland, so there is no historical evidence that the Portuguese dog reached Avalon. The only possible contact in the earliest days could have been ship-to-ship; yet because the countries fished in different areas, this isn't likely.

In 1576, a book written originally in Latin called *Of English Dogges — The Diversities, The Names, The Nature and The Properties*, divides hunting dogs into two varieties. "There be two sorts. The first findeth game on the land. The other findeth game on the water." This is all the book says on the subject except that nets were used in connection with waterfowl hunting.

It is not until 1721 in Nicholas Cox's book, *The Gentleman's Recreation: In Four Parts, Hunting, Hawking, Fowling, Fishing*, that we get more information. The frontispiece of the book provides a very graphic illustration of how the English used nets and live decoys for land birds and nets, decoys, dogs, and a blind for waterfowl. As the drawing shows: for land birds, caged live birds acted as callers to bring the flight birds to the feeding area surrounded by nets. When the birds arrived to feed, the nets were sprung. To capture waterfowl, decoys were set out in the pond. The dog was sent in from the side opposite the nets to make the fowl move in the right direction. The drawing also shows that a horse was used as a blind; the gunner has a cloth over the horse and himself. Once the dog chases the birds in the right direction, the hunter fires his gun and the birds take off and become entangled in the net.

On making the nets the book instructs: "Let your Nets be made the smallest and strongest packthread, and the Meshes nothing near so big as those of the greater Fowl, about two Foot and a half or three Foot deep; line those Nets on both sides with false Nets, each Mesh being about a half square each Way, that as the Fowl striketh either through them or against them so the smaller Nets may pass through the great Meshes, and so streighten and entangle the Fowl."

This hunting technique was improved by adding live duck decoys. A stream inlet to a larger body of water was selected. Nets

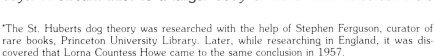

*The St. Huberts dog theory was researched with the help of Stephen Ferguson, curator of rare books, Princeton University Library. Later, while researching in England, it was discovered that Lorna Countess Howe came to the same conclusion in 1957.

The frontispiece of The Gentleman's Recreation by Nicholas Cox, shows dogs were used as waterfowl retrievers as early as 1721.

were placed on the foliage on either side. Decoys were placed in close to the stream. Trained ducks with clipped wings were set out in the open water. They were taught with food to swim towards the stream where they would be fed. They would bring with them the wild birds. Once they entered the narrowing waterway, a dog was sent in to swim behind the ducks to move them in a tight pattern over the food. Either the dog continued swimming towards them and they panicked and flew or a gun was shot to set them off and become entangled in the nets. Later, as guns and shot improved the nets were abandoned.

These hunting techniques and the dogs used were known to the men from the West Country. It follows logically that the dogs from their home country and the hunting methods of that time would have been introduced to the Avalon peninsula by the woods-men of Devon.

Middleton, in his *The Labrador Dog — Its Home and History*, sums up his discussion on the origin of the big Newfoundland dog by saying, "Even if there was a French cross in the large Newfound-land dog (Chien-dogue) there is good reason for supposing that one of the earliest ancestors must have been the hunting dog of the

Devon fishermen, which was probably the progenitor of the small Labrador of the nineteenth century and of greater antiquity than the large Newfoundland dog." Therefore, Middleton hints at the theory presented here; that the small smooth-coated dog came first, despite his original assumption that the Newfoundland came first and the Labrador was a variety of the big dog. He even suggests that the Newfoundland came from English stock.

It seems by no means impossible that even the large Newfoundland dog might have been evolved, quite independently of foreign ancestry, from the stock originally introduced into the Avalon Peninsula by the Devon settlers, who, with their great skill in woodcraft, were singularly well adapted to mould their dogs to their changing needs, and had all the resources of the West of England and the south of Ireland to draw from. Whether they made use of any dog of foreign origin in the process there does not appear to be any concrete evidence, but the beginning was made around St. John's on the east coast of the Avalon Peninsula, where the first settlers made their homes. As the small settlements gradually spread along the coast the breed of dogs which was, later, to become so famous, was to be found in a wider area; and before the end of the eighteenth century they had reached the extreme southwest of the Island and the southern coast of Labrador, and were to be found wherever the fishermen had settled.

Breeding Up Based on Need

The key to the ancestry of the big Newfoundland dog is to determine which dog was used to breed up in size from the "water dog" or St. John's dog. As the Avalon villages grew, the land workloads changed. There obviously would have been a need for dray work, to haul supplies, to move kegs of fish, to haul winter fuel. As the need for a large work dog developed, it seems logical that the men of Devon would have bred their dog up in size using their own coursing dogs or Irish Wolfhounds.

Both the Newfoundland and the Labrador are easy-going, fun-loving dogs. The personality of dogs is quite indicative of their breeders. All of the English hunting dogs, even to this day, have that same desirable personality that both dogs exhibit — another indicator that they are from the same background and bred by the same kind of people.

In the year that Colonel Hawker wrote of the quickness and running, swimming, and fighting ability of the St. John's dog, Lieutenant Edward Chappel, serving on H.M.S. Rosamond in 1813, wrote differently; "They were so gentle and good-natured that it is customary to cross the breed with an English Bulldog whereby they are rendered more fierce and surly toward strangers."

It is understandable that the writers of the early nineteenth cen-

A Case of Mistaken Identity

tury would have written about the new "import," the St. John's dog, as a subspecie of the dog that had been known for 100 years. Colonel Hawker *et al* reported their observations with no firsthand knowledge of what actually happened 3000 miles away. By the time they first came in contact with the "new" St. John's dog, hundreds of years of breeding had already taken place. Isn't it logical that this smaller dog, which was being seen for the first time, should be considered a new offshoot of the big dog that was known, was established, and had gained social status as part of the country life of the gentry? Psychologically, all was set for this interpretation, namely that the St. John's dog — the Lab's forerunner — was the lesser Newfoundland.

As we have shown, however, the Labrador's ancestor was much more likely the French St. Hubert's dog, which was brought to England well before the Devon men went to Newfoundland and which was the prime breed developed in Avalon for the survival of the early settlers.

The question arises, why didn't the men of Devon bring the dog back to England as a fishing dog? The original Devon men were not fishermen, they were hunters and woodsmen and for their purpose the dog was already in England. As far as the fishermen were concerned, the fishing technique in England was different from Newfoundland; a dog was not needed nor was ever used, not even later when the dog was brought back. Additionally, the fishermen who worked the fleet were not much more than indentured servants. The captains would have been the only ones to have the right to bring a dog back and they did, as we shall see, when it became a way to line their pockets.

The frontispiece of early editions of the Hawker book *Instructions To A Young Sportsman.*

Back on British Soil

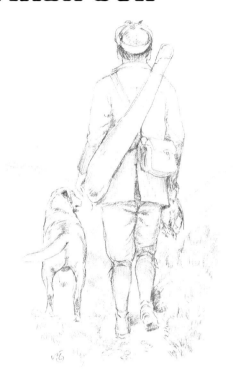

Colonel Hawker's book establishes that the St. John's dog was seen in England in 1814. Delabere Blane, a contemporary of Colonel Hawker, wrote his praise of the St. John's breed in his *Encyclopaedia of Rural Sports* in 1840.

> The St. John's breed is preferred by the sportsman on every account, being smaller, more easily managed, and sagacious in the extreme. His scenting powers also are great. Some years ago these dogs could be readily procured at Poole, and when well broken in were very valuable. Indeed, gentlemen . . . have found them so intelligent, so faithful, and so capable of general instruction, that they have given up most sporting varieties and content themselves with these; and, as we are told, found the place of the others perfectly well filled up.

First, it is apparent from Hawker's and Blane's accounts that the dogs were no longer readily procurable at Poole from 1814 to 1840. Second, Blane's use of the phrase "as we are told" implies that the sporting writers of the day still had little contact with the dog. These second-hand references continue almost to the end of the century, which indicates the dog was in the hands of only a very few sportsmen. Blane's writings show the scarcity still remained.

Why was the dog seen so rarely in England by the mid-1800s? How did the dog almost become extinct in Newfoundland?

In 1713, the Treaty of Utrecht ended the expansion of the French and gave the English full sovereignty in Newfoundland, which at that time was regarded as little more than a fishing station. The French who had settled in the area of Placentia left the island. A half-century of prosperity followed.

Released from any threat to its fishing industry, the British Navy relaxed its vigilance and departed at the end of the fishing season each fall. Without the navy to enforce the prohibition against permanent colonization, the doors were opened to the development of settlements. What the absentee British business interests had feared from the beginning of the fishing industry in the 1500s finally happened in 1750. St. John's population grew much larger than the number of migratory fishermen and changed from a fishing village into the semblance of a commercial town.

By 1800, the Newfoundland settlements had taken over a large part of the fishing industry themselves. Migratory fishermen were no longer needed because immigrants were coming to the colony in large numbers. They built their own boats, did their own fishing, and shipped the processed fish directly to the Catholic countries in southern Europe. England was gradually cut out of the deal.

England received another blow that affected the importation of the dogs from Newfoundland — America's independence, settled by the Treaty of Paris of September 3, 1783. After months of tortuous negotiations by John Adams, Benjamin Franklin and John Jay, the boundaries of the United States were fixed. In the treaty, Americans were granted fishing rights off Newfoundland. This brought added competition for the already fading British cod fishery. Fewer and fewer fishing vessels would ply the waters between Newfoundland and England.

The British business interests, not to be done in by the upstarts in Newfoundland, had already started a new industry in Labrador in the seal trade, which, according to John Hillier, Chairman of the Poole Historical Society, was started in Poole in 1773. The Treaty of Paris forced it into full swing in 1783, and the former fishing craft, now in the business of sealing, no longer touched the shores of Newfoundland. The two major seaports that lost the Newfoundland trade were Greenock in Scotland and Poole on the southern coast of England. Both were the ports of entry for the St. John's dog, particularly Poole.

Poole records also show that for some reason the volume of an average vessel's fishing catch fell off in the first decade of the nineteenth century, which further affected the number of boats sent to Newfoundland. This, added to the general reduction of shipping traffic, also decreased the number of dogs imported to England.

Colonel Hawker relates another obstacle: The fishing boat captains who brought the dogs into Poole did so in order to line their pockets with a few extra pieces of gold. As the boats arrived each

The St. John's dogs had dominant traits that were passed on. They were crossed with any dog to make it a retriever. The result here is a Black C

A Close Brush with Extinction

When the arriving captain had a dog for sale the signal was to have the dog swim ashore.

Rufus, 1832. The first drawing of the St. John's dog to appear in a sporting magazine.

Second Earl of Malmesbury

fall from Newfoundland and anchored in the harbor, the seamen would scurry over the sides into gigs and row to the quay. The dogs would be tossed overboard to swim alongside the boats — a signal for those on shore that a dog was for sale. But the British customs officers soon got wise to the trick and slapped a duty on the dogs. With the tax the captains found that it wasn't worth their trouble to bring the dogs 3000 miles across the Atlantic. Also, as we will see, there was at this time a problem in Newfoundland that would affect the supply of dogs.

This gradual slowing of trade with Newfoundland almost prevented the St. John's dog from becoming established on English soil. The problem was twofold. First, the ordinary sportsman did not have enough dogs to keep the lines pure, so he cross-bred them. Second, in those days, the average English sportsman believed that any kind of dog that would retrieve could be called a retriever, so he bred his St. John's dog out of existence. This was true for most of the nineteenth century. The shooting man bred his dog any way he wished to obtain the desired results. If he could get a dash of St. John's into the mix, all the better. As late as 1873, Dinks, Mayhew, and Hutchinson, all important dog writers of that day, wrote in *The Dog,* "A retriever is a cross-breed dog. There is no true type of them. Every person has a peculiar fancy regarding them. The best I have seen were a cross between the Labrador and Water Spaniel."

Though the name *Labrador* appears in this 1873 book, it is still not established. The dog is still called by its previous names, *St. John's* and *Newfoundland,* and by a new name, *English Retriever. Labrador* becomes common usage in about the last decade of the nineteenth century.

We are indebted to the second Earl of Malmesbury, one of the outstanding sportsmen of his day, for today's Labrador. He lived at Heron Court, which was only four miles from Poole. He was an avid hunter from 1801 until his death in 1841. Although we do not know the exact year when he obtained his first dog from Poole harbor, we do know that he used his dog from Newfoundland in 1809.

At that time the shooting sports in England were limited to the upper class. Although interest in the Lab was high, so few dogs were available because the Lab was only in the hands of a very few shooting families.

Except for the dogs that reached Heron Court, there seems to be no record of the dog between 1800 and 1835; most were apparently cross-bred out of existence. Without the second Earl's devotion to the shooting sports and this dog we might not have our friend around today.

The second Earl of Malmesbury was born in 1778 and worked in the service of his government as Under-Secretary for Foreign Affairs under Lord Canning. He married a most beautiful woman, Frances Dashwood from Lincolnshire, and had three sons. The first

CORA. A LABRADOR BITCH *Edwin Landseer*

CORA. A LABRADOR BITCH.
The Property of L. Allsopp Esq.ʳ

From the Original Picture in the possession of G Harrison Esq.ᵗ to which a prize was adjudged by the British Institution in 1823.

The 1823 legend under the print uses the name Labrador.

The first use of the name Labrador, after Colonial Hawker mentions the dog from Newfoundland, is by Edwin Landseer in his painting of "Cora. A Labrador Bitch." The 5th Duke of Buccleuch was the next one to use the name Labrador. He had the first kennel of these dogs in Scotland, and used the name Labrador in a letter which he wrote in 1839.

"Oops"

"Knickerbocker Era" **The ladies make fun of the new shooting dress.**

These are a few of the sketches that appear in the Buccleuch family game book where everyday hunting activity was recorded. The guests drew in the book the highlights of the day's shoot . . . *A dog that spilled the gun . . . A dog that would not wet his feet . . . Drinking instead of shooting on the moors . . .* in 1857.

1 P.M. useful Gyp! Oh you x x x x x x Ke!!!

The men responsible
for starting and keeping
the present day Labrador pure

The 2nd Earl of Malmesbury
1778–1841,
started the first kennel
of Labradors.

Heron Court, the Malmesbury family home was situated four miles from Poole Harbor.

The stable entrance of Heron Court leading to the kennels. This is the only place in England where the Labrador was kept pure during the early 19th century.

Although every Home ancestor's painting hangs in the ancestral home, the Hirsel in Scotland, because of his shyness, no portrait of the 10th Earl exists.

e 3rd Earl of Malmesbury
1807–1889,
continued the kennel
which was carried on
by the Buccleuchs.

The 5th Duke of Buccleuch
1806–1884,
started the first
kennel in Scotland
about 1835.

Lord John Scott
1809–1860,
the 5th Duke of
Buccleuch's brother.

The 10th Earl of Home
1769–1841,
started his kennel with the
5th Duke of Buccleuch.

The 11th Earl of Home
1799–1881,
continued his father's kennel.

The 6th Duke of Buccleuch
1831–1914,
rejuvenated the line by the
chance meeting with the
3rd Earl of Malmesbury.

The 12th Earl of Home
1834–1918,
and the 6th Duke of
Buccleuch went to the south
of England and met the 3rd Earl
of Malmesbury who gave both
men dogs from his kennel.

son became the third Earl, served as the Foreign Secretary under Disraeli and again under Darby, and continued his father's kennels.

The second Earl was a devoted hunter who kept extensive journals of his forty seasons of hunting, starting in 1801. His great-grandson, the fifth Earl, published in 1905 extracts from his exciting hunting journals: *Half a Century of Sport in Hampshire.* It was edited by F. G. Affalo, and becomes the first reference to the dog as a hunter. An entry for the 28th of December, 1809 states that his "Newfoundland dog" caught a woodcock in a brake at Avon cottage. "The bird hurt in the leg some time before could fly well but the briars arching over him prevented him from rising." On page 55, he relates that on the 30th of November, 1810, he made a double shot at a snipe and a partridge, "both of which were winged and yet, though they ran quite off, my Newfoundland dog, Ceasar, brought them both to us, one after the other."

All efforts to find the Earl's original journal or any other family documents that mention the dogs have proven fruitless.

The record of the Labrador from the early 1800s until 1882, is all a very sketchy affair. The reason is understandable; the dog was in the hands of the aristocracy, and they kept it pretty much to themselves. Of course, for the same reason the dog was saved from extinction; since the ordinary sportsman had so few St. John's dogs to breed, he was crossed out of existence. The Lab was very fortunate that his "friends" have always been influential people.

To the general sportsman and the sporting writers of the day, he was little more than hearsay. Here is what has come down to us:

• According to Thomas Bell, a contemporary of Colonel Hawker, the dogs were imported and used in the southwestern counties of England. The dog came "home" to Devon but in time was lost even there. We know from the records of the second Earl of Malmesbury that he was hunting with the dog in 1809. His kennel stayed well-stocked until his death in 1841.

THE LOADER ON A GROUSE MOOR *Ogden Pleissner*

• In 1823, Sir Edwin Landseer (1802–1873), the famous British animal artist, made a print called *Cora, A Labrador Bitch.* After Hawker's book in 1814, this seems to be the second use of the name *Labrador* in connection with a dog from Newfoundland. Landseer went on to paint oils of the great Newfoundland dog and specialized in the multi-colored variety. His paintings made them so popular that they still bear his name.

• The St. John's dog entered Scotland about 1835, when the Duke of Buccleuch started his kennel. The first time the dog was called Labrador was in 1839. Almost every book on the history of Labs mentions that in 1839 the fifth Duke of Buccleuch (1806–1884) wrote in a letter that he took his "Labrador" Moss to Naples in his yacht, and the tenth Lord Home (1769–1841) who accompanied him, took his "Labrador" Drake. Drake was bred by the Duke in 1840 according to the book *Notes on the Duke of Buccleuch's Labradors*, published by a later Duke of Buccleuch as a kennel record. Most writers have considered this the first "official" record of the dog being called by the name, *Labrador.* Today, neither the ninth Duke of Buccleuch nor the fourteenth Lord Home know the whereabouts of that letter.

• There is no record of when the Scottish Duke and his brother, Lord John Scott (1809–1860) started importing the dogs. It is assumed that they got their dogs at Greenock Harbor in Scotland, which was still carrying on some trade with Newfoundland. The date would be about 1835. Other dogs imported by the Duke were named Jock, Nell (1843), and Brandy. Brandy, as the story goes, earned his name on the high seas as he crossed the Atlantic. He went overboard into rough water to fetch a cap of one of the crew. It was two hours before he could be picked up, and he was so exhausted he had to be revived with brandy.

• In 1841, both the tenth Lord Home and the second Earl of Malmesbury died. Their kennels were continued by their sons, the eleventh Earl of Home and the third Earl of Malmesbury. Malmesbury became the major importer of the St. John's dog for the next twenty years. Between 1865 and 1875, besides Malmesbury, Montagu Guest, Lord Wimborne, and C.J. Radclyffe imported dogs through a sea captain, one Hawker, who plied a trading schooner between England and Newfoundland. Later Radclyffe's son bred the first Yellow dogs. Very little is known about the third Earl of Malmesbury during this period, except that he kept his kennel going at Heron Court, and like his father was an avid hunter.

• The earliest photograph of a Labrador was of the Duke's dog Nell, who was about twelve years old when the picture was taken in 1867. It is interesting to note the type of dog that was being bred and that she had white tips on her toes and a white muzzle. She was owned by the eleventh Earl of Home (1799–1881). His gamekeeper, Mr. J. Craw, left the service of Lord Home and

The Lab in Victorian England

Lord Home's *Nan*, born about 1855.

ord Home's *Nell*, born about 1856.

The 6th Duke of Buccleuch's, *Avon*, 1885, referred to as the ancestor of all British Labs, was bred by the 3rd Earl of Malmesbury.

went to Netherby to establish the kennels for Sir Frederick Graham, using dogs from both the Home and Buccleuch stock. During this period the Labrador started to become popular in aristocratic circles with the entry of the Duke of Hamilton, Lord Saltoun, Lord Ruthven, Lord Wimborne, Sir Wilfred Lawson, and a few others. But nearly all these strains of Labradors died out during the 1880s, and by this time there were very few Labradors left in England.

• At age seventy-five, the third Earl of Malmesbury came to the rescue. The sixth Duke of Buccleuch (1831–1914) and the twelfth Earl of Home (1834–1918) spent a number of shooting seasons as guests at Heron Court, where the waterfowl shooting was first class. It was this chance meeting with Malmesbury at Bournemouth (the seaport next to Poole), when the young Home took his friend Buccleuch to visit a sick aunt on the south coast and to partake of the best waterfowl shooting in England, which could be regarded as the stroke of luck that saved the Labrador from extinction. The two noblemen were amazed at the work of Malmesbury's dogs — the same breed as their fathers had developed. Lord Malmesbury gave some of his breed to both. These dogs carried the lines into the twentieth century. Ned (born in 1882) and Avon (born in 1885) proved to be outstanding workers. It is probable that every Labrador in Britain traces back to those two dogs.

In a letter written to the sixth Duke of Buccleuch about 1887, the Earl said, "We always called mine Labrador dogs and I have kept the breed as pure as I could from the first I had from Poole, at that time carrying on a brisk trade with Newfoundland. The real breed may be known by their having a close coat which turns the water off like oil, above all, a tail like an otter."

Shortly after the death of the Earl in 1889, his kennel died out, but his strain was carefully preserved by the sixth Duke of Buccleuch.

The historical chain through the nineteenth century links together rather neatly, but it is never even mentioned by the dog writers of that century. The names Malmesbury, Buccleuch, Scott, or Home never appear in the literature, which indicates how privately these dogs were held. Here is that chain:

The first to have the dog and keep him pure was the second Earl of Malmesbury (1778–1841).

His son the third Earl (1807–1889) kept the line going.

Independently, the fifth Duke of Buccleuch (1806–1884), his brother, Lord John Scott (1809–1860), and the tenth Lord Home (1769–1841) imported the dogs into Scotland about 1835. They all lived within a 30-mile radius and developed the Buccleuch line.

The eleventh Lord Home (1799–1881) continued his dogs, but the line phased out about the time of his death.

The sixth Duke of Buccleuch (1831–1914) and the twelfth Lord Home (1834–1918) revitalized the Buccleuch line with the dogs given to them by the aging third Earl of Malmesbury and

Langholm 1891 Dinah
Do. " Kate
Do. " Ned
Drumlanrig " Nero ♀
" + Ness. Put down July 1894
+ Was sent to Milnefield when Telfer left

1885 Avon from Lord Malmesbury
Sanquhar 1888 Trick
Lord George Scott's

1885 Dinah From Lord Malmesbury

Lord Malmesbury's Tramp — smooth coated
Lord Malmesbury's 1878 Juno — Labrador
Dan Simpson's (Preston Hall) Diver — Lord Ruthven's br...
Duke of Hamilton's 1884 Sam
Duke of Hamilton's Fan — The old Hamilton... bred
Lord Malmesbury's Nelson — Long coated Newfoun...
Lord Malmesbury's 1880 Nell — Straight coated

Langholm 1892 Bell
Do " Beg?
Do " Boss

1882 Ned From Lord Malmesbury Put down Dec 1893
Lord Malmesbury's 1877 Sweet Newfoundland.
Lord Malmesbury's 1878 Juno Labrador

Newlands 1891 Bob
Do " Hector
Bowhill " Meg
Do " Skipper.

1882 Ned above From Lord Malmesbury
1888 Dinah at Newlands sister to Trick

1885 Avon from Lord Malmesbury above
Drumlanrig 1891 Drake
Do " Kate
Do " Nibb
Jumy?
1889 Gip at Drumlanrig [crossed out] Died 1892

Lord Malmesbury's Tramp — smooth coated.
Lord Malmesbury's 1171 Juno — Labrador.
Dan Simpson's Preston Hall Diver — Lord Ruthven's bre...
Duke of Hamilton's 1884 Sam
Duke of Hamilton's Fan — The old Hamilton... breed.
1886 Nell from Lord Malmesbury
Lord Winborne's Dog — Smooth coated
Lord Malmesbury's 1882 Juno — Labrador

Drumlanrig 1892 Bess
Sanquhar " Flo. Jardine
Do " Rock Ballantyne

1882 Ned above From Lord Malmesbury
Lord Malmesbury's 1877 Sweet Newfoundland.
Lord Malmesbury's 1878 Juno Labrador

The Duke of Buccleuch's original Labrador Retrievers pedigree

Disaster in Newfoundland

John Labrador, 1904, owned by the Duke of Buccleuch.

brought them into the twentieth century. From the beginnings of the St. John's dog with the second Earl of Malmesbury, this is the mainstream of the Labrador we know today.

The seventh Duke of Buccleuch, who died in 1935, was not active, according to the present Duke of Buccleuch, in keeping the line going. But on further investigation we found that the seventh Duke was active in keeping his kennel line going. This story was pieced together from information on both sides of the Atlantic and led to finding the "missing link" in the modern history of the Lab.

In about 1930, the Duke figured he could strengthen his line of dogs by going back to Newfoundland and obtaining original stock for breeding purposes. This proved to be an almost impossible task and nearly ruined his line of dogs in Scotland. During the period 1890–1930, no dogs were imported from Newfoundland. The reasons are political and complex.

Disaster actually struck all dogs in Newfoundland twice. In 1780, Governor Edwards decided to encourage sheep raising; to cut down on the menace to the sheep he limited the ownership of dogs to no more than one per family. This decree would not have affected most breeds, as they existed in abundance elsewhere in the world. For the big Newfoundland and the water dog, however, this spelled trouble: There were only a few Newfoundlands elsewhere and at this time no St. John's dogs had been taken from the island (the underlying historical reason why both Hawker and Blaine wrote that the dogs were in short supply in England). Ironically, despite these new laws, the sheep-raising business never materialized.

Almost 100 years later, in 1885, the same thing happened again. As the islanders were developing and seeking new industry, their legislature passed an act to encourage the breeding of sheep. A heavy license was imposed on dogs. It provided a higher tax rate on females than males, and as a result the bitches of the litters were invariably destroyed. The tragedy was that after passing the Sheep Protection Act and the dog tax, again there was no attempt to raise sheep. The crowning blow came in 1895 when the English passed the British Quarantine Act, prohibiting dogs to enter Great Britain without a license and without first undergoing a strict six-month quarantine.

The Buccleuch line of dogs was carrying the Lab breed through this latter period in England; by the early 1900s the Labrador retriever was making an impact in numbers and deeds on the sporting world of England. But in Newfoundland the St. John's dog was becoming rare, and by the mid-1930s it was just about gone, as related in *The Labrador Dog,* published in 1936. Lord George Scott, who coauthored the book with Sir John Middleton and who was the son of the 6th Duke of Buccleuch (brother of the 7th Duke) wrote:

In spite of all these obstacles (the Sheep Act and the British quarantine), some breeders of Labradors (a reference to the seventh Duke of Buccleuch and Lord George Scott) have made efforts at various times to import black water dogs from Newfoundland without success until between November 1933 and 1934 [when] some dogs were obtained. Several closely resembled the type sought for in size, colour of eye, shape and texture of coat, and were water dogs. One of these dogs called "Cabot" is good looking and already the father of several litters and these dogs at present have every desirable quality both as retrievers and in appearance.

Lady Jacqueline Barlow of St. John's, Newfoundland, who is today a breeder of Labs, a member of The Labrador Club, and the recipient of a handsome, yellow, Sandrigham Chive from the Queen of England, relates a story about Middleton, which Sir Leonard Outerbridge verified and which also points out the success of the Sheep Act in practically wiping out the St. John's dog. She also reports on using Cabot at stud.

Lord George Scott

One of the early water dog stories in St. John's is told by Sir Leonard Outerbridge, one time Aide de Camp to the Newfoundland Governor, Sir John Middleton, and later Lieutenant Governor of Newfoundland himself. It's the story of Cabot.

"Lord George Scott" in 1932 wrote to Sir John in Newfoundland and asked him to look out for a dog as per description enclosed, for which he expected to pay £2. Sir John sent for his Aide, Sir Leonard, and armed with the description in question, Sir Leonard set forth to look for such a dog. Finally after a lengthy and tedious search, Sir Leonard spotted the exact dog of the Duke's description standing in the bow of a fishing boat in St. John's harbour. Asking if he could buy the dog and offering the £2, which the Skipper readily agreed to as being a princely sum, Sir Leonard stipulated that he must first get the Governor's approval by taking the dog to the government house. This being done, Sir Leonard returned to settle with the Skipper of the fishing boat, who, crafty fellow that he was, thought there was obviously more to that particular dog than had met his own eye, upped the price to FIVE pounds! A price the Duke and Lord incidentally thought excessive, and complained of for many years to Sir John Middleton. In due course the black dog now called "Cabot" (after the discoverer of Newfoundland, John Cabot) was sent to the Duke of Buccleuch.

The 7th Duke of Buccleuch

Sir Leonard quite cheerfully says this splendid specimen of a "Water Dog" had an Alsatian (German Shepherd) for a mother!

There is a sequel to this story which I cannot vouch for. When the dog was due to depart for the Buccleuch Kennels it

Lady Jacqueline Barlow and Chive, her gift from the Queen.

Sir Alec Douglas-Home at the Hirshel
He resigned his title as the 14th Earl of Home in 1963 to become Prime Minister of England.

Sir Leonard Outerbridge

was decided to provide him with a pedigree, and thinking-caps were put on. After much head scratching "Cabot" was provided with a splendid pedigree to accompany him, the Sires, grandsires, etc., being the names of all the leading politicians of the day and the Dams, etc. the ladies of the waterfront!

As Lady Barlow said, she could not vouch for the story of the pedigree, but I can vouch for this follow-up to the Cabot progeny. I stumbled onto it by accident. The fourteenth Earl of Home, Sir Alec Douglas-Home, the former Prime Minister of England, told me the following story at his home, The Hirsel, situated on the famous Scottish salmon fishing river, the Tweed.

Lord Home began by telling the story of a famous lawsuit brought to court under the title, *Tankerville vs. a dog,* a century ago. It seems that the Earl of Tankerville owned a beat on the Tweed that was being poached every day by a dog who sat on the banks of the river. The black dog sat very still and on spying a salmon he'd dive in and retrieve the fish. He never ate them, but instead piled them in a row. Tankerville lost the court case against the dog's owner, the then Lord Home. Sir Alec continued, "I had a dog once that was keen on retrieving salmon. His name was Tinto. He was given to me by the Duke of Buccleuch many years ago and his sire's name was Cabot. He loved to swim and although he was black he didn't look like a Labrador, he also had a curved tail."

When I informed Lord Home that, according to Sir Outerbridge, Cabot's dame was a German Shepherd, he thought a moment and replied, "That fits. The dog must have gotten his fishing instinct from his St. John's father and its inability to hunt from his mother. Tinto was useless as a retriever. He had no nose, couldn't find game and had no desire to hunt."

Newfoundland today is still a remote land: Rivers act as roads and travel is by boat. In some parts of the back country a dialect of Elizabethan English is still spoken.

The tax on dogs may have wiped out the dog in the more populated areas, but is seems unlikely that it could have reached all the back country.

In 1974, Lady Barlow made her own search for the Newfoundland water dog. Traveling along the south coast of Newfoundland by schooner, she found in a remote fishing village three dogs that were the original water dogs.

My investigation began fifty years after the Duke of Buccleuch tried his. I wrote to everyone in St. John's who might lead me to this dog. Which is how I got in touch with Lady Barlow in the first place. All sources seemed to lead to her. No one could come up with any other source of the dog. Lady Barlow gave me all the information she had. I wrote to Harold Melbourne, Grand Bruit, on the inaccessible south coast of Newfoundland. A year went by and

NEWFOUNDLAND WATER DOG *Richard A. Wolters*

The missing links

Lassie, the dog to the left, and his brother are the last of the original Newfoundland water dogs. He's 13 years old. They were able to survive extinction because they live in an area that is extremely remote. Grand Bruit, the picture above, is a fishing village on the western part of the South Coast. The only way to reach this fishing village is by boat. Lassie is owned by Mr. James who is in his late 80's. His father and grandfather, he recalls, always had water dogs. Since there are no females available, Lassie and his 15 year old brother are the last of the line. Their ancestors were the dogs that were taken to England and became the Labrador Retrievers. Lassie still very alert, is an excellent retriever and will come to life just like a puppy when the stick is thrown in the water.

no answer came. I wrote again and two months later I got a reply. Yes, Melbourne said, in Grand Bruit there were now two old male dogs left. They were brothers from different litters. One was fifteen and the other thirteen. As far as he knew, they were the last pure water dogs and without any females they were the last of the line. Time was running out and getting there without my own schooner was going to present a problem. The Canadian Tourist Bureau in New York didn't even know where Grand Bruit was let alone how to get there.

Finally my travel plans were made. With a map of Newfoundland in my down duck-hunting coat I boarded my first plane in New York. Three planes and an overnight ferry to Port Aux Basques later, I was within fifty miles of my destination. For the next three days I sat in the only motel in the thriving fishing village of Port Aux Basques, while a raging storm made further travel impossible.

The fourth day dawned bright and calm. I boarded the fifty-two foot fishing smack called *Northern Light*. The skipper, Morgan Durnford, who worked for the T.F. Hardy fish company, was going up the coast to collect fish. His second port of call was Grand Bruit.

The little boat hugged the coastline weaving in and out of rock formations. Often we rode inside the breakers. On shore, as far as the eye could see, was rock. With my binoculars I could pick out a few scattered pine trees five feet high and the occasional patch of brown weeds. No roads, no telegraph poles, no buildings of any sort, only a mixture of sky, rock, and water. We bobbed along hour after hour. It is hard to believe how remote these people are, but it was possible a dog could survive and stay pure in such isolation.

As the little boat plowed along, skipper Durnford told me about the water dogs that all fishermen had when they were boys. His father had them and so did his grandfather. As he said, the dogs put a lot of food on the table. The dogs were never trained; they just knew what to do. As retrievers, they brought in the downed birds, but their main job was working in the two-man dory side-by-side with the fishermen. They fished by long lines. There was a hook every yard or so. The line was put out and left on a buoy. Later the fishermen would come back and pull up the line. If upon reaching the surface a fish got off the hook by thrashing about, the dog went overboard and retrieved it. I asked him why the fishermen didn't still use the dog. He thought for a minute and said that they now had better hooks. With that he turned to his compass and studied a rock formation off the bow. I thought to myself that what the Sheep Act didn't finish off a better hook did.

We made our way around an island of rock and headed into the cove, protected and hidden from the sea by a mass of small islands. In the center of the cove was an enormous waterfall; on each side of the falls were about twenty houses painted in pastel colors. This was Grand Bruit, and all the men were waiting on the

dock as we chugged up. It was easy to spot Harold Melbourne — a black dog with a white mark on his chest sat by his side.

These are friendly people; five minutes after landing, I was seated before the finest fish dinner I'd ever eaten. Harold boasted that the fish were not out of the water twenty minutes.

I was introduced to Dan, his six-year-old dog. Dan was part Lab and his father Lassie was one of the last two pure water dogs. Because there were no more water dog females, he had bred Lassie to a Lab to keep the line going the best he could. After lunch we went out to find the old sire. He was sunning on a rock down by the water. He was old and deaf, but as soon as he saw Melbourne pick up a stick and make a throwing motion, he came to life like a Lab puppy.

He looked much like a Labrador in every way. The white on the chest and feet still comes through in some of our Labs today. He was the missing link. His ears were small just like a Lab I used to have. His head was not quite as square as some of today's show stock but you couldn't miss him for a Lab: As old as he was, he had that brainy look. His ears lay flat until they pricked up when he thought Harold was going to throw the stick for him. And when he did throw it, that fifteen-year-old fellow hit the water with style. I had gone to Newfoundland to look for the missing link in the history of the breed, but what I found was a water dog whose ancestors never made the trip back to England. Lassie did not look like today's show ring Lab, but he sure looked like many field trial and hunter's dogs I've seen.

A few other dogs in town were from the same litter of half-water-dog, half-Lab, litter mates of Mr. Melbourne's Dan. They were all black males with white markings on the chest and feet. This white chest spot is allowable in the Labrador standard and still reappears, especially in the original and older strains of Labs today.

On my return trip I stopped off at another fishing village, La Poile, only long enough for the boat to leave some mail. All the fishermen were on the dock and their dogs were with them. They were generally nondescript — yellow, long hair, pointed snouts, much smaller and with no body characteristics of the Lab. I asked one of the fishermen if there were any water dogs in the village. He just shook his head and answered, "There are some up in Grand Bruit." The only way to get to Grand Bruit, or anywhere on the south coast of Newfoundland for that matter, is by sea, which is why the dog has remained pure for so long. I'm glad I made the 2000-mile journey, but it was sad to realize, as my boat took me back to my kind of civilization, that shortly no one would ever see the Newfoundland water dog again . . . they'll be gone.

Today in England the Malmesbury line is now gone, too. The seventy-four-year-old sixth Earl of Malmesbury reminisces about his childhood. He remembers a black Lab that his father's gamekeeper

Harold Melbourne and Lassie

had. It was a wonderful dog as he recalls. When the keeper, one of the best of dog handlers, went off to war to become a gunner, the dog pined away and died. The Earl's father told him that the dog was the last they owned in the Malmesbury line. The year was 1914, exactly 100 years after Colonel Hawker wrote the first words about the St. John's variety: "He's by far the best for any kind of shooting."

Today, the Earl of Malmesbury is the Lord Lieutenant of Hampshire, the Queen's representative for the county. Over his doorway flies her flag and on his doorstep sleeps an old Lab named Dashwood. When asked about his name, the Earl smiled with a twinkle in his eyes and said, "There is a little family secret about that. We've always had Labradors and it is a family tradition that we call them by the maiden name of one of the past Earls' wives. My great, great grandmother was Lady Frances Dashwood, the wife of the second Earl of Malmesbury. Meet Dashwood." The dog stood up, wagged his tail and slowly walked to him.

All through the 1800s there were too few Labs to keep the lines pure, except in the hands of men like Malmesbury and a few other noblemen. Lack of interest for only a few years can destroy a kennel, and this is most likely what happened to bring the Lab close to extinction in the late 1870s. The third Earl of Malmesbury probably recognized this and that is why, late in his life, he gave his dogs to breeders he thought would carry on the line. Shortly after his death his kennel did disappear.

It is not clear from the records what happened to the kennels of the Duke of Buccleuch and Lord Home in the early 1880s. Records show that at the time of Malmesbury's first gifts of dogs in 1882, there were only a few available for breeding in England that were not from Heron Court. One was Sir Frederick Graham's Kielder (1872) and there was the Duke of Hamilton's stud named Sam (1884). A few Labs were held by Lord Wimborne, the Hon. Montagu Guest and C.J. Radclyffe. These dogs plus the six Labs that were given by Malmesbury and divided between Lord Home and the Duke of Buccleuch were the sole foundation, the mainstream of the Labrador that made it to the twentieth century. The Malmesbury-Home-Buccleuch line is the original stock of all black Labs today.

There were two dogs recorded that became imports after this time. One was named Hero and came from Newfoundland. It had belonged to a sea captain, and on his death in 1900 his son wanted to find a home for him. Hon. D.H. Cairne bought him for a small sum. The dog was a real "water dog" but untrained. He had a very coarse coat. The other dog was Stranger, which was bought in 1908 by Mr. W. Steuart Mensies in Norway. He saw the dog on the quay in Trondhjem. He was told that the mother had been brought over from North America in whelp. He bought the dog and had it

The 6th Earl of Malmesbury with his dog Dashwood, the statue is from Heron Court.

Stranger

shipped to England where it spent six months in quarantine before it could be used at stud. He, too, had a rough coat and was untrained. It's said that he could find game but would stand over it until it was picked up by someone.

These are the only dogs that were imported and used at stud. Actually they came a little late. In no way could they be considered important to the survival of the breed.

By 1900, the Labrador Retriever was well established once again in England. By 1903, the dog was popular enough to be recognized by the Kennel Club, and by 1908 Labradors were already starting to show their superiority in field trials. Throughout the dog's history, each time it was headed for trouble, a benefactor appeared. This time it was Hon. Arthur Holland-Hibbert, who later became the third Viscount Knutsford. In 1884, he bought his first Labrador pup, Sybil, with bloodlines from Kielder. Sybil was bred to a dog from the Malmesbury line, and that was the beginning of Knutsford's famous Munden kennel.

Viscount Knutsford

Viscount Knutsford became a great supporter of the Labrador. Through his efforts, the dog became popular and was finally recognized in 1903 by the Kennel Club as a separate breed and was given a place in the Kennel Club show. Two of his Munden dogs won awards that day. In the following year, Labradors made their first appearance in British field trials. Munden Singles was entered by Lord Knutsford, and although she did not do well that year, she did win a certificate of merit the following year in the International Gundog League's trial. In 1907, she took fourth place in the Kennel Club trials. Not only a fine hunter, Munden Singles was a handsome specimen of a dog and her progeny were outstanding in field trials. When she died in 1910 at the age of 13, she achieved the unique distinction of being stuffed and displayed as a typical specimen of her breed in the Natural History Museum in Kensington.

Early British Champions

The first Labrador to achieve real distinction in field trials was Major Maurice Portal's Flapper. In 1906, he placed second in the International Gundog League's trial and also second at the Kennel Club trial. In 1907, Flapper became a field trial champion and won the Kennel Club's All-Age Stake. Second and third place were also won by Labradors — the dog was on its way.

In 1911, another dog of great note came on the scene, Peter of Faskally, owned by Archibald Buttler. He won the International Gundog League's Championship stake, a new event in which entries were limited to dogs that had excelled in trials that year and were "contestants of the highest class." Peter's success was especially noteworthy because his handler used an entirely revolutionary method in working the dog. His system was based on methods used in training Sheep dogs, namely hand signals and whistle. Buttler's phenomenal success with this new system prompted many other retriever owners to use the same method. They achieved no

Flapper

LES ANDERSON JR.

Lord Knutsford's Munden Dogs

success with it and concluded that Mr. Buttler was a dog training genius with a profound understanding of the Labrador's mentality. His system was not tried again for almost twenty years, until Dave Elliot, a Scottish gamekeeper, used it in England and then introduced it into the United States in 1934.

Lord Knutsford had many dogs that appeared in the pedigrees of the important lines in the show ring and in field trials from the time of recognition in 1903 until the start of World War I in 1914. A few of the great old names were Munden Sixty, Munden Singles, and Munden Sovereign, a dog highly prized because of his perfect physical structure.

The war years all but destroyed many of the kennels in England and Lord Knutsford's Munden kennel became practically extinct. After the war he started again with a puppy named Munden Scarcity given to him by Lorna Countess Howe. He established a strong line once again with this dog. During the post-war years, Knutsford was very active in the Labrador Retriever Club. He was its first Chairman, a position he held from 1916 until his death in 1935. Lord Knutsford was a brilliant shot and in his seventy-ninth year was still running his own dogs in field trials. It seems that his favorite outing was the annual Gamekeepers' Stake held at Idsworth. His speech each year at the luncheon was eagerly awaited. While giving this speech in 1935 that he collapsed and died.

His very good friend Lorna Countess Howe, became Chairman of the Labrador Club upon the passing of Lord Knutsford. In her book, *The Popular Labrador Retriever*, she wrote this about him:

> To him the Labrador breed and all those who love it owe a debt of gratitude which can never be repaid. The most we can do is to try to keep the breed as he would have wished it to be — a dual purpose dog, not one from which the working and Show bench types are so entirely different as in so many breeds today.
>
> There is at the present time some danger of this. Let us beware — before it is too late. The great dogs of the past have so ably upheld both beauty and brains that we should try to keep this very high standard. What has been done can surely be maintained. I remember so well Lord Knutsford saying to me, not once but many times, that he was so proud that the Labrador had beauty and brains, and that surely people who wanted purely show dogs could seek another breed and not divide the Labrador into what might virtually be classified as dogs which were of practical use out shooting for collecting game and dogs which were purely knights of the show bench. The Labrador has proved so decisively that he can do both that it is up to those who love the breed and have its interest deeply at heart to see that this high reputation is maintained.

YELLOW LABRADOR WITH MALLARD
Les Anderson Jr.

There could be no more suitable memorial to Lord Knutsford than this, an objective he had so close to his heart.

Though Lord Knutsford was known as a great friend of the Lab, perhaps the greatest benefactor was the Countess herself. Lady Howe started working with Labradors in 1913 and was very active, along with Lord Knutsford, in organizing and started the Labrador Club in 1916. For nineteen years she was the Hon. Secretary of the Club. In 1935, when Knutsford died, she became the Chairman, a post she held until her death in 1961.

A past Chairman of the club, M. C. W. Gilliat, remembers Lady Howe's knowledge, training ability, and unequalled record of winners and placers in the Retriever Championship Stake, the highest British Retriever stake:

Lord Knutsford, the first president of the British Labrador Club.

1921 2nd, Dual Ch. Banchory Sunspeck
1922 3rd, Dual Ch. Banchory Sunspeck
1924 3rd, F.T.Ch. Balmuto Jock
1925 3rd, F.T.Ch. Balmuto Jock
1926 1st, F.T.Ch. Balmuto Jock
1927 2nd F.T.Ch. Banchory Tern
1927 3rd, F.T.Ch. Balmuto Jock
1928 1st, F.T.Ch. Balmuto Jock
1929 1st, F.T.Ch. Balmuto Jock
1930 2nd, F.T.Ch. Banchory Becky
1930 3rd, F.T.Ch. Bryngarw Flute
1931 2nd, F.T.Ch. Banchory Becky
1932 2nd, F.T.Ch. Banchory Donald
1933 2nd, Dual Ch. Banchory Painter
1934 2nd, F.T.Ch. Banchory Smiler
1935 2nd, F.T.Ch. Banchory Painter
1936 1st, F.T.Ch. Banchory Hewildo

In her book, Lady Howe wrote "Whilst I am writing about training and teaching to train I cannot leave out my Dual Ch. Banchory Bolo. I think it is only fair to such a great Labrador that he should be paid tribute to and be made known as a dog who could train and handle human beings, because through my intimate knowledge and personal devotion to him I certainly learnt more from him than he did from me."

Dual Champion Banchory Bolo became one of the most important dogs of this era. Lady Howe was a staunch believer in the dual purpose dog and her Bolo was the first to achieve this mark.

Bolo came to Lady Howe in 1918, when he was a bit more than two years old. Heartbroken about the loss of her first Labrador, Scandal of Glynn, she had decided to find the only male pup that Scandal had sired. When finally found, he'd been through sev-

Lorna Countess Howe with Lady Hill Wood, a Buccleuch, who became the third president of the British Lab Club.

Lorna Countess Howe, the second president
of the British Lab Club.

eral trainers and all had given up on him. (Lady Howe said that in
human terms "he had a really bad police record.") She was offered
the dog for nothing with the proviso that if she did not want him
later on, he should be destroyed. In his book, *Dogs You'd Like To
Meet*, Roland John, a popular dog writer of the 1930s, picks up the
story from there.

Bolo arrives Liverpool Street eleven-five.

Mrs. Quintin Dick (Lady Howe's name by former marriage) looked at her watch and saw that there was just time to
motor over to the great London railway terminus and meet the
dog: the "wild, unmanageable, stupid dog" whom nobody
wanted, despite his wonderful pedigree. His first owner had
given him away, because he had come back from some trainers of field-dogs with an evil temper which seemed to be hope-
less in one who had been bred for sport. He had in
consequence been presented as a free gift to one who er-
roneously thought he could "make something of him." This
owner had now offered to give him away again, and said that if
Mrs. Quintin Dick did not like him she was free to have him
destroyed.

And here he was at Liverpool Street Station, a Labrador
Retriever, a rebel and failure. On his nose and in his ears were
sores; his coat was unkempt, and when he was spoken to, even
in a kindly way, he growled in a surly and ill-tempered manner.
But for his muzzle it looked as if there might be serious trouble
in getting him into the motor-car, with grievous damage to
those who touched him.

Mrs. Quintin Dick looked at him dubiously. To be sure he
was of good birth, but his temper! Should he be sent back, or
should she have him destroyed immediately? A decision had
to be made quickly, and Bolo's attitude was not helpful: He did
not seem to care whether he lived or died. He looked so mis-
erable and seemed so unhappy that she was inclined to take a
risk and try to put a little sunshine into his life.

Mrs. Quintin Dick made her decision. She resolved that
she would take him down to the Banchory kennels and give
him a chance of life and happiness.

Bolo made a bad start in his new home. He always started
badly. As soon as he arrived he was taken into a spacious
room and the muzzle and chain were taken off him. After a
few minutes of liberty he was called, but refused to come. Offers of food did not appeal to him and when an effort was
made to catch him he dodged. He seemed to suspect and hate
every one in human form, and it was more than an hour before
he could be caught, when he was placed in a kennel. Some

Bolo had to be trained not to chase rabbits.

days later he was let loose out-of-doors, and again proved ill-tempered and refractory, and for two hours he eluded recapture.

Then something happened which changed the world for Bolo. His physical strength left him and he became seriously ill. No longer was he the rampant, self-sufficient Tartar of the past, but a quiet, helpless dependent, very near to death. During those days he was always gentle and responsive to kindness, and as he was nursed back to strength by Mrs. Quintin Dick he became devoted to her. At last he seemed to have found some one whom he could trust; some one who understood him and was ready to accept him for what he was. When he recovered his health he was always at her side, and it seemed possible to hope that his life would henceforth be one of serene peace and unalloyed happiness.

Autumn had now come and the guns were out, so that his mistress took Bolo out with her one day in order to see how he shaped as a sporting dog. There were many things for which he had to thank his forbears. He had inherited a natural love of retrieving, an excellent nose, and a perfect mouth. Bolo had plenty of dash. If it had been a rabbit-shoot he would have been an immensely popular dog, but it was apparent that he needed no little education in the direction of field-work with birds. Hares and rabbits had for him an attraction which was magnetic and dismaying, and he did not seem to understand that his energy and enthusiasm in coursing them was misdirected zeal.

So that it was a question of applying all the arts of training to the making of Bolo. He had the right stuff in him, but a lot of wrong stuff mixed with it needed weeding out. How was it to be done? By beating him? A moment's reflection was enough to show that this was the wrong way, for there were signs that Bolo's nature had been turned sour by chastisement, and, apart from the obvious cruelty of it, there was a danger that he might revert to his former wildness if he were so mishandled. Therefore, the rod was spared and the dog not spoiled.

Everything was going well, he was taking to his training and then it happened on the evening before the field trials took place and caused Bolo to behave like a volcano in eruption. He was always haunted by the demon of fear, and now he was at its mercy. Not paralysed into inaction but precipitated into reckless, unreasoning flight from the terror which had almost ruined his life.

This sudden breaking-back to his past was caused by a stable-boy, who cracked a heavy whip close to Bolo. What recollections it aroused in the mind of this sensitive dog may well

Banchory Bolo

Britain's outstanding sporting artist, Ward Binks, painted many of Lorna Countess Howe's dogs.

62

BANCHORY BOLO *Ward Binks*

Banchory Bob

Banchory Bolo

be imagined, for he lost all control over himself and made a lightning dash for the gateway. The gate was closed and was high, with iron spikes at the top; but Bolo, under the impelling influence of fear, lost all caution and sprang up with a tremendous leap. In a panic he fled.

Countess Howe finished the story in her book.

"Finally at midnight I gave up the search for him and went to my room, leaving the front door open. At 5 a.m. Bolo came into my room and got into his basket. When I was about to go to my bath an hour later I was horrified to see big splashes of blood on the floor. On examining Bolo I found he had two very deep wounds on his chest, a tear three inches long in his groin and his hind leg and hock torn so badly that the bone was visible. I was urged to have him destroyed but this I could not do. The nearest vet lived eight miles away and there was no telephone, so with the kennelman I put twenty-three stitches into Bolo. He was so good and lay perfectly still until it was all finished."

Once again Bolo became Lady Howe's patient. He seemed to understand that he was safe from harm with her. Field trials were out of the question that year, but the following fall he took a prize in his very first event. Within the next few weeks he accomplished the impossible by winning two first places and becoming a champion. He fared equally as well on the show bench and became the first Labrador to earn the title of Dual Champion.

Bolo was not used at stud often because he was the constant companion of Lady Howe, but in every litter he produced either a show or field trial champion. The *Field* wrote of Bolo: "If ever evidence were needed of the character of a great dog, and of his influence on the generations following him, it was to be found at the Retriever Championship Trial held at Idsworth December, 1932. Out of fourteen dogs that gained prizes eight were descended from Banchory Bolo."

Bolo's ancestry traces directly back to the Malmesbury kennels at Heron Court through Malmesbury Tramp (1878) and Malmesbury Juno (1878) who whelped Buccleuch's Avon (1885). The line goes directly through Lord Knutsford's Munden Sixty (1897) to the first great field trial champion Peter of Faskally (1908) to Bolo's sire Scandal of Glynn and then to Dual Champion Banchory Bolo.

In the *Labrador Stud Book*, C. Mackay Sanderson records that this line started forty years earlier with Malmesbury's Tramp and culminated in Banchory Bolo. But forty years is only the recorded period; unrecorded, the line goes back via Malmesbury at Heron Court for a little over a century on British soil.

THE OLD DOG *Herb Strasser*

The Lab in America

The Labrador Retriever's return trip across the Atlantic took more than 100 years. Although the American sportsman of the nineteenth century was dependent on the English for his dog stock, hunting techniques, and training methods, he soon Americanized them. Hunting did not start in America as a sport, but rather as a survival technique, and hunting with dogs predated the American Revolution.

By the mid-1800s, however, the country was more settled and had more time for sport. In the latter half of the century the pointing breeds became well established; the English Setter was the most popular followed closely by another English dog, the Pointer. With the advent of the breech load gun, upland and waterfowl hunting became a sport in which the average man could indulge. Unlike England, where hunting and trout and salmon fishing were for the gentry, hunting was not restricted to the wealthy in America; it would not have been tolerated by America's budding democratic principles. Interestingly, almost from the beginning of the shooting sports in America, the hunter who carried a fine imported English shotgun could not be distinguished by his dress from the fellow who carried a seven-dollar mail order variety.

Americans like to think of their sport as having the same tradition and heritage as the English, but although the end product was the same — game on the table — the sports were quite different. Through the latter part of the nineteenth and the early twentieth

century, American sportsmen developed setters and pointers to handle hunting in big country and heavy covers. Dogs could go all day in New England mountain covers or Pennsylvania rolling country, or go wide in Georgia flat land, and if need be, retrieve the game as well as find it. What the British refer to as "rough hunting" was a picnic compared to America's. The driven bird shoot was unnatural to our concept of shooting sports. At first glance, it was obvious that the American sport, because of our bigness, birds, cover, and land, called for a different kind of dog work.

Wherever sporting men gather, someone will eventually say, "My dog's better than yours" or words to that effect, and comparisons sparked the first dog trial in America; it was held in Memphis in 1874 for the pointing breeds. The first dog show was that same year. But retrievers were rarely viewed on the American scene.

On the Maryland shore fishermen and waterfowl hunters had developed a water dog for their specific needs. That all started in 1807 with the shipwreck of the brig *Canton* on its way to Poole, England. The two Newfoundland pups on board, possibly on their way to the second Earl of Malmesbury in Poole, are credited with being the foundation stock for the Chesapeake Bay Ducking Dog, recognized by the American Kennel Club in 1878 as the Chesapeake Bay Retriever. Just after the Civil War, another group of sportsmen in the Midwest developed a dog that became known as the American Water Spaniel. It seems to have come from the mixture of the now extinct English Water Spaniel, the Curly-Coated Retriever and a dash of Irish and Sussex Spaniels. Where they came across all these retrievers is not clear, but both home-made varieties were excellent for their specific jobs. The problem was that not many hunters felt the need for a retriever, so with both breeds we're only talking about a handful of dogs.

Reviewing the American hunting situation between the 1880s and 1930s, when the Labrador was becoming the Englishman's most popular shooting dog, the American sportsman understandably took little interest in the Labrador. What could the Labrador do for him that his own American dogs could not do? In a time when game was abundant, it was more important to the sportsman to find the game and to shoot it than to retrieve it. It just was not good management to keep a dog at heel and use the second dog only to retrieve. If need be, it made more sense for the second dog to be another pointing dog that was also broken to retrieve. That way the odds were twice as good of finding birds and collecting downed game, too.

The British never utilized the Labrador as a waterfowl dog as the Chessie was used, or as a game finder like the Springer Spaniel; two skills in which the Lab would later prove superior. There were other reasons for the sudden interest in the Lab in the 1920s and 1930s in the United States.

Another Trip across the Atlantic

The Lab was recognized in England by the Kennel Club in 1903, but it was not until 1917 that the first Lab was registered in the American Kennel Club. It was owned by Charles G. Meyer of New York. Brocklehirst Floss was a black bitch from Scotland, and most of her breeding was from the Munden kennels of Lord Knutsford. It didn't really mean much. Ten years later, in 1927, there were still only twenty-three retrievers of all kinds registered with the AKC; Chessies, Labs, Curly-Coated, Flat-Coated, and Goldens were all lumped together under the heading of "Retrievers."

In 1928, the AKC's magazine *American Kennel Gazette* ran a charming article titled "Meet The Labrador Retriever" by Dr. G. H. Monro-Home, one of the first about the Lab printed in this country.

That the Labrador is the most popular variety of retriever in the shooting field in England at the present time goes without saying when one scans the results of the retriever field trials held in the autumn of each year.

It is often to be wondered at, that this popularity has not "crossed the pond" to our friends in America, a probable reason being that setters and pointers in America are so often trained to carry out the dual duty of finding the game *before* it is shot and again *after* it is shot. . . .

What do we look for at work? First and foremost absolute obedience to word, whistle, or sign from the handler, perfectly steady at heel on all occasions, to birds rising, to fur, to birds dropping to the gun, a no-slip dog in *every* sense of the word. At the same time a dog—when shooting is going on—that shows keenness and interest in its work; be "on its toes"; alert at all times to watch the fall of a bird, be quick at going out, on command, to retrieve; show aptitude to get the lay of things, quarter its ground in a methodical way, a good nose well kept down when once the trail has been found, perseverance in sticking to a scent and following it up, boldness in the thickest of cover and in water, a clean delivery, at a gallop, right to hand, when the quest has been found, with a good tender mouth to complete the performance.

Let me illustrate what is wanted in the field by giving you a short description of a day. With such a dog as I have tried to describe—and my gun comes more ready than my pen—the keen "sport," in England, goes forth equipped with gun and cartridges . . .

The corn has all been gathered, the stubble fields are bare; potato fields and "roots"—turnips, mangold wurzels and sugar beet affording good cover—are handy to them. A plan of campaign has been thought out before the start. Partridges are their quarry. And so to the stubble fields first. The "guns" spread themselves out in line, and the good setter Nell is let go

MALLARDS COMING IN *A. Lassell Ripley*

with the wind to favor her "scent."

Every inch of ground is quartered backwards and forwards to the signal of her handler.

A hare springs up. But Nell knows her work, and ignores it. The retriever, Dan, a black Labrador, sticks firmly at heel, and a cock of his ears alone shows he has seen it.

Nell has resumed her quest. Suddenly, realizing there is something in the wind, she "steadies" in her pace and comes to a "dead point." This gives the "guns" plenty of time to come up to the "covey," which rises some twenty yards away in front of a hedge.

Two birds are dropped by the shots; the second one legs it for all it is worth to the hedge. Nell sits tight. And Dan, the retriever, is called upon to do *his* part. Not an inch does he move until told to go, and then he is off at the gallop, with a head full of brains and not sawdust!

He has taken in everything from the moment the first barrel was fired. He has marked the fall of the "runner," and with nose close to the trail is off to the hedge; through it without a thought to the briars and thorns which impede his way; into the ditch on the far side; up it for fifty yards; then to the field of potatoes where, but for a moment, he hesitates, for he has overrun the scent.

He quickly casts around; again picks up the trail; and now, with nose well down, is up to the speeding wounded bird in a few more strides; gathers it as he goes, and is around and back, at the gallop, to his proud master by the shortest and quickest route he can choose; delivers the goods to hand with a satisfied wag of the tail and a look as much as to say, "You never would have got that bird if it hadn't been for me."

Given a pat of appreciation, he is told to go and get the other bird which fell dead. He does so with the same promptness, and the same expression of delight and satisfaction on his return.

What a pleasure, what an addition to a good day's shooting, it is to see a well-trained retriever recover his birds! Dan covers himself with glory this day — it's his day out. He has not forgotten those early lessons so deeply impressed upon him in the comparatively weary and unexciting hours of puppyhood, restraining cords and dummies.

Many a tale could be told of what retrievers have done and the finds they have made. Every old "sport" can roll it out when the spirit moves him — and the "spirit" must be good! — of the best performance of the "very best dog he ever had." I think of one.

We were shooting Blue Rock pigeons on the rocky coast of Caithness. These birds frequent the numerous caves found there on the sheer precipices above the sea, leaving the caves in the morning, and returning again in the evening.

The easiest way to make a "bag" is to shoot from a boat at the mouth of the cave, but this is not always procurable and the sea may often be rough.

We did it from a projecting promontory which jutted out to sea in front of the cave, and got the birds as they were coming in. But strategy and a good "eye" were required to drop the birds on the promontory, otherwise they fell in the sea below, where no man could climb down to recover them.

I had put in a good hour's sport, and my little bitch had succeeded in collecting seven off the promontory for me. There were two down below in the sea, and Nell knew they were there. What was to be done?

I consulted my worthy henchman, a Scotch "keeper," who promptly replied it would be an "awful pity" to leave them, and suggested we should borrow a tethering rope from the nearest "croft," and with it lower the "wee bitch" down to the sea and see what she would do.

The rope was got, made fast to Nell, and we lowered her some 50 feet. She soon had the first in her mouth, and was pulled safely up, bird and all. Having done it once, she was only too keen to go down again with equal success. Truly a perfect retrieve up to hand.

But I hear a reader whisper that's a "marine" yarn. It was connected with the sea, but nevertheless it is true.

Five years later, the author sold Drinkstone Pons of Wingen to Jay F. Carlisle, which started one of the early important kennels in America. Dr. Monro-Home's dogs took best of opposite sex in the first U.S. show in 1933 and the best in show and winners in 1934.

The Lab's return to North America was actually part of a fad, a whim of the times. During the Roaring Twenties—the jazz era, the flapper society, the time of the Charleston, F. Scott Fitzgerald, and good Scotch whiskey—wealthy Americans were fascinated by the royalty of Europe. American wealth could buy anything except an official social order such as in England and Scotland. The "in" thing of the times was to have British aristocracy amongst one's friends. Nothing could be more elegant than an invitation to shoot driven grouse on the Scottish moors.

During the twenties, Americans literally imported the Scottish sport of pass shooting. Clubs like the Blooming Grove Club in Pennsylvania and the Wyandanch Club on Long Island were organized. The clubs had regular recruiters who brought in young Scottish gamekeepers, and many wealthy families turned their estates into Scottish shooting preserves. They bought guns from the finest London houses and dogs from British kennels, and raised their own

Queen Elizabeth II. The Queen keeps the largest kennel of Labradors in England today.

The Roaring Twenties

King George VI

American Shoots in the Twenties

game birds at great expense. Unlike the British Isles, where game birds were in abundance, the American supply was no way adequate for a driven shoot. It is estimated that 100,000 birds were raised on these estates to supplement the natural game.

Wealthy sportsmen went to all this trouble and expense for many reasons. They enjoyed their shooting in Scotland and wanted to enjoy the sport at home. For the most part hunting on the American scene was a very rough and "homespun" sport. In the leading pointing dog trials of the day the participants could be financiers or farmers; elegance was not one of the main attractions of the shooting sports in America. Scottish style shooting had its status symbols and one of them was the Labrador Retriever. For more than 100 years the dog was seen only in aristocratic circles in England; Kings George V and VI had owned Labradors. There would develop a certain snob appeal in importing and running Labradors.

It must be noted that at this time the Labrador had no other hunting skills than the jobs the British set for him: to work from heel, to mark game down, and to track and retrieve it. If these were the only jobs the Lab could have learned, he would not have survived in America because there was little call for a strictly land retriever. But before long the Lab proved as good a "springer" of game as the Springer Spaniel and a better water retriever than the specialist, the Chesapeake Bay Retriever. The Lab's success in America is a tribute to the dog himself rather than to his importer.

The new sport of Scottish style shooting in the 1920s was essentially a theatrical production in which the birds, the dogs, and the gamekeepers were the actors and the props. During the late 1920s and early 1930s, Robert Goelet "produced" Scottish shoots at his Glenmere estate in Chester, N.Y. The most spectacular "act" was the manufactured pass-shooting. On cue, the birds would appear overhead, giving just as fine shooting as one could get in Scotland. The first American field trial came a few years later on this Glenmere estate. Jim Cowie, one of the early Scottish gamekeepers who handled dogs for the shooting guests at Glenmere, suggests that the field trials were a by-product of these shoots.

Over 10,000 game birds were raised each year to supplement the natural game on the Goelet property, but the shooting conditions in Chester, New York were nothing like Scotland, so they had to be created. Birds were planted for walk-up hunting, what the British call "rough shooting." In traditional British pass-shooting, the birds were driven over the guns. In Scotland, a line of beaters walked across the land, pushing the birds ahead of them and finally forcing the birds to fly over the guns. In Chester, this was simulated by having ten or more "hidden" bird boys, working from gullies in the fields, throwing birds as fast as they could towards the advancing guns. The hunters used the cover in the fields in the regular walk-up manner and then had the chance to pass-shoot as they

In the early 1930s the gamekeepers got together to help each other train the dogs.

Left to right:
Dave Elliot,
    trainer for Jay Carlisle
Dog food salesman, worker
Billy Gladwin,
    trainer for Mrs. Moffatt
Jack Monroe,
    trainer for Robert Goelet
Leon Bond,
    trainer for Dr. Millbank
Ernest Wells,
    trainer for Dave Wagstaff
Alex Cummings,
    one of the old time gamekeepers
Rustle Murdock,
    trainer for Gould Remick
Laurence McQueen,
    trainer for W. K. Dick
Jasper Briggs,
    trainer for W. Averell Harriman
Tom Briggs,
    trainer and gamekeeper for W. A. Harriman

approached the area where the bird boys simulated driven conditions. Driven flight was also produced with a tower shoot. As many as thirty guns would be placed in a 300 to 400 yard circle around the tower. Hundreds of birds would be released a few at a time, and the guns would go to work. At the height of this event there was bedlam, and without dogs to retrieve the game it would have been an impossible task.

Jim Cowie recalls some of the elegance and pageantry of these weekend extravaganzas on the nearby Goelet estate. The cast of characters arrived late on Friday in their chauffeur-driven cars. The thirty or so guests would all stay in the main house. Jim would bring the dogs from the Harriman estate to help keeper Golin Macfarlane. Together, they gave the guests much variety. They might start with a tower shoot in the morning. After lunch it might be a walk-up, where small groups would hunt behind the dogs. There were plenty of birds planted out in the field plus the birds that managed to escape the barrage of the tower shoot. There would be a formal dinner that evening. The next day might start with pass-shooting at mallards that were trained to fly from the enclosed eating area on a hill to a pond below. After lunch they might have a walk-up and then a driven flight of pheasants over the guns. The day's gunning would be followed by a fine dinner and party.

The handlers had their dinner at the keeper's house and as Jim tells it, "There was always a few bottles sent down from the big house and many a good time we had . . . lying about our dogs . . . singing a few Scottish songs, and if it was really a good party somebody always tried to do a fling.

"All the gamekeepers stuck close together. We were all friends and helped each other. Once field trials started we trained together and had practice trials to help each other. The dog was the best part of our job."

The Scottish Gamekeepers

Jasper Briggs in the early thirties

Jim Cowie today

Tom Briggs was one of the first Scottish gamekeepers brought over to this country. He came to work for W. Averell Harriman in 1913. His job was to manage the estate, raise about 10,000 game birds — both pheasant for their upland preserve and ducks for the flighted mallard shoot — and to train the dozen or so pointing dogs. His son Jasper was just a young boy when the first Labrador, Peggy of Shipton, was brought to the Harriman estate from England. Through his teens, Jasper trained and worked the dogs along with his father. Today, Jasper is ready to retire from the shooting preserve business that he has been running for the last thirty years. He speaks with great respect and affection for Averell Harriman. Harriman, now in his ninetieth year, talks about Jasper as if he were still a teenager running the dogs; the admiration between them is mutual. But, as Jasper says, "The relationship between the owners of the estate and the keepers was much the same as it had been in the aristocratic society of Scotland. They were up here (he raised his hand over his head) and the keepers and dog handlers were down here (he lowered his hand to the floor)."

Jim Cowie recalled one incident when the separation of owners and handlers caused a problem. It was at a field trial on Long Island in the late 1930s. As Jim explained it, there were a lot of new people in the game. Everyone was staying at a hotel that served as the field trial headquarters. The handlers had rooms in the cottages and the owners stayed in the main building. At dinner time, it was announced that the handlers would have to eat in the kitchen. Cowie got up and announced to all the handlers, "OK, boys! Let's go. That's the end of the trial." Jim chuckled and added, "They never let us get as far as the door. And that was the last time there was ever one place for the owners and another place for the handlers. That was the end of it!"

Jim Cowie was working for Tom Briggs at the time of the first licensed field trial in 1931. He recalls that the pond was frozen, prohibiting any water tests. He started to laugh. "In those days do you know what the water work was? I'll tell you. You took your dog into a blind set up on the edge of a pond, a man threw a duck as far as he could into the open water and the dog was sent to get it. He only had to do one retrieve and swim no further than a man could throw the duck. The Chesapeake people started their trials just after the Labs did and we saw some real water work. The Chessies skunked our Labs. We had to start some serious training. We did and the Labs were soon beating the Chessies at their own game."

Until this time, the Lab had been in the hands of a few wealthy sportsmen. Now it would become the hunter's dog. Even the boys on the Eastern shore began to trade their Chessies for Labs. What might have spelled extinction for the Lab in America instead ensured its future. As only a land retriever the Lab had little future in America. As a waterfowl dog, by beating the Chesapeake, he

75

started to make his mark with the hunter.

A report of the 1933 Chesapeake trial held on the Charles Lawrence estate in *Popular Dogs* Magazine outlines the difficulty of the water work in those days, but for today's dog it would not amount to much of a test.

> The dog and his handler remain behind the blind while the boatmen out in the water release the ducks and shoot them as they fly by. The handler then shoots a blank after which he orders his dog out to retrieve. The dog jumps immediately into the water, goes through the decoys and the live ducks swimming about, marks his wounded bird and brings it in, placing it in his handler's hand. This constitutes the first test which as a rule eliminates several contenders.
>
> The second test includes a swim across the water and back, the ducks being shot on the far shore and the dog being required to mark the bird from a greater distance, swim over, get it in his mouth and swim back to hand.

According to Cowie, the Labrador Retriever trials were started because of the work of Franklin B. Lord, a prominent New York lawyer. He was the moving force behind a small group who organized the Labrador Retriever Club and had the trial licensed by the AKC. The group had plenty of precedent for the first trial, for the Scottish Club had been running trials more than twenty years.

First American Lab Trials

The first trial was under the management of the George F. Foley Dog Show Organization of Philadelphia. Although Foley suggested that they run the event on a weekend to attract a gallery, the club's spokesman, Mr. Lord, wanted no gallery; the trials would be held strictly for the participants' own amusement. So the 21st of December, 1931, a Monday, was chosen.

There were no specific tests in those first trials, as there are today. The dog work came naturally from the shooting situations. The procedure was the same used in the early British trials, basically walk-up shoots. The line consisted of two dogs with their handlers, four guns, and the two judges. Each dog would get two opportunities to retrieve. As both Jasper Briggs and Jim Cowie tell it, the line walked a specific pattern. There were plenty of birds out in the field so that there was always a chance of flushing a few birds. When a bird was put up and the guns dropped it, the line would stop. The judge would call the number of the dog that was to make the retrieve. As Cowie explains, "In those days we didn't teach the dog to mark as it is done today. Most of the time in the walking-up, the dog at heel never saw the bird fly or where it landed. Often the shooting took place in high grass cover. The technique was to send the dog downwind and he'd pick up the scent and work out the problem. If the first dog didn't come back with the bird the second dog was sent for that same bird."

On a typical shooting day, much the same procedure took place. The line would consist of six or so hunters and two dogs with handlers. The line would follow a specific course, flushing birds as they came across them in the field. Although the British field trials had walk-ups, they did not have them in the typical day's shoot.

Jasper Briggs recalls that the guns would hunt through the "staged" driven pass-shooting and go on with walk-up shooting. Then the next group of hunters would swing in towards the area of pass-shooting and take their turn at it. This same procedure was used in the dog trials. The course was specific. The line would go towards the pass-shooting area. For trials there would only be two bird boys. When the line was 100 yards ahead of the shooting area, each bird boy would throw one bird. The guns would kill the birds, but if a bird was not hit, another bird was thrown. When both birds were down, the judge called for a dog to retrieve. Whether the dog had to retrieve both birds or just one was up to the judge; however, if the dog flushed a third bird while he was hunting up a downed bird, that flushed bird, if shot by the guns, was also the dog's responsibility. He had to retrieve his flushed bird after he found and delivered the downed bird.

Each dog was given a chance at two birds, then the next two dogs and their handlers were brought to the line. They would repeat the same procedure, possibly covering a little different cover in the walk-up area, and then they would swing into the "driven pass-shooting area." All day, groups would file by the "pass-shooting."

Both Briggs and Cowie recall that bird boxes were first used in 1935. A bird was loaded into the box, which had a trap door operated with a long string. It was spring-loaded so when the door was opened the bird was catapulted into the air. The trial line and the two dogs "hunted" up to this area, and the action began when the judge called for the strings to be pulled and birds released. Cowie remembers that the exception to this was at Caumsett, the Marshall Field estate on Long Island. The birds were so abundant there that the boxes were not needed; they could even have a small driven shoot, using the bird boys as beaters.

Walk-ups were eliminated and thrown birds were first used about 1938. Cowie suggests that the change occurred because as the number of dogs increased in trials the traditional walk-up became less and less productive and the thrown-bird method proved more efficient. "At first the field trials were a by-product of the shooting," Cowie says. "There were only a few trials a year. Then the trials became a sport unto itself. As more and more people got interested in the dog work and entered their dogs into the trials we had to devise a means of getting more work done. That's when the trials became artificial. By about 1940 the change over was complete. For example, up until that time there was no such thing as a 'no bird.' Now if a dog received a runner, the dog was called off because it would take too long for him to work out the problem. We professional trainers were throwing and shooting birds as part of our training methods. It was a fast way of doing the work and that's why it was incorporated into the field trials. Instead of the line constantly moving to find the birds, the line became stationary and the dogs and birds were brought to it. It became a whole different game. Those first trials were the best."

In the January 2, 1932 issue of *Popular Dogs*, Freeman Lloyd's report provides comprehensive coverage of the first American field trial for Labs.

LABRADOR RETRIEVER CLUB HOLDS COUNTRY'S FIRST TRIALS FOR BREED

On the 8,000 acre Glenmere Court Estate of Robert Goelet took place this country's initial field trials for retrievers when the Labrador Retriever Club held forth on December 21st at Chester, N.Y., under the presidency of Mrs. Marshall Field of Huntington, L.I. Other officers of the club include Mr. Goelet and Franklin B. Lord, vice-presidents, and Wilton Lloyd-Smith, secretary and treasurer. The field stewards were W. A. Harriman, Robert G. McKay and Mr. Goelet; the official guns, Captain Paul A. Curtis, Wadsworth R. Lewis, E. Roland Harriman and Mr. Lloyd-Smith; the judges, David Wagstaff and Dr. Samuel Milbank.

Among the owners of the competing Labradors were Thomas Briggs, W. R. Coe, Mr. and Mrs. Marshall Field, Robert Goelet, Paul Hammond, H. F. Guggenheim, Dr. A. R. Lippert, Clarence H. Mackay, Douglas Marshall and Henry Root Stern. It will be gathered that the above names guarantee that the Labrador Retriever is on the highway to a very distinguished success; such support means much for the future of the breed in the Western Hemisphere.

At this meeting the birds were walked up; that is to say, the advancing line of three guns, gun attendants, the two handlers with dogs at heel, and beaters advanced in line with a gun right, centre and left. Behind strode the gallery, among whom were many women of much social distinction and affluence.

The first and second prizes in the Open All-Age Stake were won by Mrs. Marshall Field's Carl of Boghurst and Odds On. Carl was handled by Mrs. Field, and Odds On taken in hand by the head of the house. In describing the actions of these two imported Labradors bred and primarily broken in England — and kept up to the collar in their work in this country by Douglas Marshall — the field accomplishments of any retriever may be read, marked and inwardly digested by the ordinary dog owner. The education of the Labrador consists of

LABRADOR AND GREENWINGS *Bob Kuhn*

his learning that he is simply a messenger with a nose for finding out things. His is not a hunting partner for finding game for the gun to shoot. His is not to kill, but to carry a wounded bird as if it were the tenderest of creatures. He must keep his eyes wide open and his ears must listen to no sound but the still, small voice of the softest of notes emanating from his handler's buckhorn-pipe. Not a sound disturbs the air save the report of the gun. All is silence and dumb motions.

Now for the last two, three or four tests given to the judges' choices in the All-Age Stake at Glenmere. Imagine a valley with flat marshland well covered with long, dry grass and tussocks. Here and there is small brush, while a few trees of stunted growth relieve the monotony of the stretch. The bogs of the marsh that would have held snipe before the frost set in, were frozen over and cold. The scenting conditions were bad, but perhaps a little better as the sun was going down and whatever heat there was in the earth coming forth to be condensed like vapor when meeting the colder element of the night air. This atmospheric action might explain the mystery of good and bad scent: it's a home-bred formula, nevertheless. Under such conditions Mr. Field was called upon by Messrs. Wagstaff and Milbank to come along with his big, black, rangy Labrador.

Sure enough, an old cock pheasant was soon on the wing, and neatly "pricked" by the gun on the left. Odds On marked the drop, and on being ordered on, soon reached the spot of contact. But then the scent, confound it, was bad although the bird had only just trod the frozen soil. So Odds On had to be described as "slow in picking up the line" — not that any other dog would have better recognized the trail at that moment. But there it was — an apparent deficiency in the dog's olfactory powers was a failure that had to be duly recorded in the book of the public observer. However (referring to the notebook) then comes the cheerful: "At last he hit the line, carried it on and soon nailed the very strong runner. He returned at the gallop from a considerable distance beyond where the pheasant first hit the ground. In his carry Odds On had to twice leap across the small brook. The return was good and his delivery excellent." The dog did all of this work on his own accord. Mr. Field never moved a yard from where Odds On had been ordered on. Save in his slowness in picking up the line of the fallen and running winged bird, the performance had been complete in its efficiency. Odds On had displayed the talents and usefulnesses of his kind.

Now for Carl of Boghurst, son of Corona of Boghurst and Hayler's Livida, the big winner of the Glenmere Court Day; the English-bred Golden Labrador of medium size and hardly as good looking as his kennel companion, Odds On, it was

Labrador Retriever Club Holds Country's First Trials For Breed

On the 8,000 acre Glenmere Court Estate of Robert Goelet took place this country's initial field trials for Retrievers when the Labrador Retriever Club held forth on December 21st at Chester, N. Y., under the presidency of Mrs. Marshall Field of Huntington, L. I. Other officers of the club include Mr. Goelet and Franklin B. Lord, vice-presidents and Wilton

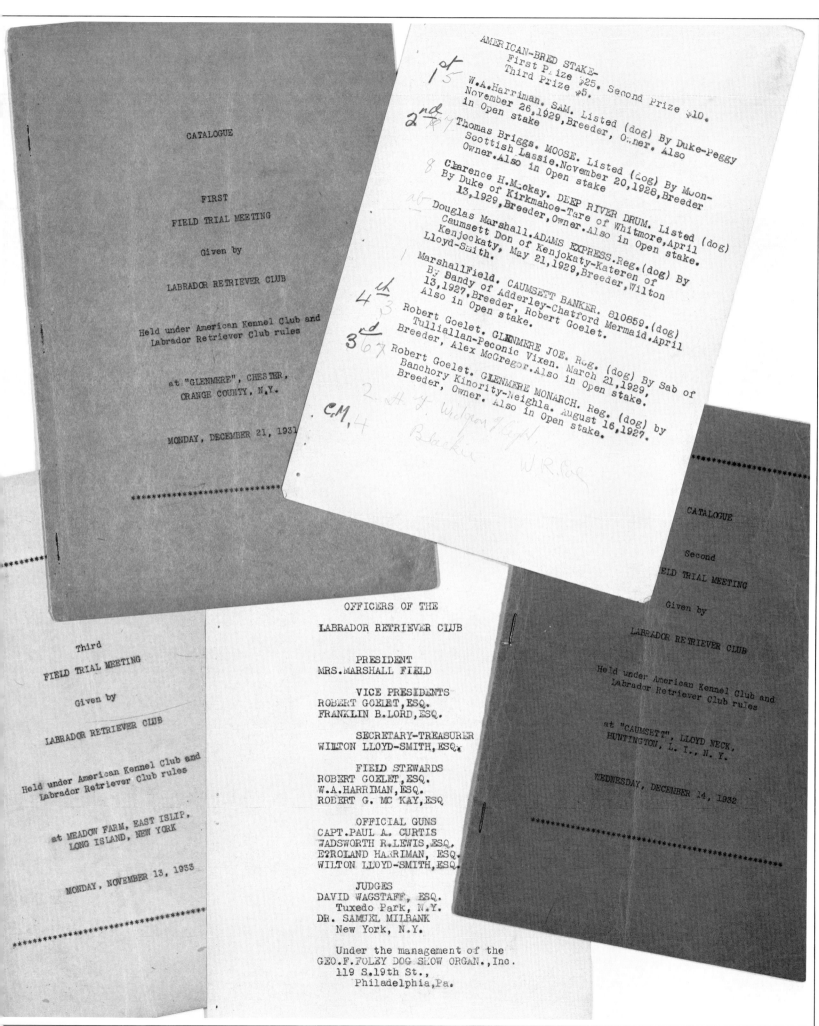

CATALOGUE

FIRST

FIELD TRIAL MEETING

Given by

LABRADOR RETRIEVER CLUB

Held under American Kennel Club and
Labrador Retriever Club rules

at "GLENMERE", CHESTER,
ORANGE COUNTY, N.Y.

MONDAY, DECEMBER 21, 1931

****

AMERICAN-BRED STAKE- Second Prize $10.
First Prize $25. Second Prize $10.
Third Prize $5.

1st 5 W.A.Harriman, SAM. Listed (dog) By Duke-Peggy
November 26,1929,Breeder, Owner. Also
in Open stake

2nd 8 y Thomas Briggs. MOOSE. Listed (dog) By Moon-
Scottish Lassie.November 20,1928,Breeder
Owner.Also in Open stake

8 Clarence H.Mackay. DEEP RIVER DRUM. Listed (dog)
By Duke of Kirkmahoe-Tare of Whitmore,April
13,1929,Breeder,Owner.Also in Open stake.

ab Douglas Marshall.ADAMS EXPRESS.Reg.(dog) By
Caumsett Don of Kenjokaty-Kateren of
Kenjockaty, May 21,1929,Breeder,Wilton
Lloyd-Smith.

1 MarshallField. CAUMSETT BANKER. 810859.(dog)
By Bandy of Adderley-Chatford Mermaid.April
13,1927,Breeder, Robert Goelet.
Also in Open stake.

4th 3 Robert Goelet. GLENMERE JOE. Reg. (dog) By Sab of
Tulliallan-Peconic Vixen. March 21,1929,
Breeder, Alex McGregor.Also in Open stake.

3rd 6 y Robert Goelet. GLENMERE MONARCH. Reg. (dog) by
Banchory Kinority-Neighla. August 16,1927,
Breeder, Owner. Also in Open stake.

CM,4   2.A.y. Widgeon/Capt.
         Blackie   W.R.Fol

Third

FIELD TRIAL MEETING

Given by

LABRADOR RETRIEVER CLUB

Held under American Kennel Club and
Labrador Retriever Club rules

at MEADOW FARM, EAST ISLIP,
LONG ISLAND, NEW YORK

MONDAY, NOVEMBER 13, 1933

****

OFFICERS OF THE

LABRADOR RETRIEVER CLUB

PRESIDENT
MRS.MARSHALL FIELD

VICE PRESIDENTS
ROBERT GOELET,ESQ.
FRANKLIN B.LORD,ESQ.

SECRETARY-TREASURER
WILTON LLOYD-SMITH,ESQ.

FIELD STEWARDS
ROBERT GOELET,ESQ.
W.A.HARRIMAN,ESQ.
ROBERT G. MC KAY,ESQ

OFFICIAL GUNS
CAPT.PAUL A. CURTIS
WADSWORTH R.LEWIS,ESQ.
E?ROLAND HARRIMAN, ESQ.
WILTON LLOYD-SMITH,ESQ.

JUDGES
DAVID WAGSTAFF, ESQ.
Tuxedo Park, N.Y.
DR. SAMUEL MILBANK
New York, N.Y.

Under the management of the
GEO.F.FOLEY DOG SHOW ORGAN.,Inc.
119 S.19th St.,
Philadelphia,Pa.

CATALOGUE

Second

FIELD TRIAL MEETING

Given by

LABRADOR RETRIEVER CLUB

Held under American Kennel Club and
Labrador Retriever Club rules

at "CAUMSETT", LLOYD NECK,
HUNTINGTON, L. I., N.Y.

WEDNESDAY, DECEMBER 14, 1932

****

Catalogs from the first three American field trials.

81

thought. Steady but ever watchful and alert to every sound or movement, marched the yellow dog on the left side of his mistress. Away out in front a cock pheasant rose with a whir of wings, and before he was many yards nearer to his prayed-for sanctuary, the wood on the western hill, he was hit and winged. He was just the sort of bird for a semi-final or final test. He took to his toes when he reached the ground, and with a low carried head disappeared into the morass. It was Carl's duty to find that fleeing pheasant. So at the judges' order Mrs. Field hied her dog away to the spot Carl had marked down. Almost in a trice the golden fawn Labrador had overtaken and lifted his pheasant. The "parcel" he carried at the balance — a safe and harmless conveyance. Scarcely a feather was ruffled. So far all was well and very pretty. But even the sagacious Carl could have made a better return! Instead of making a direct line for his fair handler, he elected to take a round-about route.

In the last of all tests Carl went out very fast for a bird he had well marked. It was a runner and the dog used his good nose for all it was worth. Thus it wasn't long before he was homeward bound through the long grass of the marshland. It was noticed that Carl's pick-up on this occasion could have had more speed; but the dash of his comeback and perfect delivery into the gloved hand had fully satisfied the demands of the judges and 'twas Carl's victory!

He headed the list that likewise proclaimed Odds On, second; Robert Goelet's Sab of Tulliallan, third and Mr. Field's May Millard and Mr. Goelet's Glenmere Joe, equal fourths. Certificates of Merit in this, the All-Age Stake, were awarded to Mr. Goelet's Niths Double, Mr. Harriman's Sam, Mr. Briggs' Moose, Mr. Goelet's Glenmere Monarch and Mr. Field's Caumsett Banker. That wonderful handler Colin Macfarlane, worked the Goelet Labradors.

The field arrangements were all that could be possibly desired in the experienced hands of Mr. James, head gamekeeper at Glenmere. A large house party was entertained at The Court, while the banquet provided for the handlers, beaters and others at the American House Hotel proved a fine harbinger of the good things of Christmastide. And the catering of the bountiful Mrs. Smyth, landlady of the old-time Inn in the far famed valley, was as generous as it was good.

The dog owners in the first American trial in 1931 were as notable as the aristocratic owners in England, and the combined wealth of these families would have been an impressive sum. They were all devoted to the new sport of retriever field trialing, and all spent a lot of money developing their kennels. They took particular pride and interest in the breeding programs supervised by their

W. Averell Harriman

Some Early American Field Champio

THE KENNEL CLUB (London)

A15329 Pedigree Certificate

SIRE: RONALD OF CANDAHAR

RALTAG
TAG OF WHITMORE 707 (FT Ch)
SQUIB OF BELVOIR

JUNE
SANDHOE JUSK 336 J
SEGUIN

DAM: GEHTA

BANCHORY BLUEE 926 CC
BANCHORY BOLO (Ch FTCh) 218 AA
BROCKLEHIRST NELL

BALBEARDIE (Ch) 209 AA
MUTO 2F2 AA
BALMUTO PINKIE

Stud Book No. (if any) 1384 JJ
Born 21 February 1927
Colour Black
Breeder Col. J. L. Sleeman
Registered by W. G. Goode as "Peg o' the Carrots"
Named changed by Mrs. E. E. Turner

I certify that the above is a true copy of the Pedigree of the
Retriever Labrador (bitch) PEGGY OF SHIPTON as recorded on the Registers of the
Kennel Club.

Signed E. Holland Buckley, Asst. Secretary

Kennel Club, 84 Piccadilly, London, W. 1

Date 3 March, 1933 SEAL

Peggy of Shipton's pedigree

gamekeepers. It was a very close-knit social group, and they were all importing the best stock they could find in England.

Perhaps the best kennel from that era was the Arden kennel. When Jasper Briggs, Jim Cowie, and Averell Harriman were asked why the Arden kennel was so famous in its day and why even to this day its record is still impressive they each answered, "Peggy of Shipton. Harriman's bitch threw champions in every litter she produced." She was bred to Mrs. Marshall Field's Odds On, then to Dr. Milbank's Raffles of Earlsmoor and these combinations produced notable progeny. Many say that Raffles and Peggy produced a standard for quality that has never been equaled in any other Labrador kennel in this country. Tom Briggs was the mastermind and Averell Harriman the proud owner.

Harriman remembers those years.

"In the twenties I wanted to get some shooting and I undertook to develop a duck drive. I had imported Thomas Briggs from Scotland in 1913. He turned out to be a very fine gamekeeper and extraordinarily good dog handler. We raised our own ducks and it was a very tough shoot. In the late twenties I imported Peggy of Shipton. A friend of mine bought her and she is the basis of the Arden Kennels. She was not a very expensive dog. Shortly afterwards they started Labrador Retriever trials on Long Island. The first trial was December 21, 1931. The trial I remember best was in 1934. We entered our dogs, all out of Peggy of Shipton. There wasn't a single litter she had that she didn't have a winner.

"The interesting story about Peggy's pups, Blind and Decoy, was that one of the rather wealthy people on Long Island bought a famous dog in England and he was going to sweep the field trials but Blind and Decoy beat him. Decoy was first and Blind second, both in the puppy trials and in the Open Class. That was the only time Blind was ever beaten in his career. Then around about '34, at the Sands Point field trial Blind won everything.

"I was one of the first to get into Labradors. I had always had a Lab. I don't know why, I just wanted to have a retriever. That was in the early 1920s. When I got Peg, we began breeding. If the first trials were 1931, it was the latter part of the twenties that Peg had her first pups. I had Labradors as a young man as a pet and to shoot grouse at Arden, and of course I shot out at my father's ranch in Idaho. I took my dog out there.

"I was so very much involved in the New Deal that I couldn't go to these field trials, but the AKC asked if they could have a field trial at my place on Long Island at Sands Point. My friends, including my brother-in-law Charley Lawrence, Marshall Field and others, thought that Blind was a great dog because he was handled by Tom Briggs. So, without my knowing it, they made the Open Class to be handled by amateurs. They called it an Amateur Open. I was going to have to handle my own dog in this trial. I never dodged a chal-

The Gallery and Contestants at the 1935 Labrador Retriever Club Trial

Marshall Field, Douglas Marshall

Harriman's Blind and Decoy

Tom Briggs, Mrs. E. Roland Harriman

Mr. and Mrs. Jay Carlisle, Mr. and Mrs. Dave Wagstaff

Buell Hollister,
Dr. Milbank, F. B. Lord

Avril Harriman with Blind,
Decoy and Sam

Tom Briggs

R. W. Morgan

Mr. and Mrs. Morgan Belmont, Mr. Carlisle, Mr. Lord,
Mr. J. Cowie, Mr. Remick, Mr. Ely and Mr. Talmage

Mrs. Marshall Field

Mr. H. Morgan, Mr. C. Lawrence, Mr. F. Lord, Mr. J. F. Carlis
Mr. D. Wagstaff, Mr. G. Remick

Catherine Starr

Dogs travel in style.

Mr. Dave Elliott

Typical Water-Work

Mr. Alfred Ely, Mr. F. B. Lord and
Mr. Carlisle

Mrs. Morgan Belmont Recieving Harriman
Trophy Jim Cowie Alfred Ely President of
Lab Club

Mrs. E. Roland Harriman.
The judge, Hon. Mrs. Joan Hill Wood
Later Lady Hill Wood. She is
now president of British Lab Club

Dr. Samuel Millbank

C. B. Lawrence
The Judge

lenge. But I thought I was caught because I had never been to a field trial in my life, although Blind had won everything, and so had my other dogs, under Tom Briggs. Blind was already a Field Champion. So, I came up to Arden on Thursday night to get to know the dog. I took Blind in the car to spend the night with me and to get to know him before going down to Sands Point on Saturday morning for the trials.

"Tom Briggs, my handler, had the most shrill whistle. He was a trainer who trained his dogs to work mostly by themselves, but if they were doing something, and he wanted to check them, he would put three fingers in his mouth and would give the shrillest blast you ever heard, and it was the only sound they would obey.

"So when I went to look at the dog and to get some advice from Tom about it, I said, 'What about whistles. Do they respond to a metal whistle?' He said, 'Oh no, only this whistle.' I said, 'Can I learn that?' He said, 'Oh yes, of course you can learn to do it.' 'How long did it take you to learn?' He said, 'Seven years.' He was a Scotsman with a straight face and a great sense of humor.

"I made up my mind that I would have to trust the dog and give him what advice I could by how I sent him out, so I asked Tom if he had any advice for me in the field trials, and he said, 'No, you know how to work dogs, work them just the way you do, send them out, so forth . . .' I said, 'Do you have any special advice?' He said, 'Yes. If there is a wind, you want to send him a little bit downwind so that he gets the scent, if he happens to go sharply in the opposite direction he will pick up the scent.' That was the only piece of advice that he gave me.

"We had these three dogs entered. Sam by that time was rather old and slow. He really was outclassed. While handling Decoy I unfortunately moved my hand a little bit and she was a very keen dog and broke. That eliminated her, so it came down to Blind.

"We had some pheasant shot in territory that was in high grass and Blind worked fine. The water test was rather easy because it was just out in the Sound and of course he did that perfectly. There was another dog that also had a perfect record — I think there were three of us that had perfect records and the judges wanted to have a rerun of these three dogs. There had been a bird shot for one of the other dogs and it was lost. They sent the second dog out there and he couldn't find the bird either and by that time it was rather late in the day, I was at it all day. I was tired and had gotten to the point where I didn't care much what happened as long as they finished. I was sitting on a stone wall, the dog lying behind me when Marshall Field called Number 4, and that was my number.

"I said, 'Well, Marshall, where is the bird?' He said, 'You see that old tree out there?' Well it looked to me as if this was quite a long way and he said, 'Somewhere in that area.' So I put my finger in my mouth, wet it and tested the wind to see how it was blowing. I

The dog on this week's cover is Blind of Arden, who won the No. 1 U.S. retriever stake of the year on Nov. 21, had his picture taken at Southampton by LIFE Photographer George Karger. A stylish black Labrador, with a sly arrogance about him, Blind is now 4, has been trained for hunting ever since he could stumble into the field. He lives on the big estate of his owner, W. Averell Harriman, near Tuxedo, N. Y., where he practices on live pheasants for half an hour every day with his handler, Jasper Briggs. For more pictures turn to page

Blind makes the cover of Life Magazine.

sent the dog way to the left of the tree, downwind. I saw him go through the broomgrass. He got to about the point where the bird was supposed to be shot, and he turned to the left instead of the right. If I'd had a whistle I would have blown it and stopped him because I figured he'd gone too far over and downwind. I couldn't conceive that he would have gotten near the bird.

"I was helpless without a whistle. Pretty soon I saw him come in in my direction and I thought, 'My God, this is terrible. He's coming back.' There he came in the grass with the bird in his mouth. I had sent him out far enough, he picked up the scent, he found the bird. So Tom's advice was the one advice that I needed and I remember Marshall Field saying, 'Well, Averell, I guess that dog really is a great dog.'

"So he won the trial, and that was a most dramatic ending. Of course later on I went to field trials. We had some at Arden. I had other dogs but the real important field trial that I went to was that one in 1934.

"Arden kennels was very big in field trials and bench shows from those early years right up to the beginning of World War II. But I gave up Labs just as the war came. I gave up because Tom Briggs was killed. He was returning from a show or a field trial—I've forgotten which. He came back late one night to Arden. There was fog in the valley as he was crossing the railroad tracks the train came along and killed him. That destroyed my interest. My kennel died with Tom Briggs.

"I kept two white dogs—one was fully white. She was called Brum after the Norse god and I had her for fourteen years. I had her when I worked for Truman, I think it was in 1950. She was with me all the time. I taught her to retrieve. I would get up from the room she would follow me, she slept in my bed and she was with me when I was Governor in Albany.

"That was 1954–59 and dogs weren't allowed in the Capitol. But she was there. She would lay under my desk all the time I was Governor. When I would go to an affair there would be hundreds of people around, I would never have a leash. She would follow me all through the crowd; Brum wouldn't leave me. She died when I was working for Kennedy. She was one of the dogs I had a great fondness for. Brum was a member of our family and was a good companion; she was really a friend.

The lifestyle of even the wealthiest families changed during the 1930s. The Great Depression reached all walks of life. The day of the fancy Scottish-type shoots became a thing of the past. The chauffeured limousines with their elegant occupants no longer lined the roads of the country estates. Four- and five-day shooting parties of driven pheasant and flighted ducks with splendid luncheons on the lawn and formal dinner parties in the evenings went the way of the speakeasy and the flapper.

Tom Briggs

Effects of the Great Depression

In some ways, the changes brought about by the depression benefited the Labrador Retriever. The dog that was imported with his gamekeeper to authenticate the shoots became the primary participant in the newest game of the wealthy—field trialing. The game, which had its start in the fashionable area near Tuxedo Park, moved to Long Island. Gameskeepers, who were now called trainers and handlers, moved along with the game. From there the sport moved west. The sport evolved much like horseracing—the owners never trained or rode; they only wanted to win. Their participation was restricted to judging. As Dave Elliott, one of the best known Scottish gamekeepers, once said, "They were after championship points for their dogs. They were not dishonest, they just didn't know much about the game or the dogs."

Of course, there was some fast shuffling. If the judges did not like the way the dogs were working, they called the test to a halt and started again with a "better" test. In October 1938, in a field trial run by the Sun Valley Field Trial Club in Idaho, only four dogs were entered to compete for championship points—all four dogs were owned by the Harrimans.

Field trial clubs in the 1930s sprang up all over the country. In 1935 the legendary publisher of *Field and Stream* Magazine, E. F. Warner, donated a trophy to be awarded annually to the "Outstanding Retriever of the Year." There seems to be no public record of the *Field and Stream* winners either in that magazine, *Popular Dogs*, or the AKC *Gazette*, which indicates just how privately this game was maintained.

The first year, 1935, saw Fld. Ch. Blind of Arden, owned by W. A. Harriman and handled by Tom Briggs, as the winner. In 1936, the award went to Fld. Ch. Dilwyne Montauk Pilot, a Chessie. The Chesapeake Bay dogs were the ones who "showed the Labrador how to swim." The Lab in those early days was a land retriever, or at least that's the way the British used the dog. Americans followed suit, so the trainers eventually had to train the dogs for serious work in the water. By the next year, the Chessies were almost out of the future. The Lab's future was secured.

In 1937, Fld. Ch. Banchory Night Light, owned by J. F. Carlisle and handled by Dave Elliot, took the *Field and Stream* prize.

In the same year, a change in the field trial rules stated, "No sticks and stones on blind retrieves." Today's field trialers find it hard to believe but before then, the Chesapeake Retriever trials allowed handlers to throw sticks and stones or even empty shell cases to direct their dogs into an area on land or water. This story has been told before, but could not be confirmed until now. Dave Elliot tells how it worked.

"Dogs worked from a blind made of wood or reeds. On command from the judge the dogs were sent. They jumped through a hole in the blind and were directed to the birds. When working from

Decoy, Blind, and Sam of Arden

Field and Stream Trophy

90

these blinds, the dogs never saw where the birds were downed by the guns. To get the dog going in the right direction an object was thrown. On land, to get the dog into heavy cover, a stick was used." Dave stopped to laugh. "On many occasions the dog came back with the stick. Over water, stones were thrown. The dog swam out to the first splash made by a stone, and to get the dog to swim further a second stone was flung ahead of him. A three-stone retrieve was a long blind. Once the dog got near the bird his nose did the rest of the job. Thus evolved the term 'a three-stoner.' "

Elliot is a feisty Scotsman who came from a line of gamekeepers; grandfather, father, and uncles before him worked at the trade. At seventeen, working on the Montrose estate in Scotland, he began training dogs. He started running them in field trials in 1929. Always an innovator with a fine understanding of dogs, Dave was fascinated by the work of sheep dogs. These Border Collies had strong rapport with their handlers and displayed a keen intelligence that Dave thought was very similar to the Labrador. Having watched many sheep dogs at work and in trials in his native Scotland, Dave believed that a similar approach would work with retrievers. So he proceeded to train his retrievers to handle in a precise manner to the whistle. Though he used this method in Scotland, he did not perfect the method until he came to this country. Handling by whistle and hand signals got Dave into trouble from the very beginning. It would take many years before his system was accepted. Now Dave is the first to say the method is overused.

After the 1935 Labrador Retriever Club field trial held on the Pierpont Estate the *Gazette* reported, "Orchardton Doris of Wingan was fourth. This import is a high-class bitch with beautiful style, great pace and very keen. She and her handler, Dave Elliot, gave a beautiful exhibition of giving and taking direction to an unmarked fall by hand and whistle, without undue disturbance of ground on either side."

Dave does not remember it that way. He recalls that the judges were annoyed with him for handling the dog, even though it was in a very precise manner, and that was why he was awarded only a fourth place.

Dave came to the Carlisle estate on Long Island in 1934. Mr. Carlisle was semi-retired and was looking for a hobby. He had been raising Dachshunds, but through shooting he became interested in the new sport of retriever field trials. He bought a few dogs and went to a field trial. His dogs did so poorly that he decided to "get someone from the old country who knew how they worked."

In those days the field trial fraternity was very small and made up of men of means. W. Averell Harriman had imported Tom Briggs for the Arden Kennel; Robert Goelet had brought in Colin MacFarlane for his Glenmere kennel. Marshall Field's kennel was called Caumsett, and Douglas Marshall handled his dogs. Other trainers who came to America and must receive credit for the early retriever training in America were Jim Cowie, Jock Munro, Martin Hogan and his sons James and Francis, and Lionel Bond. When Carlisle decided to import a handler in 1934, Lorna Countess Howe, Chairman of the Labrador Retriever Club in England, recommended Dave Elliot. Dave recalls her as a wonderful woman, if you knew how to keep your place.

For his kennel, Carlisle imported some basic English stock (including Orchardton Doris and Drinkstone Peg), which proved to be an important foundation for breeders in America. With Banchory Night Light, in 1937, Elliot won the *Field and Stream* trophy, which was then the major national event. On the infamous day, December 7, 1941, Dave qualified and ran his Hiwood Mike in the first National Retriever Trial Championship.

Elliot became more than a dog handler. He was devoted to the Labrador breed and became an important spokesman for the sport of field trialing. At the same time he tried to keep the focus of the sport on the dogs rather than the people. Through the years he was a contributor to *Field and Stream*, *Country Life*, *The Field Trial News*, and in 1952 wrote the book *Training Gun Dogs to Retrieve*.

Elliot's experience in field trials reflects the progress and changes in the American trials that were made over the years. He first ran in British trials, which have not changed from their origin in the early 1900s to the present day. Their tests are still run on live game, in the wild, under actual hunting conditions, and still limit entries to twenty-four dogs. As Elliot recalls, there was little pressure in the early American trials because of the small number of entries. As the sport's popularity increased, however, birds were planted in traps along the walk-up course, the first indication of the American democratic temperament, according to Elliot. The planted birds took some of the luck out of the game, gave the dogs a more uniform test, and allowed many more dogs to run.

Tests consisted of single retrieves. The bird trap had a string-operated, wire covering, and a man was assigned by the judge to pull the string at the propitious moment. Most often it was in cover over the dog's head, so there was still a lot of luck in the game. When a bird was released, the dog with the lowest number was called. After the retrieve, the dog stayed in the line so the judge could see if he would break (rush in out of control). After the first round the judge could call any dog. The competitors never knew how many birds would be sprung. If one dog missed, his brace-mate would be sent, and it would be very embarrassing if he "wiped your eye." The judges would reverse dogs in the next rounds, disqualifying those dogs that broke or had hard mouths.

The Labrador Club always had a pheasant drive in the Open All Age stake. All the dogs in contention were brought up to the stand. When the drive was over and the birds were down, the judge

PICKUP AT BARNEGAT BAY *Milt Weiler*

93

indicated which dog should work. Today, this test is considered a blind, but handlers then were not allowed to assist the dog; they had to hunt on their own. Elliot recalls that on his first American trial his handling of the dog was not given a very favorable reception. "Any dog that did not possess a full measure of natural ability was sorely handicapped. In those days very few handlers suffered from cold hands! They just kept their hands in their pockets! There is no question that the old dogs were better game finders than dogs today."

In these drives there was no such thing as a bad fall. Everything was considered fair game. A dog seldom had a chance to mark a bird down. He would see it in the air, and then he would be sent out to hunt. Because handling was not allowed, there was nothing else to do. But experience taught these dogs to hunt, to be self-reliant, and to follow a cripple alone.

The water part of the trial consisted of a bird shot over decoys and one shot in open water. While the dog made the first retrieve in the decoys (and the contestant prayed that the dog would not re-trieve a decoy), the open-water duck was either drifting ashore or heading out to sea, depending on which way the wind and tide were going. If the bird came towards the shore, it was just a matter of sending the dog down the shoreline; the wind would be onshore and the dog would pick up the scent. But the bird that headed out to sea was a big problem.

According to Dave Elliot, the dogs that "went to sea" finally proved to the skeptics that handling was not such a bad idea. Even the skeptics realized that a dog out searching the water, no matter how much perseverence he had, was no match for a drifting dead bird on a swift current. Some dogs that pressed on with their search were caught in a dangerous current. Elliot was able to handle his dogs onto a drifting bird with dispatch, make the retrieve, and keep him out of danger. He demonstrated that he could first handle his dog to the open-water bird and then make the simple retrieve in the decoys. But today Dave is the first one to say that we've made our dogs too mechanical and depend too much on handling.

The *Field and Stream* award continued to be the cherished retriever trial trophy until World War II, when the National Club Championship began. From 1939 to 1943, Paul Bakewell III won the trophy each year, an incredible feat. Mr. Bakewell, a business-man from St. Louis, was the first amateur to beat the professionals at their own game. It would be almost twenty years before another amateur, Richard Hecker, won the National Championship with his Labrador, Dolobran's Smoke Tail. Despite his Navy service during the war, during the decade from 1939 to 1949, Bakewell managed his dogs through seven National wins. During two of those war years the dogs were handled by professionals, Cliff Wallace and Cot-ton Pershall. But, as Bakewell recalls, a precedent had to be broken; the judges did not want to give top honors to an amateur handler.

Dave Elliot today

Amateurs Enter the Sport . . .
Paul Bakewell

94

Paul Bakewell was a good trainer and a tough competitor, as *The Milwaukee Journal* pointed out on January 12, 1943.

We do not know of an instance in national field trial history, whether among bird dogs, spaniels or retrievers, in which one man has turned in such an impressive winning streak. Bakewell—and three retrievers—have dominated the national championships since 1939 and we might add that we do not know of anyone in the field trial game with such a fierce competitive spirit as this same Bakewell. He has always been in there to win. He has been tough competition, as many Wisconsin sportsmen can tell you.

Bakewell's personal attitude in field trials has interested this reporter as much as the performance of his dogs. He is a genial and pleasant friend, but when the chips are down something steely creeps into the Bakewell eyes and his whole demeanor suggests, "All right, boys, we're friends, but I'm out here to lick you and I think I can."

Bakewell's five consecutive championships are the most remarkable because the first two, in 1939 and 1940, were won by him with a dog which he had trained and always handled himself. That meant that Amateur Bakewell was putting down his dog against the hard to beat professionals.

A lot of people thought Bakewell played too hard at winning. But that's the game, and right now you can bet that Lieut. Paul Bakewell is playing the same kind of game.

Tom Merritt, Paul Bakewell III, and Dual Champion Shed of Arden when he won his first national championship in 1942.

Maxwell Riddle, the dog writer, explained Bakewell's contributions this way in the *Cleveland Press* in 1952: "An Amateur stake is one in which the dogs are handled by their owners. However, the owners are not necessarily amateurs in the quality of their handling. Thus Bakewell is to retrieving what Bobby Jones is to golf."

Bakewell reminisces about the amateur issue today. "In going through the results of amateur stakes you will notice my practically complete absence until 1951, when I made Marvadel Black Gum an Amateur Field Champion. The reason for this was I always thought amateur stakes were for women and children and old men, as I am now, and I confined my activities to competition with the pros. However, in later years when they counted a win or placing in an amateur stake towards qualifying for the National Championship Stake, it changed that status." It was in 1951 that a win in the Amateur stake first counted toward championship points and the first National Amateur Championship was held in 1957.

Paul started with Rip, a Golden Retriever that he bought for $35. "I trained him completely, developed him my own way by trial-and-error, repetition after repetition, and made him so good he was able to win the *Field and Stream* Trophy. He won in 1939 and again in 1940, and at the time of his death in the summer of 1941 he was tied with his kennel mate, Tar of Arden, for the *Field and Stream* Trophy for a third consecutive win. Following his death I put more insistence on Tar winning, and she did take the trophy that year."

The original 1935 rules of the *Field and Stream* trials stated that the dog with the highest number of points for the year won, which meant endless campaigning from trial to trial. In 1935, there were five trials; by 1941 twenty-one trials were scattered throughout the East and Midwest. The dog that was entered in all events might not be the best, but he certainly had the best chance of winning. The competition for this trophy was strong, and to win it a dog had to run in as many trials as possible, a procedure quite expensive in both time and money, especially for the amateur handler. In at least one year the award was not settled until the last trial of the season. It became evident that what was needed was one championship stake to be held annually at the conclusion of the regular season in which proven dogs would be eligible to compete. In February 1941, Morgan Belmont, Henry Bixby, Alfred Ely, Thomas Merritt, and Walter Roesler founded the National Retriever Club; the winner of the club's trial would hold the title of National Retriever Champion of the year.

Consequently, confusion existed between the *Field and Stream* Trophy and the National Club's award. The 1941 National Club winner was King Midas of Woodend, owned by E. N. Dodge, and handled by Frank Hogan, but the *Field and Stream* Trophy had already been won by Tar of Arden, owned by Paul Bakewell and handled by Cotton Pershall. The confusion about the 1941 championship was settled by 1942. Bakewell's Shed of Arden won the new National Club Championship *and* the magazine's trophy—a feat he accomplished three times, 1942, 1943, and 1946—a never-to-be-repeated achievement. In 1942, and from then on until the *Field and Stream* Trophy was retired in 1953, it was presented along with the National Club award. Although the *Field and Stream* Trophy was retired to John Olin, whose dog King Buck won the National Championship in both 1952 and 1953, many people thought it should have been retired to seven-time winner Paul Bakewell.

A most outstanding dog bred by Tom Briggs at the Harriman's Arden kennel, Shed was a dual champion and one of the famous "fish" litter. Each dog was given the name of a fish, such as Bass, Trout, Shad, etc. Through a typographical error in the registration papers, Shad became Shed.

Paul Bakewell remembers Shed of Arden this way.

"Shed was from a litter of Arden Kennels, and in the fall of 1940 I purchased him for $250 on approval for thirty days. Once I saw him in St. Louis, I could see why he was sold; he refused to re-enter the water for a second retrieve. We had no trouble at all in overcoming this fault, and we completed the deal within the given

Shed of Arden's first field trail award.

The Arden Labs

The famous Fish Litter . . . each pup was named after a different species of fish, but Shad became Shed because of a typographical error.

Paul Bakewell with Shed of Arden as they win the national championship for the first time

time. I could tell he was a nice prospect but no more so than any other. He was a well-bodied dog and I could see he would make a good looker. I settled on him as a fine prospect, and he was worked daily from then on for the balance of his lifetime, on Sundays and holidays, without intermission.

"He took training very nicely with just a little affection and appreciation along with the necessary discipline. He made his field trial championship quickly and when I realized he was so good looking, I had Hollis Wilson take him around to a few shows in this country. This took very little time as I don't think he was ever defeated.

"I went into the navy in the fall of 1941, and he was left in St. Louis with Cotton Pershall taking over the daily work for me. In November or December 1942, I got leave and had him shipped up to Madison, Wisconsin for the National, where I handled him for his first National Championship at Lake Mendota. I still have memories of the raccoon coats and log fires, and everything iced over. It was some five or ten degrees below zero at the time, and I recall how the other dogs failed in the water tests, but Shed never refused.

"I was not able to get away from my navy duties to be at the 1943 National at Bourbon, Missouri, but Cliff Wallace handled Shed and Speed for me and they had to compete against each other, with no others working, in extra series to decide the winner. The judges selected Shed.

"That gave me the record of Rip having won the *Field and Stream* Trophy in 1939 and 1940, Tar in 1941, and Shed in 1942 and 1943. Because of the war, I could not compete in 1944, but in 1945 I ran Shed in the National. He must have made a couple of small mistakes, as he did not win. Returning from the Navy in the fall of 1945, I worked him daily in 1946 and he was an easy winner in that year's trial.

"This is as much as I can remember of my training of Shed. As

I look back on it, I think the reason he made things look so easy is that the tests used in training were considerably more difficult than those we received at the trials, both on land and water. In training he very rarely received a double but instead long triples in all types of cover, heavy and low, in a diversified area, repeatedly working on land and water.

"I was always interested in the dual-purpose dog, the looks on the bench as well as performance in a trial. Actually, I wouldn't put a dog on the bench until he had completed his field trial championship, and I thought him deserving of being a bench champion. One of the exceptions to this was my Hello Joe of Rocheltree, a Shed pup. He needed only a couple of points on the bench and a point or two in the field to complete his championships back in the forties. When the Midwest trial was held in Chicago and a bench show nearby at Skokie, Illinois, Hello Joe competed in both. When a certain water test came along, he was one of the first to complete his work. I drove him over to the show where the Labradors were being judged while the rest of the field trial test was still going on. He completed his bench championship and I took him back to the trial where he won the Open Stake, making him a field trial and a bench champion on the same day, which I think was a very unique accomplishment."

During the late 1940s and early 1950s, three men and their dogs stand out, and they were all out of St. Louis. Paul Bakewell and Shed of Arden became a legend. John Olin, of Winchester Western, became an institution with his Nilo Kennel and his famous dog, King Buck. The third man, T. W. (Cotton) Pershall, was a link between these men and their dogs. Growing up in Walnut Ridge, Arkansas, Cotton learned all about wing shooting, rabbit hounds, fox-hunting Walkers, and squirrel-treeing feists, but in the South Labradors were as foreign as Republicans. Cotton went north to St. Louis to work as a groom for Bakewell, but his groom career was a brief one. His aptitude with dogs showed loud and clear, and Bakewell soon put him to work in the new sport of retriever trials. Under Bakewell's guidance, he trained both Tar of Arden and Shed of Arden. A hitch on the West Coast with Uncle Sam during the war saw Cotton as an instructor in the K-9 Corps, training attack dogs. To this day, Cotton gives full credit to Paul Bakewell for teaching him all he knows about dog training.

After the war, Cotton trained and handled Bracken's Sweep for Dan Pomeroy of New Jersey and won his next National Championship. When Bakewell handled Marvadel Black Gum to a National Championship in 1949, it brought the total of Pershall-trained National Champions to five.

Reminiscing about his 40-year training career, he cannot recall exactly how many Field Champions he trained but he is sure it was more than fifty. He qualified four or five each year for the Nationals

THE MALLARD HUNTERS *Peter Corbin*

and nine of them became National Champions.

After a short training stint in Minnesota, Cotton broadened his horizons by visiting England to buy dogs and learn the English methods of dog training. On his return, Dan Pomeroy placed him with John Olin, who in 1951 started Nilo Kennels. Olin, now in his late eighties, recalls Pomeroy and Pershall.

"I became acquainted with Dan Pomeroy after the war. What a grand old fellow he was! He was one of the founders and one of the first directors of Bankers Trust Company in New York. He died at age 95, but I remember him telling me that he had two ambitions: to win the National Retriever Championship and to marry a beautiful woman. He accomplished both. He kind of adopted me as a son and we became very good friends. He interested me in a lot of things and that's really how I got into Labs.

"I remember in the late forties Dan Pomeroy came to me and said there was a woman in Winona, Minnesota named Mary King. Cotton Pershall worked for her. Cotton was raised down in Arkansas and he was a horse trainer. He got acquainted with Paul Bakewell and that got him into Labrador Retriever. Cotton trained practically all of the dogs that Bakewell had. Cotton and Bakewell were getting pretty edgy and Cotton left him and went up with Mary King. He was dissatisfied with her. Dan Pomeroy learned of that and told me, 'John, grab Cotton while you can. This is the best trainer in the whole game.' So I hired him. With Nilo Farms started, we had to have a dog trainer and Cotton filled that bill.

"Cotton and I never had one sour note all the time we were together. We disagreed sometimes, like when I bought King Buck. He bought Freehaven Muscles the same week. I think he paid $2500 for Freehaven Muscles and I paid $6500. Well, Bakewell cost me $1500 because I had the deal made with Bing Grunwald, who owned the dog, for $5000; Bakewell came in and had me up it to $6500, which was the highest price ever paid for a Labrador then. I got that all back when we had a Calcutta pool with the Mississippi Valley field trial people and they got George Gardner to bid King Buck for me. That pool netted $7500.

"King Buck was the greatest Labrador I've seen anywhere. The dog seemed to have almost human brains. When the going got tough, he got tougher, it was just unbelievable. That dog really was a part of me before we parted company with his death. I never had a dog that had so much affection in him. He was a real crowd-pleaser.

"The National down in Maryland, which we won in '53, was the most exciting trial I've ever seen. The dog had the trial won up to the ninth series, then he had to be handled; he mismarked a bird and Cotton had to handle him. He went through the tenth series and did a perfect job and they declared the two extra series. The eleventh series was a tough one. It was a triple mark and then a

John Olin's King Buck

100

blind through a cut out to a bay with a duck attached to a float, with waves and irregular shoreline. The bay was in a fit with good strong winds and waves. Buck nailed the three marks on the blind, he took a line, went right through the middle of that cut, and went directly to that duck with no whistle. I remember Dan Pomeroy and I were sitting in an old chicken coop watching, glued to the nest. When I saw Buck pick up that duck I almost hollered, 'Man, here it is, we've got it. There will be no other dog that will perform this, and if any does, it will be with a whistle.' That's just what happened; they had to hack the dog all the way. Buck did it without a single whistle!''

King Buck and Cotton Pershall were destined to be a team; they both had the same birthday. Cotton wasn't born in duck country, but King Buck was in 1948 at Storm Lake in northwest Iowa; he was one of a litter of eight. Timothy of Arden was the sire, owned by Ed Quinn. The dam, Alta of Banchory, had five males and three females. There was nothing spectacular about the pups, and they all received their early training from Quinn. They took to water like Lab pups usually do and showed early promise as good gun dogs. At six months of age they were all sold, and when it got down to the last two, of which King Buck was one, the price was down to $50. These were sent to their new owners in Omaha and on arrival both came down with distemper. One of the pups didn't make it. Robert Howard took his pup home and placed it in a basket next to the basement furnace.

The little retriever showed no improvement, and Howard was advised several times to have him put to sleep. For nearly a month the pup was as sick as an animal can be and remain living. But Mrs. Howard's loving attention and devotion to the sick puppy finally turned the battle.

One night Bob Howard went downstairs to have a look at him. The pup managed to stand in his basket and greet him. He knew then that he was going to make it.

Yet the effects of distemper weren't shaken off overnight. King Buck did not eat well and was very thin. When Howard took the young dog to a veterinarian, he was told that Buck had a bad heart and should not be run in the field. As if this weren't bad enough, the dog's stools were sometimes bloody, and Howard feared that his Lab might have suffered internal damage. Yet, Buck ran well. Even more important, he wanted to run. And by the time he was eighteen months old, his weight and appetite began to improve and Howard never noticed symptoms of poor health again.

In his second autumn the dog began his first field hunting. A very brainy dog, Buck was also eager and affectionate and showed no inclination of being shy or a one-man dog. He did not suddenly "come of age" as some dogs do. He won a licensed derby when he was only eighteen months old. The young dog also won first place

Cotton Pershall with a young pup
at the grave of King Buck.

in September, 1949, at the Missouri Valley Hunt Club's licensed trial in Iowa.

By this time, Howard sensed a quality of greatness in the young Labrador. He wanted to give Buck a real chance to prove himself but could not afford to run his retriever in top-flight trials. So he sold King Buck to Byron "Bing" Grunwald of Omaha for $500, with the stipulation that Howard would continue to train the Labrador and handle him in trials.

Bing Grunwald, who started in field trials in 1946 and was president of the National Amateur Club in 1961 and the National Open Club in 1964, picks up the story from there.

"In November of 1949 Bob Howard came to me and said, 'You know my first wife passed away with cancer; I remarried. This girl's name is Mildred; she's doing a fine job taking care of my two girls and now we're going to have one of our own. I would like to sell you King Buck for $500 and use the $500 to buy Mildred a special Christmas present.' I said, 'I'll just give you the $500' and I wrote him a check. He said, 'There's a catch to this. I think this dog is going to be an outstanding dog. I would like to train the dog until he's three years of age.' I said, 'Well, keep the check.' So that's the way I bought King Buck. I am bragging when I say I bought King Buck out of the kindness of my heart to help this man buy his wife a Christmas present; no one knew that he was going to be what he turned out to be.

"When the dog was three years of age we ran him in April, 1951 in a licensed trial in Lincoln, Nebraska and Bob Howard lost him on a land blind. I attended the trial and he came to me and said, 'Bing, you have done everything that you agreed to do. This dog has turned out to be a fine animal.' He said, 'You should give him to a big-time trainer and go in with him because he's going to produce good results. I think the number one trainer in the U.S. is Cotton Pershall.' I told him, 'If you can get Friday off we'll drive up to the trial at Eagle, Wisconsin and take it in and talk to Cotton.' I found out when I got there that Cotton Pershall had just gone to work for John Olin, so that limited him training for me.

"We ran the trial Saturday and Sunday. King Buck ran six series and won the trial. The first thing that happened was a man named Snuffy Beleveau, an old-time professional, came to my wife and offered me $4,000 for King Buck. That was the first offer that we had. As soon as we got back home the telephone started ringing; everybody wanted to buy the dog. A man named Mr. Kline, who won the National Open in 1956, offered me $7,500; Paul Bakewell called me and offered to send me the best brood bitch in America and a check for $5,000 for Buck. I would breed the brood bitch, raise the puppies, keep all the puppies and send the brood bitch back to him—so this was a fine offer. I just debated about it and kept thinking about Cotton Pershall, so finally a friend of mine

King Buck, the dog who became a legend.

Cotton trains King Buck.

by the name of Arthur Stores called me and had just returned from fishing with Mr. John Olin. He said, 'What are you going to do with that dog?' 'Well,' I said, 'I've had a lot of offers, but I would like to see Cotton Pershall get the dog. If they buy him, I'll take $6,500 and two male puppies from his breeding.' 'Well,' he said, 'that's a lot of money.' I said, 'I have been offered $7,500 and I have been offered this other deal. I've had seven other offers, but not that much.' He said, 'Let me call you back.'

In forty-five minutes he called me and Mr. Olin bought the dog. He said he was going to change his name to Gold Dust because they couldn't think that any dog should be worth $6,500. Mr. Olin was just opening his Nilo Kennels for field trials, so it was brand new to him. So now John Olin got the dog. Of the two puppies I received, I gave one to a friend and both of us gave them away when they were twelve months of age because they would not retrieve. King Buck was never sire of good field trial dogs."

In June, 1951, two months after Buck's third birthday, he was delivered to Cotton Pershall. There was a tacit understanding in Nilo that Freehaven Muscles was Cotton's choice, and that King Buck was Olin's dog. Both men were right. Freehaven Muscles was a fine retriever — the sort that perpetuates fine bloodlines. But King Buck — the mid-sized Labrador of the fifty-dollar puppy price — was the sort that makes history. Under Cotton's hand the maturing King Buck began to catch fire.

In spring, 1951, King Buck won a first, two seconds, and a third place. That fall he took another first, a third, and a fourth, and completed ten of eleven series of the 1951 National Championship Stake, placing high among the nation's top retrievers. He made a slow start in 1952 with a first and a third in the spring. In autumn he won a first, second, and fourth. In November he again entered the world series of retrievers at Weldon Spring, Missouri.

"King Buck seemed to have some power of knowing when the competition was really rough, and he always came through," Cotton said. "He wasn't a big dog as Labs go, but he had great style. Always quiet and well-behaved, not excitable nor flashy. He just went steadily ahead with his job, series after series, whether on land or water."

Buck put on a show at Weldon Spring. He obeyed superbly, responded sharply to commands, and made direct, perfect retrieves. Right down to the final test, when he completed the tenth series with a 225-yard water retrieve; he performed like a champion.

Of a possible 300 points, King Buck had earned 294.9. The judges were vastly impressed with the new champion and vied with each other for superlatives. "Much style and hustle, lots of guts, very sharp, perfect response. The winner without question." "In all my experience, King Buck gave the best performance throughout the trial that I have ever seen . . ."

Soon after the trophy was awarded, Olin and his dog headed for Arkansas. Olin wished to see if Buck could perform as well in flooded timber as before a field trial gallery.

When Olin and his dog arrived in Stuttgart, the "Duck Hunting Capital of the World," the National Duck Calling Championship was just ending. Buck could not have had a more enthusiastic welcome; when he was introduced as the new national champion he was given a booming ovation by the nation's finest waterfowlers.

Buck was the center of attention that night at a general rejoicing and was even offered some champagne in his silver trophy bowl. A champion athlete in training, he sensibly abstained. Olin poured out the champagne and filled the bowl with water, and after Buck had quenched his thirst the bowl was refilled with champagne and passed among the guests as a communal toast to a great dog.

One man refused the toast. "I'm not going to drink from that bowl after a *dog* used it!!" he exclaimed. At that time and place, the remark showed a signal lack of discretion. Under Olin's withering glare, the guest was invited to leave the festivities and seek more antiseptic surroundings. For a moment there was even a distinct possibility that he might find such a germ-free climate in the local emergency ward.

When Buck was taken to flooded timber for his first adventure with wild ducks and wild duck-shooting, he came typically to life. Of King Buck, Olin said: "He was one of the finest wild duck retrievers I have ever seen. In spite of his intense field trial training, he loved natural hunting. He used his head in the wild, just as in field trials. That first wild duck shoot was *his* day, every minute of it, and he made the most of it. He was beautiful to watch."

Pershall continued to polish the champion that winter and spring, and, although he was not entered in the spring trials, Buck swept the autumn campaigns with three first places. Then came his third National Championship Stake and the automatic defense of his new crown.

This contest was held at Easton, Maryland, in unseasonably warm weather—a long, tough competition that went into overtime. For the first nine series of the 1953 National the defending champion made perfect scores but was pressed closely. In the tenth series Buck needed special handling on a long marked triple, and the gap between his high scores and those of close competitors was narrowed. In the opinion of the judges, no dog finishing the tenth series had a sufficient edge to be the winner. Two additional series were called. Buck went on to win with the flawless performance that John Olin and Dan Pomeroy watched from the chicken coop. By the twelfth series it was so apparent he was the clear winner that the official announcement came as an anticlimax.

Buck was active in the national field trial campaigns for four years after that, still competing fiercely with younger dogs and es-

King Buck and John Olin won the national championship twice.

tablished champions. As late as 1957, when he was nine years old, he not only qualified for the National Championship Stake but also completed eleven series out of twelve in the "National" and nearly won another title!

During his years at Nilo, King Buck finished seventy-three of a possible seventy-five series in seven consecutive runnings of the National Championship Stake. The only series that he failed to complete in those seven "Nationals" were the eleventh series in the 1951 contest and the twelfth series in 1957.

There was still one major honor in store for the famous old champion. Maynard Reece, the famous Iowa artist whose work had already appeared on two "duck stamps," came to Nilo and did a portrait of King Buck. The 1959 federal duck stamp was a portrait of old Buck with a drake mallard in his mouth, set against a backdrop of windswept marsh grass and flaring ducks. It was the first time a dog had ever appeared on a United States stamp.

King Buck died on March 28, 1962 — just one week before his fourteenth birthday — and was placed in a small crypt at the kennels' entrance, his statue above him.

The outstanding performances of Shed of Arden and King Buck in the late forties and early fifties set the standards for the training and the running of Labradors in the field. Paul Bakewell III and John Olin, both from St. Louis, were most influential in the Labrador's progress in the U.S. By beating the professionals, Bakewell proved that the amateur was more than a dilettante. The reign of the Scottish gamekeeper was over; the "average guy" with his one or two dogs would become competitive. John Olin would be the last of a long line of wealthy men to dominate the sport. Olin's influence was much more than running dogs in trials. His vision of controlled hunting on preserves came to pass. No one knows the amount of money he spent proving and developing his ideas. Nilo Farms in Illinois became an experimental center for the development of controlled hunting techniques. The hunter's game would evolve almost into a crop; the cultivation of the game similar to the growing of produce; the harvesting was the payoff. Olin saw these preserves as the answer for a society that was quickly losing its hunting grounds.

Bakewell proved to be the first of a new breed of dog owners and Olin the end of the old guard. The story of the times can be best told by Roger Vasselais and his beautiful wife, Pert. Roger (pronounced Row-jay) started training, hunting, and field trialing his Labradors almost thirty years ago. He was in the "second wave" of Long Islanders in the sport. Marshall Field and his contemporaries were no longer participating, but a strong nucleus of wealthy sportsmen were very active.

Roger: "When we first started twenty-five or thirty years ago, there were in Long Island about ten professional handlers catering

John Olin today

The Old Ways Yield to the New

KING BUCK *Maynard Reece*

to the public, a great many in the employ of one private owner. People like the Laughlins, the Morgans, the Greenleafs, the Brokaws, the Murnanes, Louise Hooker, had their own trainers. Trainers like Bud Hedges and Ray Stodinger usually had more than one client. Today there isn't one dog trainer in all of Long Island dedicated to retrieving.

"Most of the people have died, but basically it was a hangover from the original stock of Marshall Field and the handful of people. These very rich owners would bring their dogs from England and have their private shoots. Because of the large commercial development of Long Island, the private shooting clubs have gradually disappeared.

"Back then it was a rich man's sport with some rich clubs, and people used to bring their dogs to retrieve at the driven pheasants and duck shoots. Now that's a thing of the past.

"When I started, virtually no owners ran dogs in an Open Stakes. It was exclusively professional trainers, and I was one of the few amateurs.

Pert: "Amateur Day used to be a joke. All of these people ran their dogs in the Amateur Stake, but they never trained them; they simply took it out of their professional's truck and they went up to line. Anybody who trained their own dogs could beat them sixteen ways to Sunday. Many times the dog didn't even know their owners. Amateur Day was the only time that the owners ever handled them."

Roger: "In that period, it was like a social club. We had lovely lunches at the trials or elegant tailgate parties, and we all met for dinner later at one of the better restaurants in the area. It was a very closely knit social group, older, richer than they are today, and many were in the Social Register."

Pert: "It's changed a great deal from when we first started in the game. I can remember all of the people — the Murnanes, the Greenleafs, the Humphreys, Alice Lewis, and many more would be there with their chairs and their parasols, the women doing needlepoint and watching the dogs; they had the front row section all to themselves, and it was a big social event."

Roger: "If you compare field trialing to horse racing, field trialing has never had the social status of Saratoga. You must have social entree to be in the harness game; it is not essential in the field trial game."

Pert: "Although there were certainly a great many people in Labradors who felt that way. In other words, in the old days an amateur daring to run in an Open Stake was really kind of an upstart."

Roger: "But that is a competitive thing, not a social thing."

Pert: "I'm not so sure. I remember when they had tables on the patio here at Westhampton marked Professional Handlers Only;

they didn't dare sit at the elite people's tables. And it wasn't so easy for the one-dog newcomer who didn't have a social pedigree."

Roger: "The fact is that the rich people could afford to have those pros, and the pros wouldn't sit at the table with their bosses. That's what it amounted to. Today it has become every man's game."

Pert: "Several years ago Helen Pierson (she or her husband was running the club) asked me if I'd have the judges for drinks after the tests on Friday. So I said, 'Sure, I'll be glad to.' My invitation list got bigger and bigger. Helen came to me later on and said, 'Are you having quite a few people?' I said, 'Oh yes, I've invited almost everybody, including the pros.' As if shocked, she said, 'The *pros!*' I said, 'Absolutely, they're good friends of ours.'"

Roger: "The social aspect has changed a lot. Anyone can get in the game now. They get a dog and train him themselves and run in trials. Things have changed."

Pert and Roger Vasselais

The new social order that developed after World War II brought leisure time and extra dollars to the new middle class. The average family could participate in activities that were once only for the wealthy. In a way, the change in ownership of the Labrador was similar to that of the automobile: everyone could now afford to have one.

The "revolution" was a slow and quiet one. As suburbia grew, the great estates in America and England dwindled. The Labrador became an extremely popular dog; almost everywhere, one could see a black or yellow Lab at the heels of the housewife as she pushed her cart to market. In America, from a mere handful of Labs in the thirties, there were now hundreds of thousands. The Labrador became just as at home in the family station wagon as he was in the kennel. The dog that sat at heel at a driven pheasant shoot at Long Island's exclusive South Side Club could now be found on weekends sitting with his master pass-shooting on the rocks of Long Island Sound.

The Lab's Growing Popularity

It was only natural that with the great popularity of the Labrador more and more people would gravitate to field trials. This presented no problem in most of the country because the clubs had a broad sociological base and were very democratic from their onset. The social change was felt most on Long Island, where the sport had its beginnings. By American Kennel Club regulations, the trials were open to all. Mixing a Wisconsin milkman and a Wall Street banker who belonged to a fine shooting club and had his own professional trainer was bound to have its effects. Just because they both had good dogs did not mean they had equal social status. The first things that went by the board were the after-trial banquets and social get-togethers, which became very informal and infrequent, and some newcomers had a difficult time of it.

Audrey Brokaw is truly one of the *grand dames* of the sport.

Audrey Brokaw

The Lighter Side of Social Change

She and her husband, Clifford, first entered field trials in the early 1950s. They were members of the Wyandanch Club and the Santee Club in South Carolina, which was a fine duck hunting club with beautiful marshes and excellent shooting. Today it is part of the wilderness area. Charlie Kostrewski was their dog trainer, and when Clifford Brokaw died in 1959 Charlie stayed on and trained for Audrey. Although she had never blown a whistle before then, she went on to produce twelve field trial champions, and in 1970 became the first woman to win a national event.

Audrey Brokaw is a petite, elegant woman, whose name appears in the Social Register. When she first entered into the sport of field trials, it was known as the "poor man's racing." At the time, field trials were simply an extension of the shooting community. She does not agree that newcomers to the sport had any special problems. Mrs. Brokaw has enjoyed all the people in the game and has opened her home and grounds to dog people from all parts of the country and all walks of life. She said, "I think there has been too much loose talk about the social aspect. I think people are people."

Audrey Brokaw's views of the social changes were not shared by all. As one campaigner of the sixties told it, "By the time my wife and I reached Butte, Montana with our dogs we felt that we really belonged. After their trial we were invited to the club's annual dinner as their guests. But we'd started our campaign trialing across the country in Long Island where we couldn't get as much as a 'Good morning' while airing our dogs in the designated area. One had the feeling on the Island that the pedigree of the owner was more important than that of the dog."

There were two Jack Cassidys running dogs in the East in the early sixties. One was given the handle "Good" Jack and the other "Bad." One was quiet and easy-going, and the other looked the part of "Bad Jack." Actually, Bad Jack was a very nice guy, but he was from Brooklyn, talked Brooklynese, looked like an off-duty cop, and was really a fireman. He remembers the social segregation during those years and relates the story in his own Brooklyn fashion.

"We were duck hunters and we decided we needed dogs. We picked up one of those sporting magazines and saw the Bigstone Kennel ad and Bob (Bad Jack's crane-operator friend Bob Willow) bought his first Labrador. I think he paid $40 for it. Then I bought Rip for $70. Bob's dog was called Blackie. I called the AKC to find out how I could go about training the dog and they told me to get in touch with a Mr. and Mrs. Belmont who was secretary for the Long Island Retriever Club. I called the Belmonts and they told me they were having a field trial that weekend. My dog was about ten or twelve weeks at the time. So Bob and I came out to the field trial, which was my first ever seen — it happened to be the National Amateur that was held in Long Island. When I got there I arrived with Bob Willow. We went to the National and we said we think we

YOUR SERVANT SIR *Marguerite Kirmse*

could train the dog to do this with a little time.

"With our dogs we continued hunting and training and getting into field trials. His dog is a pretty good dog. My dog was probably the wildest dog that ever lived. It had every bad habit and most people would probably give up on him.

"Rip almost made Amateur Field Champ and Blackie, Bob's $40 bitch, made Amateur Field Champ. She qualified for the National. By the time I was done I think I had 17 points with Rip, but I didn't have a win.

"I joined the Long Island Retriever Club first and then I joined the Westchester Retriever Club, which had at that time a lot of sanction trials — two days. It seemed like there was at least two trials every month during the summer until it got into the winter time. It was a place where you could come and train for what you needed; if you had intentions of going to the License trials, which were tough at the time because the people who were big into the field trials didn't really think you belonged there. It was the rich people's idea that they deserved all these licensed points and they didn't want you coming and taking them away. They were hard to get and they also had the best dogs and you had to really work a dog to beat their dogs. If you did beat them, you really earned it.

"I think the judging of trials was fair, but the placing was not fair. I had three seconds. Two were definitely firsts and one was so close that it should have gone another series to decide the winner.

"There was a whole social status thing that was going on at that time. We were beneath the people who were running the trials. Boy, was I watched! They wanted to get something on me and throw me out of the trials. The committee followed me around because they thought I was a mean dog trainer, but I was no meaner than anybody else. At the time I couldn't afford any of those electric collars and all these other devices that people were using, but if I hit a dog with a strap, I know that I would be kicked off the ground. I was warned before I got there by other people that if the dog screwed up, the field trial committee was going to watch me.

"I remember how that whole business about being watched got started. At every trial, it never failed, at every one of them the front row of the gallery was made up of a line of ladies sitting in their fancy folding chairs. These very refined, rich, old ladies were all handsome-looking, dressed in the finest field trial clothes with national pins all over their hats. They sat and watched the trial and knitted. It reminded me of *The Tale of Two Cities.* I don't know what they were knitting, but the needles were going for three whole days at every stake. They all had professional trainers and I don't think they ever had a dog in their house and of course never handled a dog. I've forgotten most of their names, but I remember the knitting.

"Well, I brought my dog up to line and Roger Vasselais had just

111

finished the test with his dog Mick. Mick was supposed to sit and honor as my Rip retrieved. At the time Mick was the highest-point Labrador in the country. Roger's dog wasn't honoring right, he was rolling on his back and my dog had to go out, pick up a duck and come right back past the honoring dog. Well, Rip comes back in and he sees this dog rolling around on his back, drops the bird, and starts going after Mick. To stop the fight I kicked Rip in the side to bust it up. These women dropped their knitting and went wild— they were going to kick me out of field trials forever. Luckily, Roger stepped in and said that I'd done the right thing. If I hadn't kicked the dog to break up the fight, his dog or somebody could have gotten hurt. Those women sure got hysterical when I kicked Rip. They'd just never been around to see their own trainers at work. They wanted me out!

"The Long Island people were not a very friendly sort. I was never invited to any of the after-trial dinners or that sort of thing. But there were a lot of exceptions. Mrs. Belmont, especially, was one of my top people. She showed me how to train dogs; I learned most of the things from her. After almost winning the Labrador Club trial and being a member of the club for ten years, I was invited down to Mr. Laughlin's kennel for a frankfurter once, and that time I thought I was starting to get in—it took me ten years to get a frankfurter in a kennel.

"Mr. Laughlin was one of the nicer people. He ran the club very nice. I don't think the Labrador will ever be the same since he's gone. It was one of the better clubs. A very exclusive club. I was asked to join the Labrador after I guess around ten years of field trialing, almost winning the club trophy. I didn't win the trial because I wasn't a member. I sent Rip to his grave without becoming a champion . . . they just couldn't give it to him, wouldn't let him have it.

"It's changed now. Most of the older people are gone, and there are new clubs and new people. It's a new breed, mostly of amateurs with one dog they train themselves. Very few people in the game have professional trainers. The pros aren't exclusive, except for Mrs. Brokaw, who still has her own private pro. She is a very nice lady, and Charlie Kostrewski, her trainer, is one of the nicest—always has a big smile, a hello for everybody.

"I had a lot of fun in my time. Those were some of the bad parts, but there were plenty of good parts. I had to work twice as hard as anyone for the little bit that I did get, but I still did it!"

Jack threw his head back and looked at the ceiling. His big mustache curved into a smile, then followed a good belly laugh. "The bad and the good seem to work together. I remember my old dog Rip got even with one of them fancy ladies all dressed up in Abercrombie and Fitch field clothes and sitting in her front row seat knittin'. It was a sanction trial and she had a bitch that was close to

Bad Jack

being in season. Her dog went out to retrieve a duck and was play-ing with it. Then she left the duck and starting having fun in the water. The judge asked me if I'd get my dog to pick up the duck. I said OK, and I ran back to the truck, got my dog, lined him up with the bird and sent him out. He got out to the bird, picked it up and he got wind of this bitch. They are in shoulder deep water; he comes over and pounced on the bitch, pumping away like hell with the duck still in his mouth. They were almost ready to breed and everybody at the trial . . . except that lady . . . was laughing like hell and rolling on the ground. She dropped her knitting and Rip got steak for supper."

BOUND FOR THE BAR *Tom Hennessey*

Herb Strasser

Training Methods...
Past and Present

In my earlier book, *Water Dog*, the three basic hunting dogs are compared. "The rabbit hound believes in his nose and the chase. The pointing dog believes in his nose and the gun. The retriever believes in his handler."

The rabbit hunter's dog is a self-hunter. You put him on the trail of a rabbit and he either goes off a-howling or you don't use him. If he won't hunt on his own accord, you can't teach him to do it. If he does go off for Brer Rabbit, he goes after him for himself. *He* wants that rabbit; he's not hunting for the gun.

The bird dog hunts for the gun. You can never teach a bird dog *to* hunt; you can only teach him *how* to hunt. He quarters the field scenting out the game. When he finds it, he stops dead in his tracks and his rigid position means that game is near. The hunter moves in for the flush and the kill.

The retriever is a different kind of hunter. The hunter finds his own game. The dog doesn't go into action until the game is down. He sits at heel during all the action. His job is then to retrieve the downed game either on land or water. He does his job directly for you and not your gun.

This is true for all retrievers, but the history of the Labrador makes him best suited for this work — indeed, any work. Perhaps no other dog has been bred to have a closer rapport with man. From his earliest days, working alongside the Devon fisherman, swimming the cold waters of Newfoundland, the Lab worked on command. He retrieved fish that sprang loose from the hook and game, fur, or feather when the fisherman took up his gun. When the Lab returned to England, his job was still to follow the directions of his handler. Today, after centuries of breeding, he still loves to carry anything he can get in his mouth. Interestingly, the Lab has not developed into a one-man dog in the same way as the Prussian dog. Working so closely with his masters for so many generations produced a dog with a strong general desire to please, which complements perfectly his natural intelligence.

The training of the retriever goes well back in the English sporting literature. One of the earliest training guides was written in 1721 by Nicholas Cox *The Gentlemen's Recreation of Fowling.* He titles a section, "How to Train a Water Dog, and the use thereof."

> For the training of this Dog, you cannot begin too soon with him; and therefore as soon as he can lap, you must teach him to lie down, not daring to stir from that Posture without Leave. Observe in his first teaching to let him eat nothing till he deserves it; and let him have no more Teachers, Feeders, Cherishers, or Correctors but one; and do not alter that Word you first use in his Information, for the Dog takes Notice of the Sound, not the Language.
>
> When you have acquainted him with the Word suitable to his lesson, you must then teach him to know the Word of Reprehension, which at first should not be used without a Jerk. You must also use Words of cherishing, to give him Encouragement when he does well: [And] in all these Words you must be constant, and let them be attended with spitting in his Mouth, or cherishing of the Hand. There is also a Word of Advice, instructing him when he does amiss.
>
> Having made him understand these several Words, you must next teach him to lead in a String or Collar orderly, not running too forward, nor hanging backward. After this you must teach him to come close at your Heels without leading; for he must not range by any Means, unless it be to beat Fowl from their Covert or to fetch the wounded.
>
> In the next Place you must teach him to fetch and carry any thing you throw out of your Hands. And first try him with the Glove, shaking it over his Head, and making him snap at it; and sometimes let him hold it in his Mouth, and strive to pull it from him; and at last throw it a little way, and let him worry it on the Ground; and so by degrees make him bring it to you, where-ever you throw it. From the Glove you must teach him to fetch Cudgels, Bags, Nets, etc.
>
> If you use him to carry dead Fowl, it will not be amiss; for by that Means he will never tear or bruise that Fowl you shoot.
>
> Having perfected this Lesson, drop something behind you,

Earliest Training Methods

116

which the Dog doth not see; and being gone a little way from it, send him back to seek it, by saying, *Back, I have lost.* If he seem amazed, point with your Finger, urging him to seek out, and leave him not till he hath done it. Then drop something at a greater distance, and make him find out that too, till you have brought him to go back a Mile.

Now you may train him up for your Gun, making him stalk after you step by step, or else couch and lie close till you have shot.

Many more necessary Rules there are, which for brevity sake I must omit.

The last use of the Water-Dog is in moulting time, when wild Fowl cast their Feathers, and are unable to fly, which is between Summer and Autumn: At this time bring your Dog to their Coverts, and hunt them out into the Stream, and there will your Nets surprize them, driving them into them; for at this time Sheep will not drive more easily. And tho' some may object, that this sickly Time is unseasonable; yet if they consider what excellent Food these Fowl will prove when cramm'd, the taking of them may be very excusable.

Many modern training manuals do not digress very far from Cox's, though he did deviate from the trainers of his era by starting the pups at such an early age. The English traditionally started their pointing dog's training at six months to one year to allow a litter to develop a hunting instinct on their own and to find the pups that showed the most promise. The time and effort was then put into the precocious ones. Cox recognized that a retriever works for his master; by starting the dog early and allowing him only one teacher, the dog will learn his work without undue force. His understanding of communicating with the pup seems very sophisticated for the time: "A dog takes notice of the sound not the language." It is also interesting that the command "Back," which is used by most handlers today to send the dog away from them, seems to have had its origin with Cox.

Captain Brown's "Play" Learning

A little over a century later, in 1829, Captain Thomas Brown, in his book, *Anecdotes of Dogs,* describes a teaching method, based on instilling in the pup a desire to play the retrieving game, that was unique for his time.

Gentlemen who have large establishments of sporting dogs generally keep one or two for the express purpose of finding lost and wounded game, and these are termed *Retrievers.* These consist of the Newfoundland dog, the great water-dog, and the large Water-Spaniel. Genuine dogs of this kind are now extremely rare in Britain . . .

When puppies are five or six months old, they should be

BLACK LABRADOR *Owen Gromme*

taught to fetch and carry as a preliminary to breaking them. This is easily done by throwing a glove or other article to them in the house, and desiring them to fetch it. With young dogs the most gentle means are certainly the best, and where any animal proves obstinate his correction should only be moderate; and if he seems much disheartened by beating, it will be best to suspend his teaching for a time, and in the interim he may be propitiated with gentle carresses.

A method which has been successfully employed in training the dogs under consideration is, to get a rabbit's skin stuffed, and begin by tossing it about in a room. When the dog, which should have a small line to his collar, takes up the skin, bring him to you by a gentle pull with the skin in his mouth; encourage him three or four times, and then take the line off. When the dog begins to enjoy this sport, take a small line and run it through a pulley fixed to the ceiling, then tie the rabbit's-skin to one end of the line and keep the other in your hand; after this fire a pistol and let the skin drop. The dog will soon become fond of the sport, and will thereafter readily bring every head of game and wild-fowl that is shot. After some proficiency is made, take two or three together into a room, fire the pistol, and order first one dog and then another to bring the skin, and with a little practice they will soon be perfect.

Should all these means prove unavailing, the task should be abandoned until he is old enough to be broken in, and he will then be better able to bear correction and to understand for what cause it is inflicted.

Recourse should next be had to throwing a piece of wood into the water, and desiring the dog to fetch it out, which he will soon do by a little practice.

John B. Johnson, in his book *The Dog and How to Break Him*, published in 1851, assumes that retrieving is a natural instinct. He states emphatically that the retriever's "proper and legitimate business is to hunt wounded or dead, not living game." From his writings he seems to have problems with some hard-mouthed dogs.

The first lesson for a young retriever may be given in company with pointer or setter pups; it is merely to be taught to keep to the heel, and drop on the firing of a gun or pistol. It must be first ascertained whether he will carry; but little doubt need be entertained on this head, as I never yet saw any dog having a cross from the Newfoundland that did not take to carrying naturally, and as if by instinct. Sometimes it will happen, though not too often, that a young dog will bite his game too hard; and this is an unfortunate circumstance. If a rabbit skin be stuffed with hard straw, with thorns intermixed, and

119

used for him to fetch and early in the first instance, it will not often happen that he will bite his game; but, should he acquire the habit, a dead bird — a pigeon, for instance — may be stuck through with sharp wires, which will prick his mouth when he attempts to squeeze too much, and may eventually cure him of a practice which will be likely to increase with age.

All dogs when urged to the pursuit of living game, such so as to acquire the habit of dropping his game as soon as he reaches you; on the contrary, it will be well to let him occasionally carry a bird or hare some distance, and encourage him to do so; and to bear in mind that it should be taken from his mouth by the hand, when it is required from him, in as gentle a manner as possible.

Some dogs acquire a wonderful sagacity in marking birds. If a retriever keeps to heel, he will, on seeing his master fire at a bird, if it does not immediately fall, soon learn to follow the bird with his eye; and in case it is supposed to be killed, he will have less difficulty retrieving with the knowledge of the flight of the bird than if he had to depend on the sense of smell alone.

An extremely important book on dog training in the second half of the nineteenth century was *Dog Breaking: The Most Expeditious, Easy, and Certain Method, Whether Great Excellence or Only Mediocrity be Required* by Colonel William Nelson Hutchinson of the Grenadier Guards. It was reprinted in many English and American editions. Hutchinson's discourse on the training of the retriever gives the reader a good notion of what should be expected of a dog and how to get it accomplished. Here, for example, is what he says about marking.

Hutchinson's Treatise

It is quite astonishing how well an old dog that retrieves knows when a bird is struck. He instantly detects any hesitation or uncertainty of movement, and for a length of time will watch its flight with the utmost eagerness, and, steadily keeping his eye on it, will as surely as yourself mark its fall. To induce a young dog to become thus observant, always let him perceive that *you* watch a wounded bird with great eagerness; his imitative instinct will soon lead him to do the same. This faculty of observation is particularly serviceable in a Water Retriever. It enables him to swim direct to the crippled bird, and, besides the saving of time, the less he is in the water in severe weather, the less likely is he to suffer from rheumatism.

As an initiatory lesson in making him observant of the flight and fall of birds, place a few pigeons, or other birds, during his absence, each in a hole covered with a tile. Afterwards come upon these spots apparently unexpectedly, and, kicking away the tiles — or, what is better, dragging them off by a previously adjusted string — shoot the birds for him to bring; it being clearly understood that he has been previously tutored into having no dread of the gun. As he will have been taught to search where bidden — nothing now remains but to take him out on a regular campaign, when the fascinating scent of game will infallibly make him search — I do not say deliver — with great eagerness. When once he then touches upon a scent, leave him entirely to himself — not a word, not a sign. Possibly his nose may not be able to follow the bird, but it is certain that yours cannot. Remain, therefore, quietly where you are until he rejoins you.

When we see a winged pheasant racing off, most of us are too apt to assist a young dog, forgetting that we thereby teach him, instead of devoting his whole attention to work out the scent, to turn to us for aid on occasions when it may be impossible to give it. When a dog is hunting *for* birds, he should frequently look to the gun for signals, but when he is *on* them he should trust to nothing but his own scenting faculties.

Need for a Comprehensive Training Manual

The popularity of the retrieving dogs increased during the latter part of the nineteenth and early twentieth century, and a new and comprehensive book on training was badly needed. The first systematic training method had still not been introduced. Many of the books at the time were mere dialogues on hunting, gamekeepers, guns, and memorable experiences in the field, with dog training experiences scattered throughout. A good example is Sir Henry Smith's book *Retrievers And How To Break Them*, written in 1898 and dedicated by special permission to His Royal Highness The Duke of York. The book makes charming reading about days in the field but leaves much to be desired when it comes to training methods.

I remember being out in Dryfesdale in October '96 with gamekeeper Michie and two of my favourites, "Doubtful" and "Dryfe": the former in her fourth season at my side, broken by myself; the latter just a year old, having the finishing touches put on by Michie. A covey of hill-partridges on the edge of the moor got up wild, and flew across a large meadow intersected by deep drains completely overgrown with long rank grass — a very puzzling place, as I well knew, for a retriever. Taking a long shot, I brought one down, and "Dryfe" was dispatched by Michie for it. She had marked the place well, and immediately picked up the scent; but the deep wet drains were too much for her, and after trying hard for a long while, she was pretty well beat. Meanwhile, "Doubtful," her tail waving slowly backwards and forwards, had been intently watching her, and every now and again looking eagerly up in my face, and saying as plainly as it could be said, "How long is my silly little granddaughter to keep pottering about there? Let me go—I'll find the bird for you." Presently a shout from Michie, "We shall lose that partridge, sir." "Get on, 'Doubtful,'" was my instantaneous reply. A badly broken dog would have made straight for the other, and the two would have careered about madly jealous, rushing after one another with their heads in the air, to the complete interruption of business and the eventual escape of the partridge; but this was not "Doubtful's" idea of work. Without taking any notice of "Dryfe," who was still persevering, and who continued to persevere on her own account, really beat but, like the British soldier, ignorant of the fact, she galloped straight to the place where the bird had fallen, and casting herself about with extraordinary rapidity, instantly disappeared, reappearing again almost immediately, some sixty or seventy yards away, with a poor little dripping partridge in her mouth—"Dryfe" soon discovering what had happened, and joining "Doubtful" to try and get a little credit to herself for the find. The inexperience of the young one and the experience of the old were to me very interesting to watch.

The requirements and hunting standards for a retriever were simple back then as compared to what is called for today. At the turn of the century, a dog that would stand at heel, then go on command, hunt, and carry game was considered a first class retriever. B. Waters in his book *Fetch and Carry*, published in America in 1895, puts it this way: "A slovenly and disobedient retriever will mar the best of sport. However willing a dog may be to obey and perform, if he does not know methods and commands, he can add little to the pleasure or success of the shooter. The hunter is commonly satisfied with too low a standard of retrieving. His own standard of sport is often not any too high. He is eager to capture regardless of method, and his eagerness many times is the source of unseemly scrambles between himself and the dog to get possession of the bird."

Although this passage conjures up a very unsophisticated picture of his fellow sportsmen, B. Waters did devise the first systematic training method. For the first time retriever training was separated into two systems, the natural method and the force system. The author defines the natural method as the amusement method. The trainer plays with the pup and begins the game of fetch at an early time. Once the dog learns to like the game he will hopefully like the more serious game of hunting. There is no play involved in the force system. Waters held a short line, choke collar in one hand and a corn cob in his other. The collar is jerked. When the dog opens his mouth to cry out, the cob is gently put in, the collar slackened and with the hand under his mouth, is induced to hold it. The dog learns by force that he must carry the object.

SUNKEN BLIND by John Cowan

123

The Waters book was quite complete in all phases of the retrieving job, advancing step-by-step from the first retrieves of game to the field retrieves on land and water. He even devoted a chapter to the finder-retriever, stating that in America hunting conditions dictate that more game would be brought to bag if the dogs did dual-purpose work. He contended that if a pointing dog could be taught to fetch, a retriever could be taught to find. Waters prophesied many events of the twentieth century, both in his dog training methods and forseeing the destruction of our natural game and the necessity for game preserves.

The first book to discuss training in the 20th century, *The Scientific Education of the Dog for the Gun*, was written by "H.H.," whose initials, it was discovered later, belonged to Holland Hibbert, the Hon. Arthur Holland-Hibbert who later became Lord Knutsford, one of the important benefactors of the Labrador Retriever. The importance of the book has been forgotten over the years because book dealers "lost" the association between the initials and the author's identity. The exact date of the book is not known, but the third edition is dated 1910.

Holland Hibbert stresses the importance of early training, a point animal behaviorists substantiated sixty years later: "If you want actual perfection, it is a *sine qua non,* in my opinion, to begin with a pup *as soon as it is weaned;* don't let someone else bring it up for you till it is three or four months old, and don't let it ever know anything of anybody else except yourself, and your task will be tenfold easier. Leave no stone unturned never to allow a pup to contract the least bad habit. To avoid these, though it wants a lot of care, is far less trouble than to cure them."

Although many of the training books that were written in the late nineteenth and early twentieth centuries were produced by sporting gentlemen, most of this period's Labradors were trained by gamekeepers and dog handlers who were not especially articulate and in some cases illiterate. Dog training methods, like the British shooting sports, were based on tradition handed down from generation to generation. Nevertheless, certain dog writers did have a lasting impact on training methods. Colonel William Hutchinson is still quoted in England more than 100 years after publication of his book, *Dog Breaking*.

In the 1930s, as the Labrador became more and more popular, new authors and books started to appear. The best known were the British authors Leslie Sprake (*The Labrador Retriever*), Rowland Johns, and Leonard E. Naylor. Although their books make interesting reading, they added little to the accumulated literature on training that already existed. Today's British authority, Peter R. A. Moxon, is also a traditionalist, which is understandable: The British have not changed their hunting methods; what is required of the Lab in Britain today is no different than what was required during

Knutsford's "Forgotten" Masterpiece

Peter Moxon, the grand old dean of British dogwriters.

Americanizing of Technique

the last century, and their methods work very well for their needs.

This has not been the case in America, where the Lab has been asked to do a lot more over the last fifty years than when the dog was first imported as part of British style shooting. The American waterfowl hunter needed a hardy dog that could stand the cold, a strong swimmer that could break the ice to make a water retrieve; these were not tweed shooting-jacket conditions in the blinds on the Eastern Shore. During the American field trials of the 1930s, the Chesapeake Bay Retriever proved he could do the job, but for the Lab the water work became so much more demanding than anything the British required that the Scottish gamekeepers who were training the dogs in the U.S. had a big job. However, it only took a year for the Lab to show that he could outswim and outclass the Chessie at his own game. The American hunter soon learned that the Lab was outstanding in every department and was an easy dog to train and live with. If the Lab had not shown its versatility so dramatically in those early years, the American Labrador might have had as difficult time of surviving as the Scottish driven shoot.

The depression and World War II changed the social and economic structure of America and also affected the training of the Labrador. As the social change gradually took hold, more people from all walks of life entered the field trials. Though the British kept trial entries to a maximum of 24 for a two-day trial and 12 for a one-day event, in America the contest was open to all comers. Trial entries increased and with so many good retrievers in the field, more emphasis was placed on training. The day of the domination of the sport by the professional trainer was fast ending. It was not just the fact that there were fewer and fewer people who could afford to run a string of dogs, but the training that was necessary for the exacting tests required the trainer to spend many, many more hours with each dog. This was something the professional could not afford to do.

Paul Bakewell, the first amateur to beat the pros consistently, discussed training during the post-war period. "Except for a fellow named Hogan I would suggest that many of the professionals were more like attendants than trainers in the way their dogs worked. Their dogs knew nothing about taking a line or taking directions. One reason I think I did well is that I could devote the proper time to each one with repetition, repetition, and repetition. The trainer of a number of dogs could not devote enough time to each individual dog to get the proper results.

"I worked the dogs every day, with no time off — Saturdays and Sundays as well as Monday, Tuesdays, etc. When I was training the dogs I would be the only one to feed and water them. They were brought in the house and spent time each evening so that we'd get to know each other better, rather than just be their trainer.

"I knew of some trainers who used to work together, which to me was a lot of damn foolishness, as I would never work with another trainer watching their dogs making mistakes. My time was too valuable."

In *The American Sporting Dogs*, edited by Eugene Connett, Bakewell contributed the most concise, step-by-step training procedure that had been written up to this time. Although he says now that many professionals were little more than attendants to their dogs, in 1948 he wrote, "The development of retrievers did not happen by chance. Without an able group of professional trainers and handlers, the game in no way would have reached its present peak." He gave credit to Tom Briggs, Harry Conklin, Martin Hogan, Orin Benson, Charlie Kostrewski, and Bill Wunderlick, and ended his praise with "More power to you! These and many more made the Labrador."

As the interest in field trials grew, the need for a book that would teach the rapidly changing requirements for the retrievers also grew. The English methods were no longer applicable to American needs. In 1949, James Lamb Free, an amateur who started training Labs in 1938, wrote *Training Your Retriever*, a step-by-step training manual for the amateur that would remain the best book on the subject for twenty-five years.

Cotton Pershall was never pleased with the changes in field trial tests that were instituted during the late 1940s to the 1960s.

"Back in the early days it made no difference if the bird was a runner or a cripple, your dog was sent for it. Today I don't think there are a half-dozen dogs that would know how to work out the problem of a runner. Unfortunately, we're eliminating all the natural ability of the dog. To this day, every dog I train is taught how to track a runner.

"We would drag a freshly killed bird and make a trail of scent. Then let the dog follow that scent by walking him a few feet, encouraging him to go a little further each day. Finally I would clip the wings of a bird and turn him loose and after I saw the bird was moving I'd take the dog towards the bird real quick so he could make the recovery. Each day I'd wait a little longer before I'd send the dog . . . they learned to track.

"We are getting too far away from real hunting conditions. Two-hundred-yard marks and three-hundred-yard blinds are not what we find very often in the natural hunting condition. We are getting too mechanical. I guess in some ways I have to blame a lot of it on myself.

"I was the first to start lining my Labs back a great distance. Here is how it came to me. One day I was working some dogs next to a bridle path trail and I had a young dog with a problem of not being able to push back deep enough. It dawned on me that if he could see the dummies he would go back and get them. Well, I just dropped some dummies down this trail, and I let him see me do it. I

Pershall's Methods

started lining him down the path to them going further each time. It wasn't any time until I could line this dog hundreds of yards down the bridle trial. I then started using paths for long side casts, back casts, and over casts to right, left. I hate to say I started it, but they've overdone the usefulness of the line.

"We're spending so much time on lining and handling we're neglecting field manners. We used to have walk-ups. We'd have three or four dogs in the line and they had to be well-mannered. While one dog worked the others had to sit at heel. Today we don't have well-mannered dogs. In fact, some that are brought to line are wild with excitement. They don't teach manners like the British do. Today we don't even really honor another dog's work. We only ask a dog to sit at heel when the next dog's birds are shot. As soon as the running dog is sent the honoring dog is excused. That's not the way it happens in hunting.

"Paul Bakewell and I were the first to use the 'baseball' set up to teach the dog to learn to handle. We drilled constantly on handling and taking a line. In many ways this changed the work of the Lab. They were certainly smart dogs and they could take the training but I'm not too sure today what these mechanical tests, long blinds, tight triples and trick tests are doing for the breed. Certainly a hunter doesn't need all this precision and it has made the training job more difficult."

Another of the grand old trainers is Charlie Kostrewski, who started in the game in 1926 on the Marshall Field estate and later worked for Jim Cowie. In 1952, Clifford Brokaw hired Charlie to run his kennel. Brokaw died in 1959 and Charlie stayed on with Mrs. Audrey Brokaw; they have been working together ever since. Charlie has the reputation in field trial circles of being a champion. Here are his ideas on training:

"If you treat your dog right and you become a team, he will not let you down. If he makes a mistake, it's an honest mistake, it's not because he's trying to cheat on you. Some fellows say, 'The dog stuck it to me.' Well, maybe he had a reason for giving it to the trainer because he was cruel to the dog. Usually dogs that you get hard on are going to get back at you somewhere along the line.

"I see no reason for a lot of the things we do at field trials today. Why should a dog have to take an angle into the water on a blind? I have to do it because the judges require it, but I don't think it should be done . . . it's unnatural for a dog and we have to force them. I try never to force a dog. Force retrieve? . . . Never!

"I'll put my dogs against any dog. If a pup drops a dummy I'll say 'Fetch,' and he'll pick it up and hold. I do it all as fun. Sure, it's sloppy for quite a while, but once they get the idea they've got it, and you've got a happy dog. It's the same in all the training, but you have to go step by step, even through the complicated lessons, so they know what you want. When you are through they know

Kostrewski on Training

Charlie Kostrewski

what you want; then if they don't do it, you can get after them.

"I never felt the need for force training to retrieve. I'll pick up a bumper if he drops it, put it in his mouth and hold it and just slap him a bit. I've seen many fellows take a dog in a barn or a shed and force retrieve him. Nine times out of ten they break the dog's spirit. Get the dog working with you and you can teach him anything."

When Dave Elliot, one of the first and best Scottish gamekeepers to work with Labradors in America, was asked what part of the dog's training field trials neglect, he responded: "Training on cripples." After all, "most of the birds we kill we can walk out ourselves and pick up by hand . . . but not the cripples! That's the weakest link in our trials. A cripple in trials is considered unfair to the dog and is a 'no bird.' What should be the most important part of the dog's work, receives the least consideration. Dogs are never trained for it because they'll never receive a cripple as a trial test. If you are going to give every dog in the trial the exact same test, there is no way a runner can be included. Besides, with the number of dogs we run in trials it would take too long for a dog to be allowed to work out the problems of tracking down a cripple."

Dave always included hunting down a cripple in his training of a young dog. He did it by using a clipped-wing duck. He would let a duck get about a fifty-yard start on a pup, and as the dog acquired experience and confidence he would give the duck a bigger lead.

In 1949, Elliot wrote:

> As the retriever trial season rolls around I cannot help but wonder what new and complicated tests will be given to try out the mechanical ability of our dogs. I use the word mechanical because that is exactly what we are developing. Our field trials call for precision in every performance, and they do not care from which end of the leash it comes. In fact, many tests are given today that call for a great deal more from the handler than the dog; it is like keeping a dog and doing the barking yourself. Such tests have forced the trainer to train his dogs to act only under his complete command; the dog is not allowed to quarter his ground as is the correct way for a retriever to work. He is not permitted to show his natural ability in hunting out a fall. Yet what would give greater pleasure to a retriever man than to watch that keen natural ability that puts the hallmark of excellence on all his dog's work? It is to be regretted that this type of work is left out of our trials. A great deal of what belongs to the dog has been placed in the handler's hands; a more artificial performance could not be demonstrated.
>
> Handlers and owners brag about how their dogs will go in a straight line for one hundred and fifty yards unless stopped by the whistle. This is seldom called for in hunting. Ninety-five per cent of your work with a retriever is accomplished within

Elliot's Ideas

128

Natural Training Methods

T. J. Linblum and Guffy

gun range, and the less whistling and handling done during a shoot will put more birds in your bag. I am sure there is nothing that will bring down more wrath on a handler's head from his fellow gunners than one who insists on blowing whistle and waving arms to pick up a stray duck while the flight is on.

The more we train our dogs to depend on that whistle and direction, the more helpless they are going to become, and it is going to show up in our breeding. We cannot expect the offspring of mechanical parents to show much natural ability. To keep our dogs from looking like complete mechanical nitwits, we will have to breed to the old river rat, whose natural ability has been given full scope; and only then will we get back to the old type of retriever who has a head and knows how to use it.

The old adage of "when in doubt, trust your dog" seems to have died a silent death with the introduction of scientific training. To be able to give a dog direction out to a fall is a great asset, but I do think that we should make it the exception instead of the rule. We should encourage and protect natural ability. We will most surely lose it if we continue to monopolize those hunting instincts that make the retriever one of conservation's greatest friends.

In *Water Dog,* I tried to bring a new approach to Labrador training. The training system outlined in that book was the result of methods devised by a team of social psychologists at the Roscoe B. Jackson Memorial Laboratory in Bar Harbor, Maine. (The research was first done for a Guide Dogs for the Blind project, and has since become the primary system used in training these dogs. The method has been very successful: previously, only 20 percent of the best bred dogs took to rigorous guide dog training; with the new method, there was a dramatic 96 percent success rate.) The system works well for the hunter or amateur trainer who has only one or two dogs to work with. It is based on the natural training method with very little force involved. The dog learns at a very early age (seven weeks) in a controlled environment and so doesn't pick up undesirable habits.

The success of the natural training method can best be told by T.J. Linblum, a young sheep rancher from Oregon. T.J. is the Cinderella story of field trials. The first dog he trained seriously became the National Open Champion.

"I loved to hunt dogs and I was going to school at Oregon State University. One of my professors knew how much I loved animals and he told me, 'You should get a dog,' and he suggested a book to me. It was *Water Dog;* I read the book and started to train a dog, which I bought from a fellow there in town. One day, a man stopped and said, 'That's a pretty nice dog. Why don't you come out to our picnic trial.' I went, ran my young dog and he won a

THE LAB *L.R. Kaatz*

green ribbon. I was thrilled. I told my wife, 'I have to have a well bred field trial dog.' I wrote to Sally McCarthy and she shipped a pup seven weeks old to the airport; my wife and I went and picked Guffy up on our first wedding anniversary.

"The first day I got Guffy I started the play work. I remember I threw that bird out; it sailed fifty yards, and when it came down Guffy had it and he carried it all the way back to me. That started his early training, developing his retrieving desire. I started teaching the basic commands as far as Sit, Heel, and Stay—and followed the ideas in *Water Dog*.

"I had run several picnic trials to prepare him for the licensed ones. He won 25 Derby points and he JAMed (Judges Award of Merit) and placed in almost *every* Derby trial for young dogs I ran him in. At two, when he was out of Derby, he won his first two Qualifying stakes, back to back; that's when I started running in major stakes. In three major stakes he qualified for his first National Amateur.

"When he was three years old he won two doubleheaders, by winning the Open All Age Stake and the Amateur All Age Stake back to back in the same weekend stakes. He competed in quite a few Nationals and became recognized as a contender in the National. He was always a consistent dog and had qualified for ten different Nationals. He won the 1979 National Open in California.

"I did all the training myself. Guffy was brought along by showing him how, and then praising him when he did it right. And when he made a mistake, I either started over from scratch or corrected him depending on the situation. When he was a young dog, I used very little correction other than telling him 'No.' As he got older, the basic tool I used to correct Guffy was a stick, a whip, and that's all I used.

"When I started Guffy at seven weeks, I worked with him in the morning for ten minutes and in the evening for twenty minutes; I gradually increased the time, until twice a day, five or six days a week, until he was about six years old. When I had the time, the sessions would be probably two hours each—quite a bit of time for one dog.

"I like to base my training on reward. When a dog does a task right, he is praised for it and he loves it. He tries to do it right. So often I have seen dogs that are corrected whether they do it right or wrong; they receive punishment before they do anything just so they know that it can happen at any time, I guess. I really don't understand it, to tell you the truth. They receive punishment even when they are being praised . . . I base my training on show and praise, teach by praise.

"The thing I don't like about the electric collar is that it is based on punishment, but I can see some beneficial things about it. It is instantaneous, and maybe it's good if you have a real severe problem and you can't get to the dog right away or he's in the water. I hope I would never use the collar the way I have seen some people use it.

"Guffy's been a real big part of my life. He's always wanted to do what I wanted him to do. Maybe it was because I started him at a very early age and made him part of the family. He has as much rights around the house as the rest of us. We respected him, and in return he wanted to please."

Dogs were always an important part of the lives of August and Louise Belmont. Augie's grandfather was the leading force behind the founding of the American Kennel Club. Louise fancied poodles and ran her own pack of beagles. When Augie and Louise got married, they lived in New York and raised pointers.

The Belmonts started to work with Labs in 1957, when Augie bought a Lab pup, Shuna Buck, for Louise through two top professional trainers on Long Island, Joe Reiser and Dave Elliot. But Louise wasn't pleased at all; she didn't think she would like the field trial game or the people in it. "And" she recalls now, "I didn't like Labradors."

With his new Chessie, Bomarc, Augie started his training routine with obedience classes. Louise started her three-year-old Shauna with Dave Elliot and Dolly Marshall. The plan was that Louise would handle the dog in the Amateur stakes, and Dolly, who was a professional, would handle in the Opens. That plan didn't work out because Louise became so involved that she decided to run her dog in all events herself. Once Louise placed in an Amateur stake, she was hooked, and from then on she and Augie worked as a team. She finished Shauna Buck, making him a Field Champion and an Amateur Field Champion. Augie did make an Amateur Field Champion out of Bomarc but felt he would have less and less success with Chesapeakes as time went on, and so he too started working with Labradors.

Louise's new Lab pup (a purchase from Wilbur Good) and Augie's first Lab, High Wind of South Bay, went out to California to start their training with Rex Carr, who had trained many champions. Laughingly Augie recalled, "I swear that young pup had four legs all of different length." "But," injected Louise, "that pup, who didn't work out, becomes important to our story." Two years later, in 1961, Wilbur Good had a great litter from Paha Sapa Chief II out of Ironwood Cherokee Chica and, because he'd always felt badly about that first strange-legged pup, wanted to replace the dog the Belmonts had given up on.

Augie felt that this new pup should be trained by Rex Carr, and Louise felt that she would rather train her dogs herself, so she gave the pup to Augie and in return Augie gave her High Wind. Louise went on to make "Windy" an Amateur and Field Champion.

Augie's new puppy, his pride and joy, lived his first six months

The Belmonts' Super Chief

The doubleheaders pin

in the Belmont home and became very much a part of the household. His favorite sleeping place that first summer was in the middle of the fireplace. He managed to jump over one of the Belmont's sleeping Chessies once too often and got bitten in the eye. That postponed for a few months his shipment to Rex Carr, but at Christmas time, when he was six months and his eye had healed, he was sent to school in California. By February, Carr called to say, "Send me a few more pups like that. He makes the sun shine brighter in my day . . . every day." That dog was Super Chief. He became the highest point winner in history. He was twice National Amateur Champion and one of those years made a doubleheader. He also won the National Open Championship. Winning three national championships was a feat only one other dog ever accomplished — Super Chief's own daughter.

"Soupy" was a wonderful dog. Augie knew from the moment he came into their home that he was something special. He was precocious and friendly with people and dogs. Later, when he was an adult, he even loved puppies. He spent half his life in California with Rex Carr and the other half living in the house with the Belmonts. There was something so outstanding about him that he even lived in Rex's home, an honor no other dog ever won for himself. There Soupy, after his initial training, would spend summers and part of the winter after the field trial season closed in California. Rex would continue his education each year until the trial season opened again, then he'd be sent East to be run by Augie. Most years, in the month of February, Augie would go out to California and work with the dog under Rex's supervision so they both would be ready for the upcoming trials.

"The way to win trials," Augie said, "was to do something spectacular, and that was the thing that would get you about Soupy. When he won his first National Amateur, there was a triple retrieve that stumped all the dogs. The first two birds were not too difficult, but the third one was through a stream, across some high grass, and into heavy woods. Soupy got up there and took the first two and thrilled the gallery by going out and nailing that third bird. I was stunned, but Rex Carr cried. Soupy could do extraordinary things that would make you gasp. Oh, he'd blow it every once in a while. He was excitable and he might creep on line, but he had a way of pulling himself out of trouble. He was no machine."

"And," added Louise, "he had a wonderful disposition and was a joy to have around the house. The amazing thing about this dog was that he could be handled equally as well by all three of us, Augie, Rex, or myself. We all trained by Rex's system but each person moves a little differently, our voices are different, and our manner is different. But this was something he seemed to take in his stride, so a lot of the credit has to go to the dog. He was great."

He proved that in his offspring too. Soupy had 53 litters and

August Belmont and Soupy, who won three national championships.

from them came 26 Field Trial Champions. The two nearest top sires, Cork of Oakwood and Paha Sapa, each had over 100 litters, and one produced eleven and the other thirteen champions. Soupy produced more than twice the champions in half the litters, an all-time record. Five of his full brothers and sisters went on to win their championships. One of them was Penrod, owned and trained by Louise.

Soupy and Penrod ran head-to-head in trials and Augie remembers fondly the late-night arguments as to who really won that day, Augie's Soupy or Louise's Penrod. But there was never any doubt about the Belmonts' single-mindedness and teamwork. Although Louise never sent any of her dogs to Rex Carr, she and her dogs did spend "vacation" time each year with him to learn his training and handling system.

Back on Long Island the teamwork started at dawn five or six days a week when they'd get up and train for a few hours before Augie had to catch his commuting train for the city. In the winter he'd put heavy clothes and rubber gear over his business suit and as Augie says, "get in one more blind or a good double, then rush like hell for the train." In the summer he'd change clothes in the car as he was driven to the railroad and as he recalls, "Always managed to be decent by the time the train got in the station."

Louise, back from the station, continued the training each day with a group of retriever people that she organized. She handled both her dogs and Augie's. Come Thursday, Louise would pack the car with dogs and coffee and drive to wherever the trial was that weekend. Friday morning she'd start running the trial with both her dogs and Augie's. Friday night, after work, Augie would jump on a plane and fly to the nearest airport, get to the motel one way or another. Saturday morning he'd take over and run the dog through the rest of the weekend. They won open stakes with Soupy this way, and as Louise says, "That was some dog to be able to work under two handlers."

So training became a most important part of their lives. Once Augie got into the sport in 1957 he never again took a vacation that didn't revolve around the training of dogs. They fell in love with the dogs but for some what different reasons. Augie loved the competition, and as Louise says, "I'm a trainer at heart. I really love training the dogs. I don't particularly care for the competition. I like the routine. I have that kind of a Germanic temperament, I guess. Augie doesn't really like to get up each morning to train, but he does it."

"We knew we had something special with Soupy," Augie asserts. "He was very precocious and we needed to have faith and determination. When he was two-and-a-half, I ran him in a number of open stakes and he did very well . . . great style. Then he went back to Rex at the end of that season. When he came back to us he'd developed a habit of popping. We think he was trying so hard

A Story of Courage

Augie and Louise Belmont working together

to please us that he'd turn and look back to me for help. We had to break him of this so I didn't run him for a year-and-a-half. I gave him no work in that time but I never doubted that he was as great as he finally proved to be. Through that whole setback I had a gut feeling he'd make it. I worried a little, but he made it."

A few years after Soupy's great wins, disaster struck the Belmonts while they were running dogs on the West Coast. Louise was completely paralyzed by an illness and spent seven months in the hospital. The only motion she could make was to blink her eyes, her only means of communication with the world. All the dogs were sent to Rex Carr; there were a new set of problems to deal with.

Through sheer willpower, Louise made a spectacular recovery. A year-and-a-half later she was back working with the dogs. Slowly, ever so slowly at first, but she was back. As Augie says, "This dog thing became very important to our lives. It was the love of training, the love of the dogs and Louise's determination that got her going again and it wasn't easy. As soon as she came home, we brought Expo, Soupy's son, back from California. Louise couldn't button buttons, but she was soon training Expo, who she'd made into a field champion before she took sick."

Dolly Reath, a friend and nurse, came with her three retrievers to live with the Belmonts. As Louise tells it, "Dolly at that time wasn't a very good trainer but was a very good nurse. She had a most inventive mind and figured ways to get me out into the field. I was teaching her to train and she taught me how to move around. Finally, when I could stand on two canes, I was working Expo. I couldn't use my hands to direct him, but he learned from my body motion what I wanted. He was a remarkable dog. We weren't too successful, but we were doing it. He was very important. He taught me that I could go on and work; he was the only dog in the world that could have done it."

Then Dolly Reath had an ingenious idea. She had a fence of stakes driven in the ground around Louise, which prevented her from falling over while she worked her dog. When both Expo and Louise gained confidence, they entered a trial, where a kitchen stool replaced the fence. The stool was attached to boards so that it could not tip over.

Augie says, "This game and the dogs have kept her going. She can't wait to get up each morning. She's organizing herself, gets out every day and I think if it weren't for the dogs she'd be watching TV or something." He stopped for a moment then continued, "It's been very important to her life . . . and to our life together. The dogs have done it . . . it's remarkable."

But what is even more remarkable is her new dog, Weege. Louise has done all the training herself except for the few weeks each year out in California "vacationing" with Rex Carr. Weege was trained to come to line and back in between Louise's leg and her cane, then sit at heel. Augie picks up the story from there: "It took guts and determination to do what she has done with that dog. You talk about success stories, that dog won the National Derby Championship and then last year qualified for the National Amateur Championship, completed it and damn near won it. The dog is already qualified for a spot in this year's Amateur Championship. She has done this all herself. That's a great dog . . . That's a great woman!"

The question is: did Rex Carr make the Belmonts or did the Belmonts make Rex Carr? The more likely answer — both happened.

After Super Chief's spectacular wins in national championships Carr's force training method was discussed heatedly by field trial people, pros and amateurs alike. Many people were appalled when they first heard of the force system that Carr honed to perfection. Traditionally, from Cox's *The Gentlemen's Recreation of Fowling* in 1721, the natural training method was stressed. Although a force system was designed by B. Waters in 1895, it took over a half-century to develop a need for Carr's "scientific" approach to training; that is, if psychology can be considered a science. Gradually, as the need for more stringent training methods developed, more and more force was used. Carr's system has carried it to the ultimate. The average hunter today does not require the exactness of performance of the field trial dog; in fact, in many real hunting conditions it can be a disadvantage.

The issue comes down to this: There are two ways to train a Lab, the natural method and the force system, and they are at opposite poles. The reader should not assume that for field trials the Carr method is the only way; T.J. Linblum, for example, trained a national champion using the natural method. It is up to the individual to decide which system best fits his or her needs, a decision that should be based on the psychological make-up of the trainer and the dog. Remember, there is a difference between a dog lover and a dog trainer. A dog *trainer* can love the dog and also train him; a dog *lover* usually ends up being trained by the dog. Some force is always used in the training situation, whether teaching a dog or a child. It is the *amount* of force that divides the two training poles.

The work required of the dog is a major consideration. A top-flight hunting dog can be trained by the natural method. Force is a faster way to train a field trial champion. There are exceptions to this general rule, but not many.

The book *Water Dog* sets up the natural system for training the hunting dog. The system starts at forty-nine days of age and develops the natural instincts of the dog and step-by-step shows the dog what is expected of him. The dog is taught by repetition, using his innate instincts to accomplish the job, and relatively little pressure is used.

At the other extreme of the training pole is the force system,

Augie Belmont and Rex Carr

Field Trials vs. Hunting

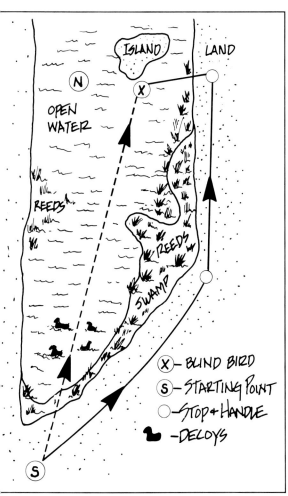

Route of the field trial dog, dotted line, compared with the hunting dog, solid line.

which some trainers feel is necessary to achieve the precision work needed in field trials. The electric collar is used to reinforce the dog's self-motivation and instill a directed motivation. The dog learns very quickly by electric sting what is—and is not—wanted. The force-train method is not an easy subject to deal with. The idea of breaking the dog's natural desire and initiative is repugnant to many people. However, you should not decide that the force system is cruel and unnecessary until you have seen it used by the expert. Then, you can decide whether you can psychologically handle it and train a Lab that way yourself.

The following test demonstrates the precision required of today's field trial dog as compared to the work done by the hunting dog. In today's field trials, blind retrieves are usually the deciding factor in proclaiming the champion. The blind is also a good test for the hunting dog, who often cannot see where a bird has fallen. In the diagram *S* marks the starting place; *X* marks where the bird is placed. (The dog does not know where the bird is, hence the name "blind.")

Both the field trial handler and the hunter must handle and send their dogs in such a way that the dogs are never out of sight, or they will not be able to receive visual directions. The hunter wants the birds retrieved and the dog back at his side as soon as possible because if more birds drop into the decoys a working dog could flair them off. In the field trial, on the other hand, the handler must demonstrate that the dog is under absolute control and will follow the handler's directions and not his own instinct.

The hunter sends his dog on the roundabout route over land because it is faster and more natural for the dog. He sends the dog to the first *O*, stops him, and gives him a new direction to the second *O*. At the second *O*, he stops the dog again and casts him into the water to swim toward the island. Once close to the bird the dog's nose will locate the bird. A smart hunting dog will then swim back to the top *O* and run the shoreline back to the hunter.

A similar retrieve by a field trial dog would eliminate him from competition. The field trial dog must follow the "line" from *S* to *X* given by the handler. In our illustration, a perfect job, worth a 10 in any judge's book, would be for the dog to "line" the bird: from point *S*, he runs across the land through the reeds, hits the water, swims through the decoys, takes a straight line to the bird, and does not need a whistle or a direction correction by the handler. On retrieving the bird, the dog swims back, coming home by water the same way he went out.

The field trial test has become less retrieving the bird than demonstrating how well the dog travels an exact line between the starting point and the bird. If he deviates even 10 or 15 degrees, the handler must stop the dog and give a hand signal to put him back on the exact course. The trick is to make the dog enter the water

SECOND SEASON *Bob Abbett*

on the correct angle rather than on the "square" (perpendicular to the shoreline), which automatically puts him on the wrong line when he starts to swim. The field trial dog must be broken of this natural instinct and taught to enter at any angle.

The better the dogs in the field trial, the more acute the angle of the tests. The reason for this is obvious: in a national event with eighty fine dogs all working like machines, the tests must be made very difficult to find the winner. In the diagrammed test, the spit of land that protrudes into the water near the first O is a natural place for the dog to go on shore and either start to hunt or run through the shallow water along the edge. The judge, however, instructs the handler not to allow the dog on that spit. The dog who has swum to point N (even with just one whistle and one handle) will get a lower score than the dog who stayed on a very close course and took three whistles. Agree or not, these are the rules of the game.

Both the field trial dog and the hunting dog are taught common techniques: both are taught to ignore the decoys and to stop on whistle, turn and take the next direction by hand signal. In the case of the hunter's dog, however, it is acceptable if he swims directly to point N, stops at that point on command, and takes an "over" command to the right to get the bird. The hunter does not need the dog to take the precise line. He does not want to stand out there, waving his arms and blowing his whistle. He wants to hunt and fill his limit and no ducks are going to be coming in with all that activity going on anyway. That field trials are digressing too far from actual hunting conditions may be a valid argument, but the point here is that the dogs must respond like machines to make it in the field trial game.

The late Charles Morgan, one of the great retriever trainers, said, "Trials today are decided on water blinds. It narrows down to what they call threading the needle, and to get a dog to do that calls for harsh treatment, a terrible training—almost brutal training."

In "Water Dogs and Devil Dogs" (*Field and Stream*, February 1978), an article on D.L. Walters, one of the leading trainers in the country, Bill Tarrant compares the training of retrievers to the training of marines.

A water dog has to be more concerned in staying beside me than anything that is going to happen to him out there. I know. I've been there. I've been a water dog. Actually they call us Devil Dogs. We were Marines. Devil Dog didn't stand for the hell we could mete out. It stood for the hell we had to take. When our drill instructors finished with us, our platoon leader could order us into the jaws of hell and we'd go. Nothing out there could equal the wrath and peril of what we were leaving behind. We were whip-run dogs who were running to the enemy for relief.

But it's the damndest thing. I swear, when it's all done, and you're force-broke, as the saying goes, you'll make the best Marine, or water dog, there ever was. Oh, some dogs and boots fold. I remember the kid in our training platoon who climbed on top of the barracks and jumped to the concrete grinder with a seabag on each shoulder. He broke both legs. He jumped for a discharge. He bolted.

If man or dog can't take the pressure they'll do that, bolt or fold.

But there is this . . . when force-broke, you will go get the enemy or the bird, on command. Man or dog, you can be depended on. And in the end, it makes a man or dog out of you. It did me. But I had a choice. I joined. The retriever doesn't. And I guess that's what sticks in the craw. It's more important that men win wars than that dogs win blue ribbons.

The electric collar is a radio-controlled buzzer and shock device. The handler carries the transmitter, which has two buttons. One button produces only a buzzing sound; the other button produces first the buzzing noise and then the shock. The dog wears the battery-operated, waterproof receiver on his collar. When some dogs first receive the shock, they respond with practically no reaction; others respond as though they have been stung by a bee. Once any Lab realizes that the shock is associated with the command "No," they react strongly, the shock has a real bite. Sometimes dogs are introduced to the collar with a cattle prod that produces a much heavier shock. After the dog learns that the buzzer and shock mean "No," the buzzer alone will produce the desired results.

Using tools of force is not new. The early training literature mentions choke collars, spike collars, and whips, and all trainers used them to some degree. (John Olin jokes that he thought Cotton Pershall used force from time to time but was smart enough to never let him see it.) One of the worst abuses of force is overtraining; constantly being at the dog can take the initiative out of an animal and practically destroy him mentally.

B-B guns, sling shots, and even shotguns are regularly used in the force-training method. For the dog that cannot learn to wait until ordered to retrieve and "breaks from line" when a bird is shot, the B-B gun and sling shot are used to "teach" him line manners. A helper stands behind the dog, and if the dog goes before he is released, he is stung on the rump. Pete Jones, president of the Labrador Retriever Club, condones the use of shotguns in training. "I consider the shotgun the most humane method for training a dog to stop on whistle. I use the lightest shot possible and an open choke gun. The dog learns very quickly and then I'd only have to do it once or twice a year if they start to slip . . . just as a reminder. Here is how I do it and it has proved effective.

Force Training Methods

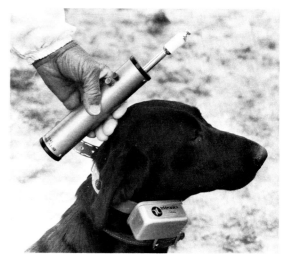

The Electric Collar, one button for sound, and one for sound and shock.

"You pace off your 60 yards and put up a marker. Then you send the dog, and at 60 yards you blow the whistle. This is where it gets tricky. If the dog continues to run after you blow the whistle, you then pull the trigger — but due to the reaction time from your eyes to your brain, and then to your finger, and the action of pulling the trigger and the shot getting there, you are shooting at that dog from about 70 or 80 yards. As I've always laughingly said, you can shoot at me for a small fee at that distance."

When it comes to the use of the electric collar, Rex Carr from Escalon, California is the undisputed master. In 1946, recuperating from war wounds, he happened to read an article in *Life* magazine about Paul Bakewell and Labradors. Rex wrote to Bakewell, who sent him in return a letter about the dogs and a copy of *Retriever Gun Dogs* by William Brown. That was Carr's beginning with the retrieving breeds.

In the post-World War II era Rex's achievements in training dogs for field trials have been unparalled. He is not sure how many of his dogs have qualified for the National Amateur and the National Open stakes, but he guesses that the number is more than fifty. Five have become national champions. Instead of training dogs and running them in trials himself, as was the custom of the other trainers, Rex trained the *owners* to run their own dogs in the trials. Though most professionals felt that the amateur was cluttering up the field and only making extra problems for the dog and the trainer, Rex believed that if the amateur owner could be trained as well as the dog, the dog would do better because of the one-to-one relationship. In 1980, 23 percent of the dogs in the National Amateur Championship were Carr-trained, which has to make the skeptic take notice. Because of his training method with the electric collar, Carr created a controversy that can be heard at practically every field trial. But as Carr says, "If it is not successful, there is no controversy. One-by-one, my critics traipse through my door to learn my method and pick my brain."

Judy Weikel, Rex's star pupil, is considered by many Lab experts to be the best trainer in America today. In the ten years she has been in the sport she has produced seven field trial champions. Five other retrievers she trained and then sold have also become field trial champions.

"Rex loves most animals and has a terrifically keen insight into them," Weikel says about her teacher. "He is most of all a student of dogs, an observer of their behavior, of what they do naturally, and what their qualities are. The thing that makes Rex different than a lot of other professionals is that he loves to teach people in addition to training dogs. A lot of dog trainers are not interested in training people, but Rex is. He loves to work with dogs; he just gets fascinated by the extremely high-quality animal, so he gets a lot of people attracted to him.

Judy Weikel and friend

DAWN ON THE DUCK MARSH *Ogden Pleissner*

"As I understand Rex, he feels that the collar is the most effective way to train dogs because you can fit the timing of the correction to the mistake. Studies in psychology with laboratory dogs show if you can get the interval of the correction down to about a half-second after the incident occurs, you can communicate to the dog more readily what the mistake is, as opposed to running out or calling the dog in to reprimand or correct him. There is such a time lag between the mistake and the correction that it is harder to communicate to the dog what the mistake was.

"Rex's whole training method is based on teaching the dog through repetition and then reinforcing the correction with the collar. The dog is not corrected for a mistake unless the dog knows that he has made a mistake, so there has to be some repetition and some other ways of communicating with the dog to get the basic lessons taught. This is where most people get in trouble with the collar because they try to take too many short cuts, and they try to teach with the collar rather than reinforce with it. The big fault of the collar as a general tool is that it is too easy to use, too easy to correct the dog, and so people correct the dog too much. They correct it for every mistake they make — no animal can take that.

"I think Rex would agree that in the hands of someone who knows what he or she is doing, it is the most humane way of training because you can communicate easily and you are doing no physical harm to the dog, which happens in other forms of training. It is a much better method of training for soft, sensitive dogs because the communication is so quick and they receive so much less punishment in the long run. The timing of it is so much more accurate. It is also better with tough, hard dogs because they are brutalized so much in other forms of training that you are risking physical damage to the dog before you can communicate with him.

"Some have tried to compare what we do with the collar to the dog with what the Marines do with the young man. The Marines pretty much take out self-motivation and give them directed-motivation. I don't really feel the collar does that because the biggest reward to a Labrador is not praise, it is retrieving."

But if you're making him force-retrieve, isn't that a directed-motivation instead of a natural motivation?

"Right, but if there were no natural motivation to retrieve serving as a positive reinforcement, it would be very hard to train them under any method. Unlike the Marines, we do not try to take away their individuality. We're seeking out the dog that wants to please and wants to do these things. We're trying to communicate to the dog a set of right and wrong. They have no moral values and we're trying to give them a set of moral values relative to the retriever game. So, by repetition and reinforcing with the collar, we're just instilling a set of values. It's right to go into the water, it's wrong to break from line, that kind of thing."

143

Rex Carr insists that a dog trained properly with the electric collar will perform his job with enthusiasm.

Rex Carr's facilities at Escalon are ideal—not only the spacious physical facilities and young dedicated helpers, but also every kind of cover imaginable and a "homemade" series of ponds constructed to lay out every kind of water and land test. Yard training is the first drill, and the dog does not go on to retrieving until his first lessons are firmly set. Then the dog goes through a series of drills that step-by-step take him up through very advanced work. All the drills have special names: Wagon wheel, extended wagon wheel, Chinese drill, T, and double T. Rex Carr describes his system.

"We introduce the dog to the electric collar in the kennel, a large building with fifteen kennels on each side and a wide hallway that is actually a room between them. There is a door in the back that leads to a fenced-in yard. The dog's own kennel is there and the door is left open; so is the back door to the yard.

"The dog has been well started on HEEL, SIT, and HERE commands. We put a leash with a chain collar on the dog and the electric collar. If the dog will HEEL, SIT, and HERE without any pressure of the collar, then we introduce the first shock. I'm using a two-button collar that gives you sound when you press the green button, or sound and shock when you press the red button; the sound always precedes the shock. Now I pick one command out of that HERE, SIT, HEEL drill to introduce the shock. Let's start with HERE, then tell the dog to HEEL, and on command SIT. After giving the command HERE, not before, I press the sound-shock button and proceed with more commands—HEEL, SIT—without any pressure, and if that goes well, repeat the shock.

"I get every kind of a response from the shock that a dog can give you. At first, very often, some will sit and wag their tails. Some will scream bloody murder, grit their teeth, and a tough dog will just sit there and he couldn't care less and you have the type of dog that will clam up. I exert enough pressure to get him in the condition where he wants to get away from it all, to bolt!

"After I have introduced the shock to the dog, in a lot of cases

The Escalon Drills

Rex starts a pup playing retrieve at a young age.

When he grows up, he receives the force training method

Force retrieve: The dog is commanded to retrieve, then he is made to retrieve and at the same time receives the sting of the whip.

I can cause this desire to escape with the green button, sound only. There's no point in going to the electricity if I can get the result with the sound. If the dog does not respond to the sound so that he won't obey the HERE command, introduce some more electricity. The response I want is obedience to the command. If I say HERE, they should come; if I say SIT, they should sit; if I say HEEL, they should heel. When they get this shock and it upsets them and they don't respond to the command because of being upset, being burned, then we want them to run.

"We work into whatever pressure is necessary to cause the dog to try to run from this chamber through one of the 'escape' routes. One will be his own kennel door or the doors in the back of the chamber so that he can go outside into a fenced-in area, or into the seat of the truck or under the truck parked in the yard, but he can't get away from the electric shock. Throughout this the command HERE is given. The dog soon learns that the only place he can be without being 'burned' is by the handler's side, with the handler, at heel. He learns to do the command, that it is the only safe way.

"We give the dog enough shock to cause him to escape. There are degrees of shock that we can give a dog. We don't give them a full shock at first, but we try to give them enough shock to cause the escape response so we can teach him not to. Once he learns this, he'll never bolt in the field."

Dana Brown, a professional trained by Carr, deals with her clients the same way he does; she teaches them to train and run

Rex Carr's training grounds allow him to set up any type of a hunting or field trial situation

146

dog learns that no matter what the
...litions are, he must retrieve.

their own dogs. We asked her how the collar is used specifically in the training.

"People always ask why you would discipline a dog or 'burn' a dog when he is doing the right action. But that's what we mean by force-training. People will say, 'I have never had to force my dog to go into the water because he just naturally went in.' That's beside the point. We don't wait until the day that it's awfully cold and the dog decides not to go in, so you have to run down there and prod him and beat him up and make him go.

"There are five steps to teaching each new command by force. *Step 1.* You explain the meaning of the command. After the dog is performing the command,

Step 2. You apply pressure, such as the collar.

Step 3. You remove the pressure.

Step 4. You apply praise.

Step 5. You remove the praise.

"There are reasons for doing each one of those things.

"Most people forget Step 1, or they don't do a thorough job on it, and this is where they get into difficulty with the collar, especially because the dog needs to know what is expected of him.

"Applying pressure (Step 2) imbeds the command in the dog's mind in a memorable manner so that if you are forcing the dog on BACK and he is already going, he knows what BACK means. Now if you command BACK and give him the electricity on that morning when you point him at the water from a far distance and you say BACK, it's remembering the pressure that makes the dog do it.

"The third step (removing the pressure) is done because the dog still has to do the command without being made to do it; they have to do it on their own. Then you apply the praise. Because some dogs can't tolerate praise too well, they are going to take advantage of you and not do it any more. They need to learn to handle that, to learn to do it even though you are praising them. Then, the last step is important; you remove the praise and the dog should do the command for the sake of the work, not for personal praise."

It is not the purpose here to make a judgment. It is our purpose to make a fair explanation of the electric collar because it has become and will be part of the training experience of the Labrador. There is little need for this precise training with the hunter's dog.

As we have seen, the Lab has had the ability for centuries to take to his training — no matter what the system — and to come out of it with his tail wagging.

Breeding:
His Past...His Future

History seems to have dictated the early breeding "program" of the Lab's ancestors in Newfoundland. The wide range of temperature in Newfoundland, from well below zero in the winter to more than 80 degrees in the summer, was much more rigorous than the temperatures of England. The severe living conditions made survival itself the driving force for both man and dog. The philosophy for both was: if you want to eat, you have to work. Breeding records from this era are nonexistent, of course, but breeding animals for specific work duties was nothing new for the English at that time.

The Darwinian concept of "survival of the fittest" explains the development of a basically strong breed of dog in Newfoundland in a relatively short time. Darwin, much interested in the Newfoundland dogs, observed in *The Variations of Animals and Plants under Domestication* that cold climate is an important factor in producing strong breeds.

Darwin's study of the abandoned settlement of the Falkland Islands, off the eastern coast of South America, showed that hereditary change in animals like the horse and cattle was a very slow process, but dogs, with a more primitive and generalized structure, have greater capacity for variation. He cited evidence of this in the domestic dog and the shortness of time required to alter the type in any way that fashion or utility dictates.

Darwin's theories seem to support the fact that a dog brought into an isolated area will conform to the environment quickly if that environment is within certain bounds. He pointed out that cold conditions are favorable to increase the strength and size of dogs. For example, species of the wolf, generally believed to be the origin of the domestic dog, are bigger and stronger in the sub-Arctic latitudes than those in the warmer, more southern latitudes. Darwin also pointed out that the Newfoundland dogs that were taken to Australia in the 1860s survived and thrived handsomely, but those taken to India did not live long.

Newfoundland provided ideal conditions for the development of a strong breed of dog. According to Darwin, modifications in domesticated animals exposed to changed conditions for a prolonged period appear to be more marked in a more severe climate. They will either adapt to the environment by becoming stronger or they will die out. Because the dog brought to Newfoundland was a working tool who had to justify his own keep, his breeding became a practical matter. Those dogs that could take the necessary training, those that were the best swimmers and could survive the workload, were bred to produce another generation of workers.

Whatever the men of Devon did in breeding this dog to work as a fishing dog most of the year and as a hunting dog during the winter, they did it well. The small water dog had dominant traits that it passed on to its progeny, despite the fact that working ability was the dog's most desired trait. All of the writers of the early and mid-nineteenth century describe the dog from Newfoundland as having characteristics desirable for the retrieving dog. One must realize that most of the English hunters during this period did not consider the retrieving dogs as any one specific breed. In 1850, "Dinks," the sporting dog writer of his day, stated in his book *The Sportsman's Vade Mecum,* "The retriever is a cross breed dog. There is no true type of them. Every person has a peculiar fancy regarding them. The great object is to have them tolerably small, compatible with endurance."

As late as 1872, a reader of the magazine *The Field* wrote, "Sir, can any of your readers settle the question as to what the retriever really should be? If I am in error in supposing him to be bred from judicious crossing of the Irish Water Spaniel, Setter, and Newfoundland, I should be most happy to be corrected by yourself or some experienced breeder."

The most respected of the nineteenth century writers was Dr. J. H. Walsh, who wrote under the name "Stonehenge." Here is what he said about the breeding of the retriever.

> No distinct recognized breed of retrievers exists, unless we make an exception in favour of the liver-coloured Irish Water Spaniel, the rough Russian, and the Deerhound. Many well-known sportsmen, possess their own breed of dogs, used for retrieving from land or water; but there is no established breed.

Early Newfoundland Breeding

UP TO MISCHIEF *Russ Johnson*

Good retrievers are to be found of all breeds.

An English Retriever, whether smooth or curly-coated, should be black or black-and-tan, or black with tabby or brindled legs, the brindled legs being indicative of the Labrador origin. We give the preference, from experience, to the flat-coated or short-coated small St. John's or Labrador breed. These breeds we believe to be identical. The small St. John's has marvellous intelligence, a great aptitude for learning to carry, a soft mouth, great strength, and he is a good swimmer. If there is any cross at all in this breed it should be the setter cross.

We have observed that the Newfoundland (the small Labrador) possesses those qualities in a marked degree, but in a general way he is too bulky for the purpose. For some masters he is too large to be a constant companion, or to be easily taken from place to place. We believe *judicious* crossing will improve and call out excellent qualities, and that his size may be diminished by selection, without too great a sacrifice of strength. We believe the Newfoundland to be the best dog to breed from, because he is as good in the water as on land, and will dive like an otter if need be.

We believe, however, the size of the Newfoundland must be reduced by the selection of the smallest specimens in litters, and that it will be a work of time to obtain these desiderata — economy in keep or food, portability, and yet strength and activity, combined with sense.

We can deduce that Stonehenge had little or no contact with the pure-bred Labrador between 1867 and 1886 when the five editions of his book were published. He was the only writer to describe the dog as too big for the job. We cannot be sure, of course, if he was seeing the Newfoundland or a product of crossbreeding, a common practice that started as soon as the dog arrived in England. As discussed in Section 3, only a few aristocratic families kept the dog pure, and so few dogs were brought to Poole after 1814 that there wasn't enough stock for the average hunter to keep a line going.

Stonehenge's references to color are interesting. Brindled legs, he wrote, were indicative of the Lab origin; all other writers of the time referred to the St. John's or Lab as jet black. He also mentions that the Foxhound and Greyhound were crossbred with the Newfoundland dogs to produce English Retrievers. He is the only writer who says that a few of the St. John's dogs that arrived at Poole were liver-hued.

The liver-hued reference raises the question of where the recessive yellow came from in today's Labrador. It has been suggested that the yellow came from the foxhound or other outcrosses, but this is not a correct reading of the history of the breed. Today's

Origins of the Yellow Lab

The Lab Reaches England

Labs are a result of the direct line through the Malmesbury and Buccleuch lines (see Section 3), and no outcrossing or intermixing reached these dogs after they arrived in England. Therefore, the recessive yellow must have come from the imported dogs from Newfoundland. Although Stonehenge was the first to report that liver-hued St. John's dogs arrived at Poole, Colonel Hawker stated in his first edition, "He is oftener black than of other color." So, on the east side of the Atlantic we do have a record of colors besides black arriving from the west.

But we have even better evidence that the dogs of Newfoundland carried recessive yellow: The story of the English brig *Canton,* homeward bound from Newfoundland and headed for Poole, that was shipwrecked off the coast of Maryland. Two pups that were aboard the brig became the foundation stock for the Chesapeake Bay Retriever. One of the pups was jet black and the other had a brown coat, described as rust red by Frank Forester in his *Manual For Young Sportsmen,* in 1856. The rust red is the recessive yellow showing up.

If the dogs entered England with the recessive color, where did it come from? There are two possible sources, either of which or both could be the true one. The original St. Hubert's dog imported into England from France, as the sixteenth-century writing states, was most commonly black but was known to be all colors, even white (as we have today). Or this recessive color could be indicative of the genes carried by the dogs used in Newfoundland to increase the St. John's water dog to the large-size Newfoundland dray dog. The color of the first Newfoundland dogs that reached England were not black as we know them today. They were multi-colored, liver and white, black and white, and even pure yellow. From that interbreeding, both dogs, large and small, could have carried the recessive yellow.

A color plate in Sydenham Edwards' *Cynographia Brittanica,* published in 1800, shows one of the dogs as solid yellow, which establishes that the big Newfoundland carried the yellow trait and legitimizes it as a color in the pure breed. Today, that yellow color is recessive.

Artist Sir Edwin Landseer (1802–1873), became the champion of the multicolored Newfoundland, and as far as color was concerned was given to using artistic license as he saw fit. (The multicolored dog today carries his name, the Landseer.) While the artist was painting his white-bodied, multicolored dogs, the English were breeding the color out and establishing a solid black dog. In 1840, after a trip to Newfoundland, Charles Hamilton Smith's *Naturalists' Library* described the true Newfoundland as black and tan. Only thirty years later Stonehenge wrote that the purest specimens were pure black with a gloss on their coats so intense that it reflected light like a mirror. The color change happened so quickly that in the

This print from Edward's book, published in 1800, demonstrates that the Newfoundland dog carries the recessive yellow gene.

first edition of Stonehenge's book he did not even mention a "black Newfoundland." The black variety he called the "Lesser Labrador" and he showed it in a sketch. In the second edition that sketch is captioned "Large Labrador." In the third edition he finally wrote about the black Newfoundland as the true breed and deplored the unsoundness of the Landseer.

There seems to be no doubt that the St. John's dog reached England with recessive yellow in his genes. The 1887 letter that the third Earl of Malmesbury sent to the sixth Duke of Buccleuch stated in regard to breeding: "We always call mine Labrador dogs, and I have kept the breed as pure as I could from the first I had from Poole. . . ." There is no record of what happened to yellow dogs through this period. The records of the restocking of the Buccleuch kennels from the Malmesbury line mentioned only blacks. It has to be assumed that if off-color puppies arrived they were not appreciated and consequently done away with.

The mainstream of the dogs were black until the turn of the twentieth century. The yellow color fad started with Ben of Hyde, whelped in 1899 (Kennel Club #55698), owned by Major C. E. Radclyffe. He was bred from two black parents, Neptune and Dutchess; Neptune was owned by the Major. Ben and Neptune were descendants of Turk, who arrived from Newfoundland in 1871 and was the last dog imported by the Major's father, Mr. C. J. Radclyffe. Six generations were bred until Ben arrived. Major Radclyffe was ten years old when Turk died. He remembered him this way: "Turk was short in the legs, with a broad head and chest. His coat was thicker underneath than that seen on show-bench Labradors today. He had a small white patch on his chest, and his ears were inclined to be pricked, unlike the flat ears seen today."

Ben of Hyde born 1899, started the line of Yellow Labradors.

The Yellow Lab Strives for Acceptance

Mrs. Wormald's successfully field trialed Yellow Labradors.

The black line stems from the Malmesbury dogs in the beginning of the nineteenth century and carried on by Buccleuch and Home. The yellow fad was started by Radclyffe, Montagu Guest and Lord Wimborne, who were breeding on a smaller scale than Buccleuch. Ben's sire, Neptune, was a Guest dog, and all dogs in that line, four generations back to Turk, were carefully bred from the Radclyffe stock. Ben's dame, Duchess, was bred by Lord Wimborne. Her resulting litter, in early 1899, included two whelps, a dog (Ben) and a bitch (Juno), both yellow — the first on record. Subsequently, when they were both bred, all of Juno's pups were black and most of Ben's were yellow. The yellow fad had started.

When black bitches from the best kennels were bred to Ben of Hyde at the turn of the century, the breeders did not understand genetics. The yellow trait was not dominant, of course; it had to come from both sides. Unknown to their owners, the black bitches must have carried the recessive yellow, but Ben was given the credit for producing numerous yellow puppies.

The most prominent kennel besides the Radclyffe's Zelstone was Mrs. Arthur Wormald's kennel, Knaith. About 1910, Mrs. Wormald became one of the staunchest supporters of the yellow. By 1913, the first yellow bench show was held at Olympia. After World War I many strong British kennels dealing only in yellows were established, and the dog's popularity grew all through the 1920s and 1930s. New kennel names like Hawesburn, Braeroy, and Folkingham appeared. Dr. Stanton's yellow Folkingham Labradors won scores of Open stakes in field trials during the 1920s.

Gaining general acceptance for the yellow dogs was not easy, however. M.C.W. Gilliat, the retired chairman of the Labrador Club of England, tells the story of Mrs. Wormald's first entry in a Crufts show at the old Crystal Palace. "She took her yellow dog to the stand where the Labradors were congregated and was told by the steward that she was in the wrong place. He told her she should go to where the Golden Retrievers were being shown. She insisted that she was in the correct place, whereupon the steward insisted she was wrong." Gilliat chuckled as he recalled the ensuing scene. "She drew herself up to her tallest, looked down at her opponent and said, 'My man! You do not know your dogs!' She proceeded into the ring and took a third place."

As early as 1908, a yellow Lab won a field trial award, but acceptance was slow. In 1925, the Yellow Labrador Retriever Club was formed to persuade the Kennel Club to establish two distinct registers, black and yellow, each having its own standard. Lady Howe, however, put an end to that movement. As she wrote in her her book, "The absurdity of this idea can perhaps be more easily understood when I point out that at that time a dog, Ch Beningbrough Tangle, winner of 18 Challenge Certificates, was black in color. Also winning at that time was his own son (from a black

155

mother) Banchory Tawny, which was, as his name denotes, a yellow, and was, at one show, Reserve to his father for the Challenge Certificate. Tangle was the son of Dual Champion Banchory Bolo, who was, as far as I can trace, entirely black bred, as was Tawny's mother. The Kennel Club, using these facts, in wisdom refused to grant a separate registration for blacks and yellows."

From the start, the yellows had very loyal supporters. King George VI was a great admirer of them and had many fine yellow dogs. Lord Knutsford, who formed the Labrador Club, rebutted claims that the yellow was a "chance-bred" dog, with "The Labrador is no 'come-by-chance' breed but one firmly established with a fixed type." Yellow owners worked hard with their dogs and two Dual Champions were produced, one by Mr. Edgar Winter and the other by Mrs. Wormald.

After World War II the yellow's popularity exploded in England. Today, although blacks predominate in British field trials, in the show rings they are outnumbered by yellows ten to one. The American scene today is similar to the British. The yellow is very popular on the bench and as a pet, but the overwhelming number of hunters and field trialers prefer the black.

The origin of chocolate and liver-hued Labs should be no more of a mystery than the yellows. As stated, the recessive dull red color was probably carried by one of the Newfoundland pups shipwrecked off the coast of Maryland in 1807.

Although Major Radclyffe's Ben of Hyde was given credit for starting the yellow line, colors other than black did appear before that time in the Malmesbury-Buccleuch line. In 1892, two liver-colored pups were born at the Buccleuch kennels in Scotland. Although the third Earl of Malmesbury was dead, the Duke of Buccleuch wrote to Heron Court to see if his descendents could shed any light on this strange arrival of two non-black pups. The keepers of the Malmesbury dogs could give no information on the matter. Of course, now we know that the recessive yellow had finally shown up in the line.

Today, chocolate is no longer a rarity and is becoming more and more of an accepted Lab trait. Chocolates started with two important British kennels owned by Sir Ian Walker, Bart, and Mr. J. G. Severn in the late 1930s, and we'll be seeing more and more chocolates on the bench.

In the American show ring blacks now comprise only about 40 percent of the Labs entered. The pet market has become an important factor in color. During the 1960s, everyone wanted that "different" dog, and the market bred for yellow to meet the demand. In the 1980s, the chocolates are entering the market in greater numbers; again the "different" dog is in demand.

Breeding for "popular demand" can lead to problems, however. About the time the Lab was introduced to America, Lord

King George VI was a great supporter of the yellow line.

Chocolate and Liver-Hued Labs

First Lab Show Ring in America

Knutsford, who founded the Labrador Club in England, and Countess Howe, the first secretary of the club, warned that the Lab should be kept a dual purpose dog, "not one from which the working and show bench types are so entirely different as in so many breeds." With the Lab's popularity growth, today, more than ever their warning should be heeded. Hopefully, it is not too late.

Is the Lab becoming so popular in the U.S. that his best traits and skills are being bred out of existence? Need we be reminded of the fate of the Cocker Spaniel, who has become a nasty little thing, or the high-strung Irish Setter whose original color was red and white or orange and white, not solid red? Some early setters had black-edged ears. Today, neither dog could hunt his way out of a pen of pheasants. There are now two separate English Setters, the hunter and the show dog, and neither can do the other's job.

One Lab was registered in America in 1917; today, there are almost 50,000 registered annually and about one million total registered and unregistered Labs in the U.S., most of which are pets. The qualities of biddability, trainability, and willingness have developed from generations of being a worker, but these attributes are not necessarily carried on through the show ring or the pet market. What will happen when most Labs will never see a game bird fly?

Breeding has split into two factions, each concerned with preserving different Lab traits: the show ring, concerned primarily with looks and petlike traits, and the field trial/hunting faction, breeding for work and hunting abilities.

The sport of showing Labradors in the U.S. had its humble beginnings in the garage of Marshall Field's town house on 76th Street in the swanky east side of New York in 1933. From that show the sport has grown to 832 shows in 1979. Colin Macfarlane, the Scottish trainer for Robert Goelet's Glenmere estate, reported on the first Field show for *Popular Dogs* magazine.

The Labrador Retriever Club held its first annual specialty show May 19th in New York City. Mrs. Marshall Field, president of the club, judged, David Wagstaff and Benjamin Moore were the stewards, the Foley Organization managed, and everything went like clockwork. Thirty-three dogs making 62 entries with three braces and one team were a good turnout for the first show. Mrs. Field had a class lot of dogs to go over, but one could not say that the garage where the show was held was an ideal place. It was too narrow and the light was poor. It is safe to say that had the show been held in the open or in a good lighted hall, the judge would have marked her card differently in one or two classes. However, this lady has the correct type in her eye and will be called upon again.

It is no surprise that the winners were the same as the partici-

FIRST OUTING *Douglas Van Howd*

pants in the first field trials: F.B. Lord, Kathleen Starr, Robert Goelet, W.A. Harriman, Charles Laurance, Wilton Lloyd Smith, Henry Root Stern, and William M. Decker. The thirty-three dogs and twenty-four owners were the whole Labrador game then. The dogs were the owners' working dogs, and they held the show to determine the best-looking. Today, a few thousand dogs are in field trialing and three times as many are exhibited in the show ring.

Training a dog for the show ring is a relatively easy job compared to field trials training. The most difficult part is teaching the dog to stand in an unnatural and uncomfortable position for a minute or so. The dog's feet must be lined up, both front and rear, and his head pulled up. The dog has to learn to have his tail pulled out straight. The average dog will want to sit when his tail is pulled. He has to learn to pull against the tail to give a tight look. If training starts when the dog is young, it is not difficult for him to learn to hold this stiff position. The dog must learn to walk on the leash with his head up. He can't lag, lunge, or sniff. He has to move smartly without breaking from a trot into a canter. It is a good idea to practice positioning the dog in front of a full-length mirror so that the handler can see what the judge sees.

The handler has more to learn than the dog. The dog's eyebrows and tail have to be trimmed. His nails have to be trimmed so

Training and Judging for the Show Ring

158

the paws appear like a round cap and not a long hare foot. Most kennel clubs have handling classes, and the dog should go to obedience school since he must be well-mannered in the ring.

In the show ring the judge will direct the handler on what he wants the dog to do. Criteria for judging Labs, outlined by national club standards appears on page 165.

George Bragaw, who judged the Labradors at the Westminster Kennel Club 1980 bench show at Madison Square Garden, was asked: "Do you think the show people have a responsibility to change their breeding methods to meet more closely the needs of field trial and hunting people?"

"I don't see any reason for that," he said. "The show people and the field trial people have sports unto themselves, but there is a problem between them on this point of what is good and what is bad. The problem could be stated very simply. There is a show every weekend of the year. There is a field trial every weekend of the year. There is no longer the opportunity (and I guess even the inclination) to try both field and bench because of the extent of the competitiveness in each area. They become worlds of their own. It has to do with the competition for people's time.

"I know you can take any Labrador puppy and if you bring him along right, and it doesn't take a lot of work, you could have a first class field dog, but not a first class field *trial* dog because that's another kettle of fish.

"By and large, Labrador clubs encourage working with their dogs; they have some matches and training sessions where the dogs are introduced to birds and shot pigeons. They are preserving the fundamental instincts. You've got to remember 90 to 95 percent of the breed is in the hands of people who never go near a show or a field trial. The closest they get to know what happens in these events is *Wide World of Sports*. If that continues, I'm not sure where it all ends up.

"I think there is a need for some kind of competition, a training, or an event. The sort of things the average guy can train his dog to do in the back yard, with a neighbor or friend. Field trials as a sport are for the wealthy. It's something that the average person who owns a dog really cannot participate in. I suggest we have some sort of meaningful accomplishment—whether you give it a certificate or if you give it ribbons isn't important. It seems to me you can do the same thing for training a retriever that you do in an obedience ring, where a dog can be measured against a written standard of performance of work that would be good enough to get him by in a day's work in the field.

"Before a dog becomes a show champion he must pass a meaningful test. I see nothing wrong with a dog being able and asked to demonstrate somehow what he was meant to do and bred to do before he could be called a champion.

Breeding for the Ring
... A Reexamination

Mrs. Marshall Field Judges Labrador Retriever Show In New York City

The Labrador Retriever Club held its first annual specialty show May 18th, in New York City. Mrs. Marshall Field, president of the club, judged, David Wagstaff and Benjamin Moore were the stewards, the Foley Organization managed, and everything went like clockwork. Thirty-three dogs making 62 entries with three braces and one team were a good turnout for the first show. Mrs. Field had a class lot of dogs to go ov-

"The Labrador working certificate, as set down by the national club, doesn't really require too much training. It is based on instinct and shows that the dog is not gun-shy and will go out and pick up things whether they be dead or alive. The dog must make one retrieve on land and two in the water. The second water retrieve must be immediately after the first water retrieve to make sure he is not water-shy. The dog can be held while the shot is fired and until the game has fallen; he does not have to deliver the game to hand but must bring it back to within an acceptable distance. This is what is expected of a six-month-old puppy in a field trial. To get the certificate the dog has to be tested by a director of the Labrador Club or a field trial judge.

"That test doesn't prove much. When I go in the field, I want a dog that can mark downed game, take a good line to it, will hunt on his own when he gets out there and a dog that will handle by hand and whistle commands.

"In the ring you are looking for a substantial dog, a well-boned dog, a dog who has the look that suggests the qualities you would need in a good field dog—eager, alert, intelligent, a dog who has muscular strength, who has the coat and the endurance to be able to work well in difficult marshes. In the ring we can only look and try to make these judgments."

Miriam Kinsella, a well-known English show judge, has been breeding Labradors since 1946 and now has a line of ten generations of her own breeding. She has a small kennel, named Brentchase. She is chairman of the Labrador Club breed council, and secretary of the East Anglia Labrador Club, which has 450 members. She judges at least once a year at a major show in England and many other countries, including the U.S. We asked Miriam if the show people should breed the Lab more to the working ideal. She replied:

"As to the show Labrador versus the field Labrador, there is always a controversy in our country. Unfortunately, they have drifted very far apart. We haven't gone as far as the spaniels have, or working springers or cockers. There are English Cockers for show and quite honestly the ones used for work are completely different.

"The Lab hasn't gone as far, and the show people do try to keep alive the working instinct through training classes. Our Club runs them once a month; they are very elementary. We give training classes for beginners, nothing very elaborate, but it keeps the instinct of the dog going.

"A good 40 percent of show people try to do something, at some stage, as far as training goes. If you go to the other side, the trial and working people, 95 percent of them don't care at all what their dogs look like—if it's fast and does what they want; it doesn't matter if it looks like a Greyhound. This is where we come up against a difficulty. If only they would try to improve the looks of

George Bragaw judges Labrador Retrievers at the Westminister Kennel Club, Madison Square Garden.

***The Show Lab vs.
The Field Trial Lab***

their dogs. The old school, particularly, is very, very prejudiced against anything to do with the show dogs.

"Some of the show dogs are too heavy, that's quite true. But you see, I think the field trial people have really got away from the main purpose of the Labrador gun dog. Your gun dog is first and foremost a man's dog to take out when he goes shooting—it is a shooting dog. These high-powered field trial dogs are very, very fast, but they are not dogs that even those owners would take out on a day's shooting; they are not the ideal dog for picking up. The majority of these top field trial dogs are not your top working dogs. This is where I think they are coming a bit unstuck. If you want to win in the trials, you've got to have speed at the present time; it's the fashionable thing. They need too much handling; they take too much holding—you can't control them. If you were shooting, it wouldn't be the dog that would sit by your stick quietly all day. Half-way through the day you would have lost the majority of those field trial dogs; they are much too highly strung. Conditions in a field trial are not the same conditions as on the shooting field. The shooting man will attend a formal shoot and he will have his dog sitting at heel. That dog will be under his full control. If it is an excellent dog, it will sit there without any lead. If it is a little bit hot, it will be pegged and that dog will stay there until it is asked to retrieve after the drive is over.

"There was a very fine dog which belonged to Lord Rank (Sir Arthur Rank, the film producer of the 1930s). He kept a good kennel of gun dogs of all kinds and he had this very famous dog, a Field Trial Champion, called Scotney Petal, who was a black dog, rather a big heavy dog and also a slow dog. All of the field trial people hated this dog and said, 'It's not worthy of being a Field Trial Champion, it's useless, it's a rotten dog.' But this dog always used to come through because he was slow, he was a plodder and he never missed a bird. He would work his way slowly, methodically, using his own brain. His handler used to stand back and let this dog get on with it. This is a good example of what I consider a very, very good working dog, because he always came back with what he was sent for. These fast ones would rush out and mush around and they might be lucky, they might fall over a bird.

"I don't think there is an answer to this two-way problem. Human nature being what it is, the show people will go on producing whatever they need in the show world and the field trial people will go on producing what they really need in the field trial.

"We have to attend a field trial with our show dogs to get tested for working certificates. It's a big mess. The judges don't really want to take the time. I say let's forget the certificate, let's cancel the whole thing out, because nine times out of ten it's not worth the paper it's written on. It's aggravating to the field trial committee and it is aggravating to the show field. Let's have Show

Champion and let's have Field Trial Champion."

The pointing dog people have handled the matter of separate breeding by succumbing to the split. The show people register their dogs with the American Kennel Club and hold their shows under AKC license. The field trial people register their dogs with the Field Dog Stud Book and run trials under their auspices. These requirements make certain decisions a lot easier. For example, if someone wants a show dog, he or she knows where to get it, and the same is true for the hunter and field trialer. Those who want a pet can go to either market: the show dogs are generally bigger and handsomer, the field dogs are generally better hunters.

Almost all Labradors, on the other hand, are registered with the American Kennel Club, which makes no distinction between field stock and show stock. In the case of the English Setter one can look at the dogs and even the uneducated eye can see the difference. This is not true as yet with the Labrador, and we hope it won't happen. But with the trial people going one way and the show people another, the odds are that it will happen unless the show people seriously consider the needs of the hunter and keep the breed dual purpose.

The fact is this: the standards the show people use for the Lab originated in England in 1916 when the British club was formed. These standards, which have been only slightly altered, can be interpreted in different ways, much like a beauty contest. The girl who won the Miss America contest in 1925 might not even be a finalist today because our ideas of beauty have changed. In the same way, the standards for the Labrador, though based on work as well as looks, may not reflect changes that have taken place since then. After all, Americans have not been hunting British-style for over forty years. The British have not changed their methods of hunting and their 65-year-old standard is still good. The American hunter, on the other hand, needs and has developed a harder-going dog.

When George Bragaw was asked, "Why are English judges brought to America to judge American dogs when the British don't know what American needs are?" his answer was simple: "If a club wants to have a successful show with a big entry, the British judge will draw them in. It might be snob appeal, but the club will make money and the handlers and owners will love it."

Miriam Kinsella said, "When I judge in the U.S., I use the American standard. It doesn't matter where I'm judging, I read the appropriate breed standard the night before. When I'm in America I check very carefully for the differences . . . there are not a lot of differences."

There are differences between the show ring and the field and they are as distinct as night and day. The American hunter has to have a dog that can do the difficult job of working a swamp all day, running through hummocks or working like a springer and quarter-

Miriam Kinsella, a British breeder and show judge.

162

READY TO GO *Diana Charles*

Two Different Dogs

ing the field for upland game. The American dog working a duck blind has a harder job than the British dog sitting at heel at a peg and retrieving when the driven birds are down, or walking at heel until the game is flushed and shot. Is it any wonder that the American hunter and field trialer has turned his back on the show dogs whose owners constantly return to England for their breeding stock, while the British show dog is getting further and further from British hunting needs?

Commander Peter Whitehead, Secretary of Trials for the Labrador Club in England, says about the English problem: "Of the eleven regional Labrador clubs in England, I believe the original one, The Labrador Club, is the only one that really tries to keep the working side of the Labs together with the show side, although after the war they became very, very far apart — and some say that they are getting still further apart. I think on the whole they are not getting any further apart, but I don't think they are getting much nearer. We in this club appreciate the fact that the dog first of all must work, and after that it's nice to have the right conformation . . . things like feet and lengths of body, which is so awfully important so the dog can put its head down to pick up a bird and use its nose along the ground if necessary. Show dogs are usually too

163

stubby and fat. A field trial dog must run flat out with its nose on the deck. He has to be *every* inch a working dog. True, so many of the very top field-trialing dogs are far too high for the average man to shoot over. They are not shooting-dog material in that respect, so the average man really can't shoot and control the dog at the same time. But most of the hunters realize that if the field trial didn't take place the blood lines of what they are really after would not be there. They wouldn't get what they need from the show ring.

"In the last ten or twelve years a lot of show people have become very interested in the working of the Labrador, probably because of the working tests and the various classes they can go to. Therefore they have bred their show dogs to Field Trial Champions, or dogs that distinguish themselves in the field. Some of this has paid off, inasmuch as they have had a nice-looking working dog that is docile and easily trained and so forth. Some of it has not worked out; they have come up with a hard-headed show dog coupled with a swift, fast field trial dog which has been nothing else but a perfect nuisance from the very first day. It hasn't done anybody any good — but then that is breeding, isn't it?"

For almost twenty-five years Mrs. Helen Warwick, author of *The Complete Labrador Retriever,* has been recognized in American show circles as "Mrs. Labrador Retriever." She wrote a column for more than twenty years in the *AKC Gazette* and was influential in breeding circles. Her husband, James, was a director of the Labrador Retriever Club. The club was basically field-trial-oriented, but James Warwick was the club's representative dealing in show ring matters. Although the Warwicks did not run in trials, they were important in the show ring. As director-in-charge of show business for the "mother" club, Jim was often called upon by other Labrador clubs to help select judges, and Helen had the ear of the breeder and show handlers. Helen has also judged hundreds of shows.

Helen feels that the 1916 standard should be the basic one for the breed. She said, "The standard has never been changed, except that the height was changed at one time; the show height was a little high. This is the standard; the Americans copied the English standard." When asked if it was important whether a British judge who comes to America should know how the American dog is used in the field, she answered, "No, in the show ring they divorce it completely from work; it is just for looks and nothing else. It's just for show. They don't even say, 'Can this dog pick up a dummy?' No judge does that; it is just judging as they see them physically.

"It boils down to how you interpret the standard, of course. You can interpret it in many ways. You can have six or seven kennels of very good type, and all the types — just considering looks — can be very different but still conform to the standard. One judge will say, 'I prefer this type to another.' You might even say, in field trials, 'I like a certain dog's work; I like the way it works better than

Lt. Com. Peter Whitehead of the British Labrador Field Trial Club.

OFFICIAL STANDARD FOR THE LABRADOR RETRIEVER

General Appearance—The general appearance of the Labrador should be that of a strongly built, short-coupled, very active dog. He should be fairly wide over the loins, and strong and muscular in the hindquarters. The coat should be close, short, dense and free from feather.

Head—The skull should be wide, giving brain room; there should be a slight stop, *i.e.* the brow should be slightly pronounced, so that the skull is not absolutely in a straight line with the nose. The head should be clean-cut and free from fleshy cheeks. The jaws should be long and powerful and free from snipiness; the nose should be wide and the nostrils well developed. Teeth should be strong and regular, with a level mouth. The ears should hang moderately close to the head, rather far back, should be set somewhat low and not be large and heavy. The eyes should be of a medium size, expressing great intelligence and good temper, and can be brown, yellow or black, but brown or black is preferred.

Neck and Chest—The neck should be medium length, powerful and not throaty. The shoulders should be long and sloping. The chest must be of good width and depth, the ribs well sprung and the loins wide and strong, stifles well turned, and the hindquarters well developed and of great power.

Legs and Feet—The legs must be straight from the shoulder to ground, and the feet compact with toes well arched, and pads well developed; the hocks should be well bent, and the dog must neither be cowhocked nor be too wide behind; in fact, he must stand and move true all round on legs and feet. Legs should be of medium length, showing good bone and muscle, but no so short as to be out of balance with rest of body. In fact, a dog well balanced in all points is preferable to one with outstanding good qualities and defects.

Tail—The tail is a distinctive feature of the breed; it should be very thick towards the base, gradually tapering towards the tip, of medium length, should be free from any feathering, and should be clothed thickly all round with the Labrador's short, thick, dense coat, thus giving that peculiar "rounded" appearance which has been described as the "otter" tail. The tail may be carried gaily but should not curl over the back.

Coat—The coat is another very distinctive feature; it should be short, very dense and without wave, and should give a fairly hard feeling to the hand.

Color—The colors are black, yellow, or chocolate and are evaluated as follows:

(a) **Blacks:** All black, with a small white spot on chest permissible. Eyes to be of medium size, expressing intelligence and good temper, preferably brown or hazel, although black or yellow is permissible.

(b) **Yellows:** Yellows may vary in color from fox-red to light cream with variations in the shading of the coat on ears, the underparts of the dog, or beneath the tail. A small white spot on chest is permissible. Eye coloring and expression should be the same as that of the blacks, with black or dark brown eye rims. The nose should also be black or dark brown, although "fading" to pink in winter weather is not serious. A "Dudley" nose (pink without pigmentation) should be penalized.

(c) **Chocolates:** Shades ranging from light sedge to chocolate. A small white spot on chest is permissible. Eyes to be light brown to clear yellow. Nose and eye-rim pigmentation dark brown or liver colored. "Fading" to pink in winter weather not serious. "Dudley" nose should be penalized.

Movement—Movement should be free and effortless. The forelegs should be strong, straight and true, and correctly placed. Watching a dog move towards one, there should be no signs of elbows being out in front, but neatly held to the body with legs not too close together, and moving straight forward without pacing or weaving. Upon viewing the dog from the rear, one should get the impression that the hind legs, which should be well muscled and not cow-hocked, move as nearly parallel as possible, with hocks doing their full share of work and flexing well, thus giving the appearance of power and strength.

Approximate Weights of Dogs and Bitches in Working Condition—Dogs—60 to 75 pounds; bitches—55 to 70 pounds.

Height at Shoulders—Dogs—22½ inches to 24½ inches; bitches—21½ inches to 23½ inches.

Approved April 9, 1957

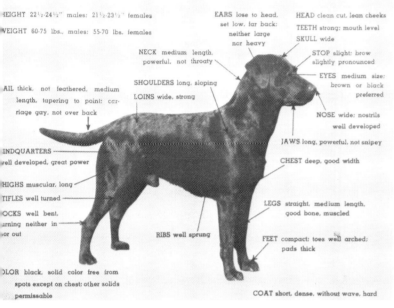

Labrador Retriever

HEIGHT 22½-24½" males; 21½-23½" females
WEIGHT 60-75 lbs., males; 55-70 lbs. females

EARS lose to head, set low, far back; neither large nor heavy

HEAD clean cut, lean cheeks
TEETH strong; mouth level
SKULL wide

NECK medium length, powerful, not throaty

STOP slight; brow slightly pronounced

SHOULDERS long, sloping
LOINS wide, strong

EYES medium size; brown or black preferred

TAIL thick, not feathered, medium length, tapering to point; carriage gay, not over back

NOSE wide; nostrils well developed

JAWS long, powerful, not snipey

HINDQUARTERS well developed, great power

CHEST deep, good width

THIGHS muscular, long
STIFLES well turned
HOCKS well bent, turning neither in nor out

RIBS well sprung

LEGS straight, medium length, good bone, muscled

FEET compact; toes well arched; pads thick

COLOR black, solid color free from spots except on chest; other solids permissable

COAT short, dense, without wave, hard

the way others do.' Yet they might be accomplishing the same thing. I don't agree that the standard is wrong. It is wordy, and as I say, people interpret it differently; even the show dogs, the good ones, are not right for hunting dogs and many could not compete in a trial. A standard cannot say too much about how a dog should behave; we all know that."

Mrs. Warwick feels that Americans should continue to "go back to the source" and continue to import the British dog to strengthen the stock. The British Lab, however, has been bred for appearance, since very few are used for hunting. The dog the standard was written for is now gone, by the choice of the British show people. The new look, a short-coupled, stockier dog, imported along with the British judges, has had a substantial influence on American dogs. Even Mrs. Warwick agrees that very few English Labradors are used for hunting today, but that does not seem to matter. In America, that is not the case. Waterfowl hunting is increasing and more and more upland game hunters are using the Lab. If anything is changing here in this country it is that the pointing dog has become less popular because upland game land in certain sections of the country is becoming harder and harder to find. Without birds it is more difficult to maintain a pointing dog at his peak of training. Labradors can be trained and kept happy with dummies and fewer birds are needed to do a good job.

Today, it is an almost impossible task to breed dual champions. The show ring has dominance, and the growing pet market has handsome Labradors sitting in the back of station wagons, losing their skills. If Americans keep developing the show ring dog to conform to British standards, field trialers and hunters will have to go their own way with their own, separate, breeding programs.

Solving the Breeding Controversy

Many people were interviewed for this chapter, and a pattern emerged from all the interviews that points to a lack of communication between field-trial and the show people. Both factions speak in exaggerated terms about each other: The field-trial people say that show dogs are too short of neck, backs too short so that they can't move well, too much bone and too heavy; they are not built to hunt and can't, etc. The show people say that the working field-trial dog is too leggy, snipey headed, too fast, too high-strung, doesn't even resemble a Labrador, etc. For the good of the Labrador both sides should reassess their positions. There are *two* main types of competition in which to measure the success of breeding programs, the show ring and field trials. The show standard depicts an ideal structure for a particular job, just as there is an ideal physique for a basketball player, a football linesman, or a long-distance runner. It would be easy to put twelve men in a ring and by looking at them judge which would make the best basketball player. Whether the man who is 6' 8" has the inclination to play basketball is obviously another matter, just as there are dogs that appear they can do the

BOX LUNCH? *Tara Moore*

job but don't have the inclination to hunt.

As we have seen, in America and in England the first field trials and the first shows were run by the same people with the same dogs. Today the two groups are miles apart in both countries and the breeding programs are going in opposite directions.

What is the solution?

To try to put this all in perspective we interviewed Helen Ginnel, who for thirty years has run her kennel, Whygin, in Bedford Hills, New York. She is active both in the show ring and in the fields. On the show side her Labs have won the best in breed at Westminster five times and best of opposite sex three. She twice won the National Specialty, the most important American show event. She is a director of the Labrador Club and head of its show committee. On the field trial side she bred Whygin Cork Coot, who won the National Open twice. For fifteen years she trained and ran her own dogs in field trials and was an officer and the motivating force behind the Westchester Retriever Club. She has been a field trial judge and a show judge. More than 1500 bench champions and thirty field trial champions go back to her line of twenty-four generations, starting with the dual champions of the thirties. Helen is an avid hunter and a fine field shot. She is also a director of the Guide Dogs for the Blind, and not only is she an advisor to their breeding program, but her stock is the base of that program.

Helen feels that if breeding continues on its present course, we will end up with two separate dogs in about twenty years. "The American field Lab is always going to remain great, and he's going to get better and better, and probably he's going to get better and better looking. But he probably will not look like the Lab that will be winning on the bench in twenty years. The problem is not the standard set down for the dog, it's the interpretation. The people who are importing the typical English show lines will produce a totally different dog than we have seen in the past.

"The written standard is not accurate enough and there are too many words like *medium* in it that can't be measured. It's really up to the judges. If judges put up dogs with certain qualities, the people are going to breed for what they think will win. So change comes about according to the fads in judging. At the present time the tendency is toward the British pet. Less than 5 percent of the British Labs are used in the field and their field stock is miles away from what the English show dog looks like. *Bone* and *substance* have become very popular words in the British ring. They might be helpful, possibly, if we were going to use the dog for pulling heavy objects. But they are breeding the athletic ability right out of the dog. The problem is that we have put a tremendous emphasis on the English breeder/judge, who is really judging his own product. He has very little knowledge of what the dog does in America or, according to many, in England. I believe that all judges should be

Helen Ginnel owner of the Whygin Kennel, bred Whygin Cork's Coot, who won the national championship twice.

NEW FRIEND, OLD FRIEND *Herb Strasser*

required to attend our trials so they could see what our dogs do. Then they could put up a dog as winner who could hunt, if the owner wished, and do it stylishly."

According to Helen's thinking, the situation now is analogous to putting twelve men in a ring and asking a judge to pick the best basketball player — only the judge does not know what the game is.

"Through our hunting and field trials, we have produced a dog who can take an unbelievable amount of training and is probably one of the most sophisticated animals in the world today, as far as what he is required to do and what he can do happily. The show people are on an English kick. The best Labs are in America, and they have been since the early 1930s, when the English dog was truly dual purpose, which is no longer the case. The English standard was written for that early working dog, but they have gotten away from it. Their field trial and shooting people also have to breed their own working line. But their show dog is the dog the American show people are importing and introducing into our lines.

We seem to have a myth that whatever is imported must be better. There is a mystique about English breeders, yet their dogs are not being worked. It does not mean, if this keeps up, that we will destroy our dog, because our dog will stay in the hands of the field trialer and hunter and get better and better. What it does mean is that we will end up with two breeds, the pet and the worker."

One will be a good looking pet but with uncertain temperament and disposition since these qualities are not considered in the ring, and the other a beautiful working machine and a marvelous companion.

Another myth should be straightened out. Field trial dogs as a general rule are not high-strung and difficult to handle. The field trial people are breeding a dog that has a tremendous amount of biddability and the ability to take training. The high-strung idiot isn't going to get anywhere in trials *or* the show ring. The greatest number of field trial people in this country are now amateurs who have one or two dogs. The proof that they are not high-strung is that those dogs double as pets. Again the problem is communication. Too many people make judgments on hearsay. If they would go to a licensed field trial and see the dogs work, and also see the dogs back at the cars before or after they run, they would be surprised at how ordinary and pet-like they are. The average person interested in the Lab owes it to himself and the dog to see what is meant by brains, by biddability, what the dog can accomplish and how easy it is to train a Lab. Even many hunters lack knowledge about their dogs and use only a fraction of their potential. The people who are breeding this dog should see the dog work.

"Then there is another myth," Helen added. "Many show people and some hunters object to speed. Somehow they equate speed with being high-strung, and somehow equate slow with having brains. No dog will win a field trial without brains, and you can get fast, crazy dogs but they will get nowhere. In the hunting field a fast dog is a real asset. The faster a shot bird is picked up the less trailing is going to have to be done. If a bird is a cripple, a fast dog is more apt to get him than a slow plodder. A dog can be fast, have a good nose and not over-run his nose. If scent is bad, he will slow down. If he is going to run in circles to pick up the scent, he'll make fast circles. There is no real advantage to lack of speed . . . just go to any field trial and see them work! There are only two reasons a dog is slow, either lack of interest and natural drive, or his conformation won't allow him to move out. 'Fast' does not mean missing birds, it does not mean hunting wide, wild, or out of control; it means doing a job efficiently, and it's a joy to watch. Speed is one of the reasons we have gotten as far as we have in developing the Lab for field trials and hunting."

"The big joke is to hear the English show breeders talk about their own high-strung field trial dogs. If you ever saw a British field

A Myth Questioned

Champion Whygin Gold Bullion and Helen Ginnel winning "best of breed" in 1961 Westminster Show

trial, you would see how well-behaved their dogs are. That is one thing we could learn from the British. Their dogs have incredible manners. But the English show breeders know nothing about their own field dogs, let alone ours."

Helen told the story of an Englishman she met at one of our trials. He said, "Your dogs are just another example of what you people in the Colonies do with the sports we teach you. We stick to tradition and now your dogs will run circles around ours. It's just like sailing. We teach you the sport and we haven't been able to get the America's Cup back for over a century."

Helen believes that dual-purpose breeding is still possible. All of her show champions have produced licensed field trial winners and good hunting dogs. Her field trial and show dogs have always been identical. This same stock that produced for the ring and the field has also produced more than 500 working guide dogs. Her field champions have sired working guide dogs, which negates the theory that field trial dogs are too high-strung and too difficult to be handled by the hunter.

For the future of the Labrador the show people and field trial people must cooperate to create a standard by which they can breed a sound beautiful animal. The show people should attend licensed trials to observe for themselves some of the beautiful Labs entered. It is a lot easier to breed for conformation than it is to breed for the desire to please, the desire and ability to work, and just sheer brains. The show people must realize that to keep those traits in all our Labs the breeding must include field trial stock.

Where does the credit belong, starting 400 years ago, for the breeding of this strong dog? Was it with the men of Devon who never, before or after, developed another dog? Was their special need just an accident of the time and place? It is possible, *but* only part of the credit goes to them. Most likely Darwin had the answer; (1) it was an isolated area where there was no other breed to interfere with the development of the fittest, (2) a subarctic area where strong breeds tend to develop, (3) a lucky stroke of genetics, and (4) the specific needs of the men of Devon and the fishermen of Newfoundland . . . this combination gave us the Labrador Retriever.

Field Trials:
Both Sides of the Atlantic

On both sides of the Atlantic, the Lab has been required to do very different jobs working for the gun, and so very different field trials have evolved in England and America. Thus, comparing the English and American becomes difficult. Even a head-to-head competition would be difficult to arrange because the tests would have to satisfy both sportsmen, and their requirements are in many cases diametrically opposed. The British want their dogs to work on their own and admit that there is a 50 percent chance of luck in their trials, whereas the Americans try to take all the luck out of the game and expect the dogs to work on their own only when the situation requires it.

The English and American trials are very different. The British trials are run between October and January during the shooting season, and only natural game is used. The land is donated to the club for the one- or two-day event by the owner of the estate. The guns are invited by the owner of the estate, and he supplies the beaters, game carriers, workers, and facilities to transport the people and dogs. All the game is retained by the estate except for a brace of birds given to each gun at the end of the day. The land covers many square miles and the amount of pheasant per acre would bring tears to the American hunter's eye.

The trial is divided into two hunting situations, the walk-up and the drive. In the walk-up, a line of handlers proceeds with dogs, guns, judges, beaters, and number carriers (who display the number of the dog working to the gallery that follows the line). In the drive, pass-shooting, the dogs are sat at heel next to their handlers. They are placed in a semi-circle, in a position to see all the guns who are spread out across the field. On command, the beaters go through the field, and the birds are flushed, fly over the guns, and are shot. After the drive a horn is blown to stop all shooting, and the dogs are sent one at a time to make specific retrieves.

The walk-up comprises at least 80 percent of the trial, although most of the sportsman's shooting in Britain is done by drive. The British feel the walk-up is a better way to test the dogs; the runner or crippled bird is the most important part of the dog's work.

Our host and commentator at the Labrador Club Trials and the National Championships was Peter Whitehead, Secretary of Trials for the Labrador Club in England. As Whitehead says, "After all, 50 percent of the gun dog's job in England is retrieving a runner, which is one thing a man cannot do at all. The Lab is an absolute master at tracking a bird by scent for as much as 200, 300 or 400 yards."

In the walk-up, the cripple can be dealt with much more dispatch than on a drive. Here is how it works: There will be as many as 25 to 35 people in the line, according to the width of the field, and three or four judges. Each judge handles two dogs at a time, one on either side. Each judge will have two guns, one on the outside of each dog. Beaters and one cardholder for each judge make up the rest of the line. There are usually three kinds of fields: beet, turnip, and kale. Beet and turnip are much easier to work than the kale, which can be so high that you can't see the dog working. Sometimes they will also use wooded cover with heavy underbrush, much like American grouse hunting. On signal the line moves forward, and when a bird is flushed and shot the whole line stops. The judges decide which of them will take the fall. Then that judge orders one of his two dogs to make the retrieve. Each dog will have two retrieves under his judge, then be retired to the gallery to wait his turn to run for the other judges. The retrieves are not long by American standards.

The amazing thing about the English Labs is that they never step away from their place at heel. They make no noise and show no excitement until they are sent, and then they move out with enthusiasm. A dog is allowed to hunt the area thoroughly. If, in the judge's opinion, the dog is not on mark, he will have the dog brought back by whistle. There are times when the judge will allow the dog to be re-sent. If the dog does not come up with the bird, that judge sends his other dog. If the second dog finds the bird, the first dog is eliminated; his eye was wiped. If the second dog has no success, more dogs are tried. If the bird is lost and not found by any dog in the line, the first dog is out of the trial but not the other dogs. If the fourth dog finds the bird, the three preceding dogs are eliminated. A dog is not expected to make double or triple re-

The British Field Trial

Peter Whitehead has qualified for the British National Championship 3 times.

trieves, but if two birds are shot at the same time, the first dog must remember both marks because he will be sent for a specific bird.

The second dog must mark both falls also because he will be sent for the other bird. After each dog has had two retrieves a new handler and dog come into the line as the first handler is retired. One-day trials accommodate 12 dogs, and in a two-day event 24 dogs will compete. Although more might qualify for the trial, only 12 or 24 names are drawn from the hat.

On the walk-up tests the birds are flushed only a few yards ahead of the line, and a 60 yard retrieve is more than average. The problem for the dog is that at times the action comes fast and furious, and in the fields the cover is uniform and the depth of the fall is hard to mark. No one, including the judges, knows how far or where the birds move to once they are down. Bill Meldrum, the Queen's trainer, lost his dog in the National Championships on just such a situation. An easy bird was dropped 35 yards in front of the line. His dog was given a few casts to find it, with no luck. Three other dogs were tested for that bird and all failed. As Meldrum said, "It was the luck of the draw." His dog was eliminated because he had first chance at the bird, and his dog should have tracked the bird when it moved off. Scenting conditions were not too good that day; but that is the game. The other dogs were not penalized.

The driven tests are the most spectacular to see. At the Championship stake, the invited guns of Sir Joshua Rowley were some of the best shots in England. On the walk-up they missed what most American hunters would consider more than their share because they shoot driven birds practically all the time. The going-away pheasant that has not attained its full speed gave them trouble, but the pass-shooting at full tilt was superb. The dogs were placed in the open. The guns stood at "pegs," positions around the field. Each man had a loader to slip shells into his gun. The birds were flushed by the beaters who sang and clucked as they beat the brush. As the birds started to fly out, none got past the ring of guns. Once the judges had enough birds down the horn was blown. The dogs were sent to retrieve. One at a time, each dog was given a turn. Again it became the luck of the draw. There were eight dogs left in the trial and this was the last test. Four birds fell in a small area behind one gun. The first dog had one of four to find, the second dog, one of three, the third one of two, and the last dog had a hard hunt to find the last bird. The other dogs had different kinds of hunts and three of them had to be handled to their birds.

After each retrieve the judge inspected the bird to see that the dog did not have a hard mouth and the bird was not damaged. When I asked Peter Whitehead what the judges consider eliminating faults, he said, "In my opinion, the best trial is three-quarters walking-up and one-quarter driving. It is necessary to have driving because walking-up doesn't test a dog as to whether it is going to whine (make noise) at a drive. Drives do not test the steadiness of a dog while he's sitting on his bottom by his gun. If you are walking-up, the dogs are on all fours instead of sitting, and that is a good test for running-in, a major eliminating fault.

"Running-in means going before it's time. You call it breaking. The other faults are hard mouth, whining or squeaking on a drive, going spare, as we say, which means the dog is not under control, is wild and not answering the whistle. A dog that is going spare is a bit more than that — it's gone wild and has started to self-hunt and is no longer under control. If this happens for long, a judge will call it out. Also, switching birds might perhaps be an eliminating fault . . . picking up one bird, dropping it and picking up another. They are the main faults."

Commenting on the dog work, Peter said, "We use the whistle, but I think not as much as you do in your trials. It is used for both training and controlling our dogs. There is no doubt that we can put a whistle-conscious dog on a sixpence at a hundred yards.

"If a bird is down and the dog is not near it, the handler at that point can give his dog direction to that bird by whistle. Once the judge sends the dog out, the handler has complete discretion as to how to handle his dog. He is told where the bird is or he sees it and it is then up to the handler with his whistle to handle his dog to that bird, or at least downwind of the bird.

"I would say marking is very nearly 50 percent of a good dog's work because it saves so much handling and so much whistling and waving around and everything else. This is tested very beautifully in the walk-up because when walking-up, dogs will mark, whereas at a drive there may be 30 birds around and he in fact is sent for the one he doesn't see; marking doesn't come into it. Marking is important. If the dog doesn't see, the handler is told by the judge that there was a bird shot and it fell by that tree 60 or 100 yards away, get your dog out there and get that bird. Then, of course, handling comes in and this is done entirely by whistle, although the human voice is used occasionally. There are commands like 'Over' for jumping and 'Hi-lorst,' which orders your dog to hunt in that area. Usually our field trial dogs don't sit at the stop whistle — some do, but in the Open Stakes they don't, simply because all you want to do is stop your dog to get him to stand by for its next direction. The fact of sitting produces one more stage, and it is perhaps not so quick, so a dog usually turns around on all fours and looks at you; you then give him the order 'Go back' or 'Get out,' or hand signal to the left or to the right. By this means you can put a dog pretty accurately on a patch 100 yards or more away.

"In a field trial, the dog is never required to do doubles or triples, but he has to remember where each fell so when it's his turn he'll know where the bird is. In 90 percent of the walk-ups, only one bird is shot at a time. If two or three birds are downed, the dog is

Land and Water Tests

never required to get them all because of the usefulness of being able to wipe another dog's eye with the next bird. Another reason you don't send one dog out for two or three birds is merely that you have six dogs in the line and it's time that some other dog was tested. You don't want to watch only that one, and also the first dog might have had one hell of a hunt for the first bird — particularly if it had been a runner — and as a result he might come back a bit tired and wouldn't want to be sent out again immediately for a second or a third bird. This doesn't often happen because I'm rather afraid that the one thing that field trials do not test is stamina. The reason is that time doesn't allow stamina to be tested in a field trial. A dog will probably work harder on a shooting day than in a field trial.

"When it comes to water tests, unfortunately, not every field trial has water because it is in the kind offices of the host, who gives his ground from his own generosity to the field trial society, and frequently there isn't any water. When there is water, full use is made of it towards the end of the trial. The reason is that a fewer number of dogs are left in the end in what we call the run-off. Then maybe up to a half-dozen dogs, the only dogs left, are brought out for the judges to see, and from which they will make their awards at the end. So a good way of doing it is to do the water work with a drive over water — either over a river or into a lake — or loch in Scotland.

"Sometimes for the water work only — if it is not possible to have a drive into a lake or across a lake — it is considered fair to place dead birds across a body of water but not often. This is a blind retrieve. The judge tells the handler approximately where the bird is and the dog then has to swim across the water and the dog is handled to the bird . . . but all dogs don't get this test. The judges have a hard time because each dog is not doing the same work. This is where the element of luck comes in. Some really good dogs have reportedly bad luck, but it is quite uncanny how the best dogs do come to the top if they are run long enough."

Just as the English have designed their field trials around a normal day's shooting, Americans have done much the same thing. The main difference is that instead of pass-shooting and rough shooting, the walk-up, the day's shooting in America is based primarily on waterfowl shooting because a high percentage of American field trialers are duck hunters. Like the English, Americans have also modified the field trial game to make the testing of the dog the prime objective. According to Nelson Sills, a long-time duck hunter and field trialer, there are more than 100 field trial clubs. Nelson has won the National Amateur Championship and is currently the eastern vice president of the Labrador Club and a director of the American Kennel Club. Nelson feels that the main American field trial problem is sheer numbers. Whereas the British limit their trials to 24 dogs, more than 100 dogs sometimes participate in U.S. stakes.

Nelson Sills, a duck hunter who won the National Amateur Championship, is a senior field trial judge.

THE AMBUSH *Chet Reneson*

The American Field Trial

Thus, the judges have had to make the tests more and more difficult to eliminate the dogs. As the judges make the tests tougher, the dogs learn to handle them.

The field trial club organizes the trial completely, including: selecting the judges, finding good land with fields and water, supplying the committees (usually about fifty workers), and selecting a gun captain. It takes many months of work to put on a good trial. Charlie Smith, a potato farmer from Long Island and one of the senior gun captains, says, "When I put a team in the field, I've got the best guns in that part of the country. I expect them to be able to drop a bird on a dime and they can do it. But I don't want just good guns, I want fellows who are interested in the dogs and their work."

Unlike the British trials, the test is set up in one area and all the dogs are given the same test. The judges test the dogs in four areas: (1) land marks, the dog's ability to remember where as many as three birds have been shot, and where they have fallen, and the ability to retrieve them without help from the handler; (2) combining the marks on land and water; (3) blind retrieves, in which the dog is handled to the bird on land, and (4) blinds on water.

Nelson says, "Field trials are strictly a process of elimination. We have no luck in the game as the British have. We try to make the game as even for each dog as is humanly possible. Each dog tested has to do the exact test that the dog prior to him has done."

The judges select the field and set up the test. It might start with three birds. Wind direction, terrain, and cover are all considered. The retrieves average 100 yards. The "line" (starting point) can be compared to home plate, with the three retrieves first, second, and third base; the distance and angles of the bases are up to the judges. Three teams of guns and bird boys take their places at those "bases." The test may consist of any combination of live and dead birds the judges select. (Dead birds are used to conserve the number of birds needed for a trial. In a national event, with 80 dogs and 10 series, we are talking about thousands of head of game.) The judges remain in one spot, behind the line. For a dead bird, one gun shoots a popper (blank), and the bird boy throws a dead bird at a spot the judge elects. For a flier, a bird boy stands between a gun team of two and throws a live pheasant; the guns shoot the bird, trying to have it land as near as possible to the same spot each time. If the bird flies too far out of the area, the judges may call it a "no bird." In the case of a no bird, the handler and his dog get a rerun, usually after three other dogs have been tested.

The judges call the dogs to line one at a time. The dog walks at heel and is commanded to sit. The handler takes his place next to the dog, and the test starts. Nelson describes what happens. "The handler tries as much as possible to assist the dog, pointing out the guns in the field for him. When he is ready, with the dog sitting quietly by his side, he signals to the judge for the birds. At that point, the handler can no longer say anything to the dog; he must stand there with his hands by his side. The judge, by raising his hand or his judge's book, signals to the guns the order to commence shooting the birds. When the birds are down, the handler is given his number, which means he is now allowed to send his dog to retrieve. Prior to this point, if his dog were to break for the fall he is thrown out for unsteadiness, which is a mandatory elimination from the field trial. Once he is given his number, the handler, at his own discretion, can pick out any of the birds that are down in any order he chooses to pick them up. There is no rule that says he has to get the last bird down first. It is entirely up to him. Then the dog is sent."

Basically, the dogs are judged on remembering the location of the birds, taking the straightest line with the least amount of hunting and disturbing the least amount of ground, and retrieving these birds to hand. Speed is a factor only insofar as most judges appreciate style and perhaps award a dog a few extra points for displaying great style; at the same time, a dog that is reasonably slow and yet shows very keen memory will score nearly as well. Once the dog has completed his last retrieve, the judge may or may not—depending on the test—ask the handler and dog to stay on line and "honor" (observe the birds that are shot for) the next dog. The honoring dog must remain steady until the next dog has been launched for his retrieves.

The two kinds of blind retrieves, one on land and one on water, evolve from waterfowl hunting, where the dog is in the duck blind and cannot see the hit birds or where they landed. Blind retrieves on land are not always *only* on land; they may also be through some water, through ditches and small ponds, and many times involve two or three blinds done back-to-back. There are all sorts of water blinds: some are across points of land, some are around points, some are one-side blinds where there is a very delicate shoreline on one side and open water on the other, and some are through a channel with land on both sides and the dog must not go on shore, a strong temptation. A channel blind might be as long as 200 yards and might seem an unrealistic test. To that thought Nelson answers: "I've hunted ducks many times in marsh where the bird fell into an acre of high cover. It would be impossible to control my dog through the high marsh reeds where I couldn't see him. If I put the dog down the channel to the spot opposite where the bird fell, then I can cast the dog into the marsh and make it easy and faster for him to come up with the bird."

Nelson, who has judged more than 100 major stakes and was voted "Judge of the Year" in 1976, explains how to work the blind. "You bring your dog to line and you set the dog down. You line your dog to that blind by trying to line up the dog's head and his spine and his tail pointing in the direction you want him to go and

The coveted American hatpins

Blind Retrieves

by putting your hand over the dog's head and issuing the command to go. The dog takes off in the line you have given him and if he deviates more than about 15 degrees from that line you blow the whistle. When you blow the whistle, the dog is supposed to stop smartly, turn, look at you and ask you 'Which way do you want me to go?' Through hand signals—by overs to the left, overs to the right or diagonally back 45°, left, right or straight back, whatever the case may be—you now direct your dog to the bird.''

The judges are interested in the dogs that have taken the most precise lines, who have used the fewest whistles to pick up the bird, and have taken true cast, whether overs, backs, or diagonals.

There is an old axiom popular in the field-trial game: "Out of sight, out of mind," as far as judges are concerned. Generally, when you are working on any test, whether it is a blind retrieve or a marking test, the dog should be in sight at all times; after all, a judge can't judge what he can't see, and the handler can't handle what he can't see.

Nelson Sills believes that the Lab has a great future: "I think definitely the Lab can go further; I don't think that we have begun to tap the abilities these dogs have. It used to be that you would do double marks and you thought the dog was very good to do that, and then it got so triple marks were commonplace . . . you thought, gee, how can a dog remember three birds? No longer is it rare to see a quadruple mark; the dogs seem to mark four as well as they do two or three. We have no idea where this is going to end up. It wouldn't surprise me to go to a trial and see a dog picking up five birds, or even six. It is a matter of what you can do with the time allotted. Twenty years ago, a 100 yard blind retrieve would be a long one. Now we are finding blind retrieves of 200 and 250 yards. It used to be the case that two blind retrieves, on a very tight angle, was almost unheard of, and now it is commonplace. It used to be almost impossible to cast your dog into a strong wind; now these dogs are being taught to cast into winds. It used to be thought that when you did water blinds, your dog had to go into the water on the square. Now you are never going to see a water entry in a field trial where you square into the water; most of them are at very narrow angles into the water, and you're disappointed when your dog doesn't take that acute angle, because you work and you train and you know he has the ability to do it.

"We really haven't tapped the full resources of these dogs and there are plenty of areas to advance with them."

Comparisons between the American Lab with the English Lab are difficult to make. Englishman Peter Whitehead says "I don't think it would be quite so difficult for our dogs to compete in your field trials, as for your dogs to compete in ours. Yours have had no experience at all on cripples, and the handling would be slightly different, mainly that you never require your dogs to walk at heel

British vs. American Labs

during a field trial; sometimes I have known a dog to be an hour and twenty minutes in the line walking-up without having a single bird. Now that's a very, very strong test for any dog. With birds being shot and shooting going on all the way around, a dog has to walk quietly at heel for over an hour without getting a single retrieve. I think that, temperament-wise, is what would worry your dogs perhaps a lot more.

"I think that in the handling your dogs are absolute machines; they are not thinking for themselves, but it is fantastic to see. However, if you start making these dogs into machines, they will never do the jobs that are really required in the shooting field, which are, after all, the ones that man can't do at all, however good his eyes and legs are.

"Which is the best dog is hard to say. We never use our dogs to flush game, you do. You do not have driven game where the dog sits at heel until the action is over. Your dog sits in a blind or on a punt and has to remember three or more downed fowl and many of those birds are blinds. In your trials you do not require the dog to track and solve the problem of a cripple. To settle it, I'd have to say that for the work we both require, we've both got the best possible dog to do the job at hand."

Nelson Sill's comments on the American and British dogs:

"I don't know a great deal about the British field trials other than what I've read. Some day I would like to observe some of their trials first-hand. Shooting in this country and shooting in England have become entirely different, so I'm sure that an entirely different type of animal is needed. I have no idea how American dogs could do in England. I don't see any reason why they couldn't do extremely well. Certainly, some of our dogs are absolutely superb markers and some of them are just mechanical robots in their handling, and I don't care where a bird is, you can get your animal to pick it up. I know very little about how a British dog would do in this country, except to go back into the early sixties when Bill Laughlin, the president of the Labrador Club, and Lou Greenleaf, one of our top dog owners, brought over what were then considered fine English field trial dogs and turned them over to American professional trainers. Without exception, I have never seen one of these dogs compete successfully in our American trials.

"I think the American dogs could be very successful in England. I'll only say that because it is rare to go to a field trial when the guns don't shoot a cripple, and the judges want the bird taken out of the bird field; on just hundreds of such occasions I've seen people take their dog down to where the bird is known to have hit the ground, and I've seen that dog start trailing. I've seen him pick the bird up 200, 300 yards away from where the bird went down.

"I've seen some of my own dogs that I have trained over the years, that really didn't display evidence of a very good nose at all,

LABRADOR WITH PHEASANT *Richard Amundsen*

183

British Field Trials have been run the same way for eighty years

British trials are made up of two parts, the walk-up and pass-shooting. In the walk-up the birds are flushed ahead of the moving line of guns, dogs, handlers and beaters. This makes up more than three-quarters of their trial. Although it is not typical of their hunting situation, it gives them the best way of testing their dogs. Most retrieves are singles and the average dis-

tance is about sixty yards. If the game is wounded, the dog is required to track him down. Pass-shooting simulates the true use of the dog in the classical British style of shooting. The dog sits quietly at heel as the birds are shot. Then the dog is sent to retrieve. British field trials are upland game oriented.

Bill Meldrum, the Queen's trainer, handles his dog to a fall during the walk up.
The British do not handle their dogs with the same precision as the Americans.

THE WALK-UP
The line consists of judges, each handling two dogs with a gun on either side of the dogs. The number of beaters depends on the width of the field. The gallery follows at a distance out of the line of action.

At times the cover is very heavy, and the judges help the handler by pointing out where they believe the game is down.

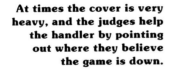

Each judge handles two dogs in the line. After two retrieves, another dog is brought into the line. Competitors follow the action.

Farm carts transport all personnel and dogs to different areas on the estate.

The gallery follows the action on foot, and are confined to a safe location.

Water entries in British trials are not common. Dog is not expected to have a spectacular entry.

Before the pass shooting starts, the dogs must sit with their handler and wait until the beaters work the adjacent fields.

A judge sees only part of dog's work. Each time a dog works for a different judge.

The card carrier displays the number of the dog being tested.

Bird "boys" gather 1000 or so retrieved game, property of estate owner.

Every piece of game must be inspected by an official to see that the game is not damaged, and the dog does not have a *hard mouth*.

Although the dogs are not allowed to chase hare, they must retrieve them if they are shot.

When the shooting starts, the dogs may not move or whine.

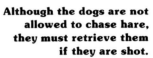

Dogs are sent without giving them a line. On blind retrieves the dog is stopped by whistle 20 yards or so out and put on course with hand signals.

The judges announce the winners, then everyone thanks the landowners who supplied the workers, guns and game.

MARKS
This is a triple retrieve. All dogs get the exact same test. Memory is very important.

American Field Trials

take as much luck out of the game as possible.

American field trials are made up of two parts; *marks*. . . the dog sees where the birds are down, and *blind retrieves*. . . the dog does not know where the bird is. Marked retrieves are usually one, two, or three birds. The dog must remember the exact fall and find the mark on his own. For blind retrieves, the dog is given a line by the handler. The dog may not vary off this line by more than about fifteen degrees. If he does, the handler must stop the dog and give him a hand signal to put him back on the line to the bird.

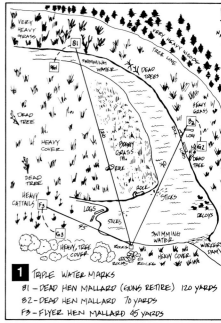

1 TRIPLE WATER MARKS
B1 – DEAD HEN MALLARD (GUNS RETIRE) 120 YARDS
B2 – DEAD HEN MALLARD 70 YARDS
F3 – FLYER HEN MALLARD 45 YARDS

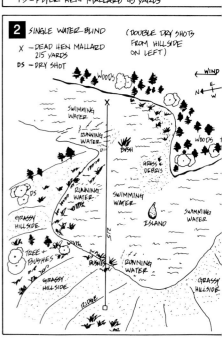

2 SINGLE WATER-BLIND   (DOUBLE DRY SHOTS FROM HILLSIDE ON LEFT)
X – DEAD HEN MALLARD 215 YARDS
DS – DRY SHOT

Each test or series is run from one starting place or line. Two judges, seated in forward chairs, keep running records of the dog's performances. Another judge, raising his arm, signals for birds to be shot. The handler on left, will do this test. The other dog must sit and "honor" the working dog. He may not whine or move. The marshall, seated behind judges, see that everything runs smoothly. Americans can run as many as 100 dogs a day in this way.

The diagrams explain the tests shown in the top two pictures.

BLINDS

Blind retrieves are where trials are won and lost. Dogs must be under absolute control, as in this case, judges can insist that the dog does not touch any land.

The dog is given a line. When he deviates from it, he is stopped by whistle and given a new direction. Americans are much more precise in handling their dogs than the British.

Before a test series begins, a test dog is run, and all the handlers watch from this vantage point to decide how to run their dogs.

189

Given a line, a dog is expected to stay on it through regular terrain or water until he scents the downed bird.

To save time, the next dog on line is held in a "blind" so he can't see test

A dog must "honor" . . . sit on line while bird is shot . . . then is released when working dog starts test.

Shooters are so accurate that they can drop a bird on an exact spot each time, insuring a uniform test for each dog.

The gallery from its stationary vantage point, has a much easier time than the British.

Bird "boys" replenish the field as retrieves are made.

As many as fifty workers are required to put on an American field trial.

American field trials are water fowl oriented.

Dogs come to trials in cars, station wagons, fitted vans, or specially built kennel trucks.

When the sun goes down, the dog talk continues.

but others have had some of the most incredible noses that I have ever seen, in that they could scent a dummy or bird 150 yards away, which is unbelievable. It is those dogs I have hunted myself; I have put them out in marsh trailing cripples and have seen them come back with some of the most difficult hunts in trailing cripples. Our field trials are just not set up for that particular type of test. There is no way to get uniformity. We try to put on the same test for each and every dog in the field trial, rather than have it a matter of luck that one dog is trailing a bird for 20 yards and another one might be trailing it for 300 yards, which is a real inequity when you are trying to score one dog against the others.''

It's an interesting experience for an American to see a British field trial. In comparison their trials are low key. At the time of the year that they hold their trials the days become very short. They gather at the estate at nine A.M., and by the time they move the participants, dogs and the gallery to the first hunting area, you have a ten o'clock start. They break for lunch and take everyone back to the cars for a tailgate snack and tea and then move out again by hay wagon if the distances are far. By four o'clock the sun is getting low and the shooting stops.

The British field trials are well-ordered, calm events, and this is reflected in the dogs and their work. The dogs are the best mannered I have ever seen. They never, but never, stray from heel. One can sense that these dogs have never been force-trained. The rapport between the dogs and their handlers is impressive. The dogs never take their eyes off their handlers. After lunch breaks, when they all return to the trials by hay wagon, dogs and participants are jammed together. Most of the dogs sit with their heads in their handlers' laps and go to sleep.

On one occasion, during a driven shoot, a bird landed one yard in front of a dog. It slid along the ground and lodged between the dog's front paws. The dog never moved. He looked up at his handler; the judge came over and picked the bird up. The rule states that no dog may retrieve until the shooting is over.

American field trialers have said that the British dogs are not aggressive enough. For American needs that might be so, but the British, like their trials, are not in a hurry. They are more interested in seeing a dog figure out a tough problem than in getting the bird to hand. Competition is ingrained in most Americans; one gets the feeling that the British are less interested in winning than in participating in their sport. No one gets upset if a gun misses a bird and the judges give a dog every possible opportunity to be successful, even if it means holding up the line for twenty minutes. Even the handlers' whistles make a soft sound. They use a Staghorn whistle without a pea or ball in it. They tweet at their dogs, whereas the American whistle "shouts" a command. Though the British object to Americans using the whistle as much as we do, it seemed to me

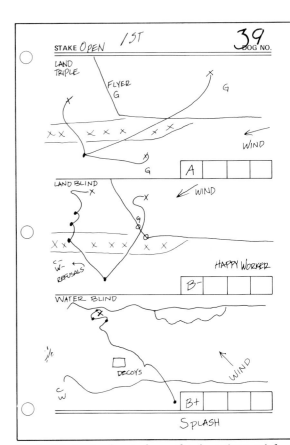

Typical judge's sheets from the American trial.

Above is a very good score on three different series. The judge marks the progress of the dog. In the land triple, the dog had three perfect marks. In the land blind, the dog had three whistles (dots). The dog handled in the right direction. On the second blind, he needed no whistles. In the water blind, the dog got to the area without a whistle

An American Impression

Bill Meldrum walks Queen Elizabeth's dogs at Sandringham House.

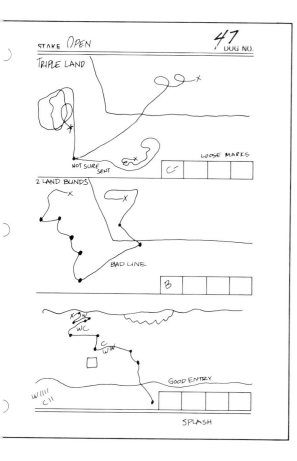

STAKE *OPEN*   *47* DOG NO.

TRIPLE LAND

LOOSE MARKS

NOT SURE SENT

2 LAND BLINDS

BAD LINE

GOOD ENTRY

SPLASH

and needed three whistles and changes of direction to pick up the bird's scent. The dog at right had a much harder time finding the three marked triples on land. On the two land blinds the dog took many whistles and his line was not good. The same thing applies for the water blind.

Sandringham Kennels house forty Labradors.

that they use the whistle as much or more than Americans do, and they get more whistle refusals than Americans would tolerate.

Many British handlers were not as good as the dogs, but that same problem exists in the U.S. also. The dogs, although passive at heel, were aggressive while hunting. Their tails wagged like sixty, and they worked and reworked a piece of cover until every inch was covered, and they seemed to enjoy it. The great difference in handling is that once an American blows the whistle, the dog must be under the handler's control. The British operate differently, moving their dogs to a position downwind and then letting the dogs hunt. I felt that the dogs did not respond to the whistle with enough precision. Later, when I visited the Queen's kennels at Sandringham House, I expressed this opinion to Bill Meldrum, the Queen's trainer. He went to the kennel behind his cottage and took out five dogs. We walked to a field and he asked me, "Which dog do you want me to use?" I chose Sandringham Salt, the dog he had run in the National Championships earlier in the week. He put the dog through a display of handling that any American would have applauded. When I asked him why he hadn't done that during the trial, he answered, "That's not what the judges want to see. They want to see the dog work on his own."

One situation I could not understand. Unfortunately my host, Peter Whitehead, had not seen it, so he could not comment on it afterwards. The dog in question had done very fine work all day. It had wiped the eye of a few dogs and was a good marker. On the drive, the last event of the trial, the dog was sent for a blind retrieve in flat field that had very sparse cover. The distance was no more than 80 yards, and the dog had to cross a river (the Test River, one of the world's great fly-fishing streams) that was about 20 yards wide. The dog was sent from the bank. It took two whistles to get him on the other side. Then the dog had a series of whistle refusals that would have eliminated him in our trials. The handler finally stopped whistling and by self-hunting the dog stumbled on the bird, which was even in plain sight of the gallery. This dog received a third place in the trial, and I can only assume it did that well because it was such an outstanding tracker and that poor handling was not enough to overbalance that skill.

The British do not direct the dog by lining up his body in the desired direction. They wave their hand and off the dog goes. They will start whistling to their dogs at about 20 yards and cast the dog in the new direction, then let the dog hunt. If the dog tracks a runner down and retrieves it, he does not seem to be penalized for the handling to mark. It appeared to this observer that marking was secondary to tracking. The British theory is that getting the bird is the important thing and you are in luck if you get a runner and your dog works out the problem with his nose, especially if you are second dog on the bird and wipe the preceding dog's eye.

I was given permission to walk in the line at all the trials I attended. One trial illustrated the British game plan very well. We hadn't walked ten feet before three birds were flushed. My estimate was that before we finished with that beet field sixty birds were flushed, which means there was a lot of scent all over the place. We could see the pheasants running ahead of our line. A bird went up and flew off to the right and was dropped only twenty yards ahead of the line. It was too close for a dog to retrieve from the right side, so a dog was sent from the far left of the line. The handler sent his dog and then blew his whistle to cast the dog to the fall. Obviously, the dog had not seen the bird go, since the field was at least 200 yards wide. The dog arrived in the area but could not come up with the bird. He started to make long casts and, as far as I could see, got completely out of the area. In America, that dog would have been out of the competition. I could not understand why the handler, who used his whistle to get the dog into the right area to start his hunt, was not using his whistle to bring the dog back to the area; I asked the handler next to me why.

"First of all," he said, "there is a lot of game scent all over the ground. The dog doesn't know that the bird was hit hard, so he is trailing the scent he comes across." I asked why the handler was not helping the dog, and he answered that the judges wanted to see the dog work the problem out for himself.

And that is what finally happened. After a long hunt the dog came back to the original area and found the bird. Everyone agreed that this was a good job. A perfect mark would have been better, but that was impossible from where the dog was at the time the bird was shot. Handling would have proved that the dog could obey his master, but as it turned out, the dog worked the problem out himself—and that is really the essence of British field trials.

After the first day I smugly thought to myself that American dogs could beat the pants off the English dogs. With more experience I realized that in a British trial American dogs would be like over-wound toys. American field trialers push their dogs much further than the British. But we can't apply our standards to their game because the judging is entirely different. Enter the best British dog in an American trial and he'd be skunked. Enter the best American dog in an English trial and he'd have his eye wiped. After I learned more about the British game I concluded that field trials on both sides of the Atlantic could learn much from each other. For the game the British play, the British Lab is the best possible dog. He's a keen dog who seems to love two things—his handler and hunting. I can't score him down because he doesn't do it our way. But I can score the British high on their trials. Underneath the sloppy rubber rain coats and field gear, they even dress well for the occasion. It is a Ladies' and Gentlemen's game, and one gets the feeling that they enjoy the sport of it all.

A Last Word

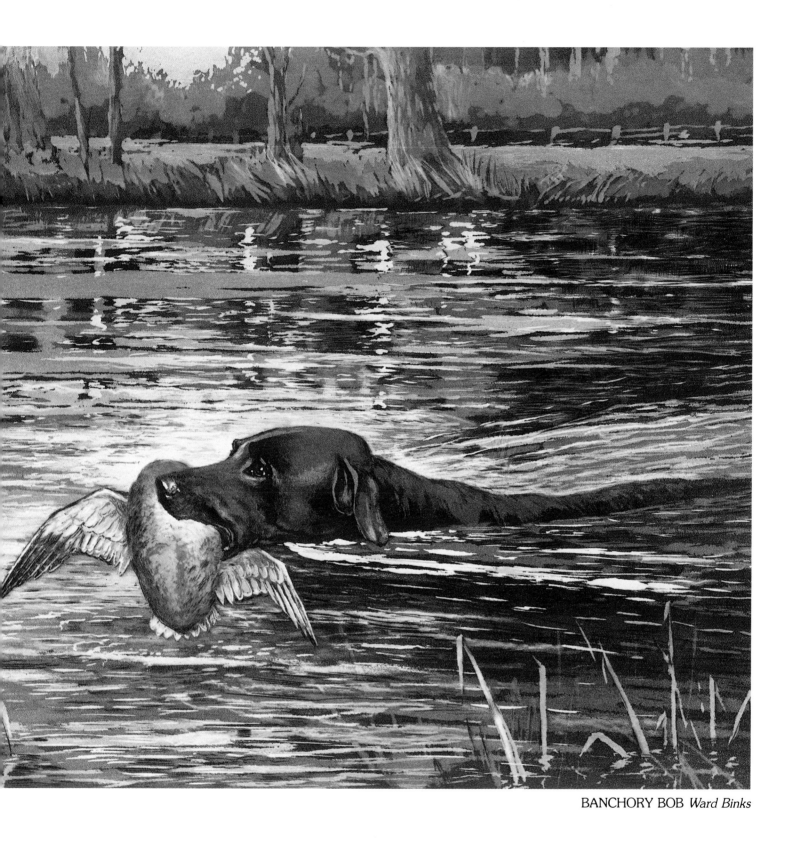

BANCHORY BOB *Ward Binks*

Into the Twenty-First Century

The research to trace this history of the Labrador Retriever was a fascinating experience. It took me back through time some 500 years to about the time of Columbus, and continued up to the year 1980, when the work was finished and the book written. That part of the book can stand on its own, as is. Now, 11 years later, however, a new chapter is needed to bring the story up to date. The decade of the 1980s brought a major development in the Labrador's history that cannot go untold.

A Look at the AKC

To understand what has happened to the Labrador in the last decade, one must recognize what has happened to the American Kennel Club, the national registry of dogs. A year after the first pointing-dog field trial in this country, over 100 years ago now, the AKC registry was formed. The aim of the founding fathers was to preserve the animals in their purest form, both in conformation and for work. The handful of men, under the leadership of August Belmont, would turn over in their graves if they could come back to see their dogs and what their own organization has done in the name of preservation. The most pathetic example has been the English Setter, their favorite, who was the king of hunting dogs at the end of the nineteenth century when the AKC was founded. Today, and for many years in the recent past, with rare exceptions the AKC registered English Setter has lost its ability to hunt, and the AKC standard, a present-day fad, has given the dog a magnificent yet useless coat for any kind of field work.

The beautiful AKC English Setter does not stand alone as a worthless hunting dog. Historically, over the years, *every* dog that has become popular through the show ring has been turned away from its work, be it a hunting or non-hunting breed.

Let's look at the last 30 years. Before 1960 the Irish Setter was 27th on the American "Hit Parade" and was already showing signs of losing its ability to hunt. In 1965, the dog moved up to 21st place, and in the next five years he became 11th in popularity. In just three more years, 1973, the Irish climbed to become the third best-selling dog in the nation. Because of being bred for a growing pet market over the years, the Irish was turned from a fine hunting dog into a high-strung, blooming idiot.

The Poodle's story is possibly the saddest of them all. It is a well-established fact that the Poodle was the first retriever in Britain, and its ancestors can be traced to the early development of retrievers in England.* From being a rugged water dog, it has been turned into a sissy with ribbons in its pom pom, taken from the duck marsh, put into the boudoir, and sprayed with cologne. For 24 of the 31 years since 1960, the Poodle has been the most popular dog in the country. For the past seven years, the dog that replaced the Poodle as number one has been the Cocker Spaniel. Known when I was a boy as the elder gentleman's hunting dog, today the Cocker can't smell his way to the meat counter in a supermarket.

Popularity means big bucks to breeders. Winning in the show ring equates to pet market sales. Breed for conformation alone to satisfy the market, without regard for work, and working ability is lost. It has never failed to happen. Why is this allowed to occur? Because the founding fathers of the American Kennel Club made a mistake. They could not have foreseen that the pet market would become such big business, so they followed the example of the British Kennel Club. Now, by the AKC's own constitution, the organization is a club of clubs. Each breed club makes its own standards. The AKC has no jurisdiction or policing authority over what the club produces, unlike kennel clubs in Continental Europe, where the national clubs control the development of a breed. In Europe, if a dog starts to lose its working ability or fails to meet its conformation standards, the national organization sends the breed club back to the drawing board.

The dogs are tested under simulated hunting conditions, as realistic as possible.

Money, politics, and fads produce our dogs today. The dog may be man's best friend, but the reverse does not hold true.

Where does the Labrador Retriever fit into this story? In 1964, when I published a book called *Water Dog*, there were 10,340 Labs registered that year in the country. With each following year the dog gained greater acceptance. In 1980, when the original edition of this book was published, the figure had risen to 52,398. Eleven years later, the Lab is going over the 100,000 mark. Even more

* See R. A. Wolters, *Duck Dogs* (New York: Dutton, 1990), p. 124.

frightening for the breed, the Lab will probably become the most popular dog in the country in 1991, replacing the Cocker Spaniel as number one. The Cocker will lose his popularity crown and be relegated to second place. He will still be classified as a Sporting Breed dog, but unfortunately without a crown and without the ability to hunt. What a price to pay!

In the early 1980s the handwriting was on the wall. The Labrador Retriever was climbing to the top . . . and to be next on the "hit" list. The Irish was sent off to the nut house, the Cocker to be a lap dog, the Poodle to the boudoir—the Labrador to suburbia in the station wagon.

But for the Labrador Retriever, as you will see, it didn't happen that way. As we have pointed out, each time in the dog's earlier history when he was about to get into trouble, the aristocracy—queens, dukes, lords and America's wealthiest tycoons—were there to help him out. This time it was the little guy, the hunter, who saved his own dog. The story is so important for the Lab's future that it becomes a crucial part of its history.

The Labrador, then, is about to become the favorite dog in the nation with the general public, but for many years now it has already been the most popular hunting dog. Unfortunately, the American Kennel Club did not make real provision for the Lab's future as a hunter. The breeding program for the hunter's best dog has literally been taken away from him, as you will see. As we have already noted, in the 1930s the Labrador demonstrated two qualities: his great ability as a water dog and his "baby sitting" temperament and personality. Although the dog started out in this country with the wealthiest of our business community, very quickly he was taken into Joe Hunter's duck blind and became a member of Joe's family. In a word, he replaced the Chesapeake Bay Retriever. It took Joe Hunter 50 years to get organized finally to protect his dog, and in the intervening years his dog, as a hunter, was practically on the endangered species list.

How this took place is very understandable. Just because the Lab had such a family-oriented disposition, and because he was sponsored in this country by the socially prominent, he became a status symbol. It did not take long for the show ring people to jump on the bandwagon and sell the dog to the station wagon set. The Lab was bred for the pet market: work be damned. In the fifties the yellow Lab became a fad. Things went downhill fast. Breeding for color alone proved disastrous. It is absolutely true that a yellow dog from working stock is just as good as the black. The yellow color is caused by a recessive gene. Breeding year after year with no regard for work, but only for dogs that carried yellow genes to produce yellow pups (because they commanded a better price), can only lead to trouble—a dog that is a retriever in name only. It will look like a Labrador, but it won't have the drive to work as a

The Hunter's Problem

Bred with the instinct and trained to use it.

retriever. In the 1970s the fad turned to chocolate. This is just a narrower slice of the yellow gene, and the brown dogs had a slimmer sliver of working ability in them. While this was all going on, the black Labradors were not faring too well either at the hands of the pet market, fed by the show ring. Sheer numbers got in the way. Too many breeders, as well as the station wagon public, were not concerned about hunting. All they cared about was looks. No way can you constantly, year after year, breed a dog for looks and conformation alone and expect the working ability to stay in his genes. Even the black dog was headed for trouble. Just read Darwin. This was not a case of the survival of the fittest: it was an artificial survival of fads.

What happened to the Lab is a two-sided story. One side almost destroyed the dog, but the other saved it. This is first of all a story of what took place behind the scenes in the Labrador Retriever Club. As you will recall, the club had the dog recognized by the AKC and ran the first field trial in the same year, 1931. The founders of that club were devoted to the dog's ability as a hunter. That was what field trials were all about. But the bylaws of the AKC required the Labrador club also to conduct show ring events for conformation. For the club membership this was a necessary evil—something that had to be done, so they did it with their "left hand."

To understand what was about to happen, we must go back to England to see how the Lab was faring. It had been the second most popular dog there for many years but rarely hunted. To hunt in the United States, all you have to do is to put down your bucks and buy a state license. Not so in England. There, only the aristocracy and the wealthy hunt. Ninety percent of the British Labs

never *see* feathers in their lives. As in the United States, the English Labrador today is a product of the show ring and has become useless as a field dog. The British hunter would not even consider using one of these show dogs for the gun. The relatively few hunters have kept an excellent strain of working Labs going for the field, but keep in mind that they are very few.

A similar situation was happening in our country. AKC-licensed field trials, having gotten their start with the Labrador Retriever Club, were also perpetuating a strain of working Lab, but as in England, their numbers were very small. After 60 years there are still less than 2000 people in that sport today. Field trials started as a rich man's game and it still is that. But it's important to repeat that, small as the numbers of these dogs were, the AKC-licensed field trials kept the hunting work in the dog as the show ring was taking it out.

Paying no real attention to the show ring activities, the more influential members of the Labrador club expended their energies in building up the nucleus of the licensed field trial game with clubs all over the country. Preoccupied with what they considered more important business, the Labrador Retriever Club turned the show ring events over to one of its board members, socially prominent James Warwick and his wife, Helen.

The Warwicks were a very classy couple who spent half of their time each year in England. They were true Anglophiles and very interested in show ring and breeding activities on both sides of the Atlantic. Jim and Helen became the power behind the scene. Jim was director in charge of show activities, and for over 20 years Helen wrote a column on retriever matters for the *AKC Gazette*, the most important breed magazine of its day. Here is the way their game plan worked: If a club wanted to hold an important show, it *might* be a good idea to contact the Labrador Retriever Club's show director to get his opinion on a Labrador judge. Actually, this way Helen and Jim selected the judges. If it was an important specialty they *might* take the assignment themselves. If not they named others on their approval list. With the "right" judges, your show *might* be written up in the *AKC Gazette*. Participants in the show business soon learned from reading Helen's column that the British dog was the paragon of Labradors. And if you wanted your dogs to make their mark and win in the ring it *might* be good to get some English bloodlines into your stock. The Warwicks knew all the British breeders and just *might* be able to arrange the sale of the right dog on their next trip to England. Those same British breeders, friends of the Warwicks, became the judges for our U.S. show events. That meant they were both selling dogs here and judging them here, a very questionable procedure. If you were an American judge and wanted a good write-up in the *AKC Gazette* for the show world to read, and wanted more judging assignments, it *might* be to your advantage to pay a lot of attention to the dogs with that British look. If a club wanted to import British judges, and entertain them in this country, the Warwicks *might* arrange it. In return the British *might* be just as proud to have the Warwicks be their all-expense-paid judges and reciprocate the entertaining. The Warwicks controlled the game on both sides of the Atlantic. The disastrous part of all this was that the British judges did not hunt their dogs in England, never hunted in the United States, yet they were interpreting a standard for a dog whose job they did not know. (Reread the interview with Helen Warwick on page 164.) The English show stock was no longer a hunter. It had what the British call substance or "bone." It was stocky, stubby, with a head so blocky, and muzzle and neck so short, that it would be a battle royal between such a dog and a wounded goose—and most American hunters would put their money on the goose. It was not just a matter of lack of hunting skill: the fads in conformation that developed *might* kill such a dog with a hard day's work on our Eastern Shore. The biggest problem dogs have with man is that power, money, politics, and lack of knowledge get in the way of sensible breeding.

The show and field trial people went their separate ways in spite of the Labrador club's written standard. The show people referred to the field trial dog as a "whippet"; the field trial people referred to the show dog as a "pig." One field trialer said when asked about the written standard, "If I could find a black monkey who could mark down three birds, take a line, run a snappy blind, and guarantee me a win, I'd register him as a Lab and run 'im!"

Lately the Labrador club has finally come to its senses and had a committee rewrite the Labrador conformation standard. The new standard was to satisfy both the show and the field people. Helen Ginnel (page 168) was the leading force. The committee submitted a standard that worked well for an American hunting dog and for American hunting conditions. The show people raised such a ruckus that the AKC decided not to accept the new standard. Because it is the show people who bring in the big money, AKC listened to them. Helen told me just before sickness took her away that she sent the standard back to the AKC and told them that by their own constitution they had no say in the matter. The standard is the work of the breed club, and it stands as is! With her strong presence gone, it is hard to say what will transpire. My guess is that the showpeople will win. Once again the hunting dog will suffer. But as you will now see, whatever happens in the show ring in the next century won't affect the hunter. Let them go their own way.

While all this has been going on, there is another big Labrador world out there. There are 17 million hunters in the United States who have no interest in the show ring. They couldn't care less about AKC-licensed field trials and could not afford them even if they did. The field trial dog could not come close to supplying the

Where Does the Hunter Get Working Stock?

202

A working pup. . . . It all starts here.

Enter the Cavalry

G. Ray Arnett and Lab friend. "There is no better waterfowl conservationist than a well-trained Labrador Retriever," Ray Arnett says. "It was with this in mind that I encouraged Richard Wolters to launch NAHRA. Using that splendid organization and a bit of dedication and effort on the part of the owner, every waterfowl and upland hunter can have a retriever that will virtually eliminate the waste of unretrieved game birds, and greatly increase the hunter's enjoyment of a day in the field."

hunter's demand, and those pups are expensive. Unfortunately, the hunters were not organized in the early 1980s. They did not know the guys in the next county who were hunters, let alone what dogs they had. If a hunter wanted a hunting pup and none was available through his hunting cronies (whose dogs were not that great), his only source was the Sunday newspaper. "Registered AKC Labrador pups for sale." Almost all of them were show stock.

Was the Labrador as a hunting dog going down the drain? Was he following, because of his ill-fated popularity, the AKC English, the Irish, Poodle, and Cocker, the destruction of the Brittany? Go down the list further if you wish. Historically, it was about to happen because no dog had ever beaten the popularity rap—until *Now!*

For years, writers like Bill Tarrant of *Field and Stream* have protested field trials. The dogs were trained to thread a needle. They were no longer hunting dogs. The reason was simple to understand. In an AKC-licensed field trial the judges must find and place dogs first, second, third, fourth out of a field of a hundred or more. The dogs were all so good that the judges made the tests harder and harder in order to find the winners. The dogs were then trained to beat the judges. The judges then set out to beat the dogs. The dogs won again. Over years of this unfortunate, vicious cycle of testing, the dogs were required to do tasks that no hunter needed done. Field trials, using birds and guns, became an obedience game unto itself. That does not mean that it should be knocked. Those in the game love it and should. There have probably been 100 dogs in the country that have been exceptional, and many still are. It costs many, many thousands of dollars to get a dog to that level of training. Those dogs can become very valuable. Field trialer Mary Howley has a great bitch named Candlewoods Tanks A Lot who is for sale. Tanks broke all Derby records and at 27 months of age was an AFC and FC Champion. At three years and four months she became the National Open Field Trial Champion and repeated that accomplishment a year later . . . winning two National Championships back to back! Tanks is for sale for $500,000.00. At this writing an offer has been made.

The field trial game kept the working instinct in the dog, but the average hunter never had a chance in that game. Writers from time to time complained in the name of Joe the hunter, but the editors of the outdoor magazines would not allow their writers to harp on the subject, so nothing was accomplished.

Gun Dog magazine, then edited and published by David Meisner, came on the scene in the fall of 1981. I was asked to write the Retriever column. Like the rest of the outdoor magazines, we too objected to the senseless direction of field trials and the show ring. But these issues did not become a once-in-a-while subject. The magazine hit it hard and constantly. Articles were published as to what the AKC should do but didn't do. The mail flowed in. The readers stood up and cheered. They wanted a place and a means to train their dogs. I am not sure they knew it, but they wanted their hunting dog back from the places the AKC had relegated it to—the show ring, licensed field trials—with no place for the hunter and his dog in their program.

Meisner, a good publisher, saw what was happening to circulation and said, "Go at it!" That gave me carte blanche as a writer, but little did I know the headaches that would produce. It all seemed to get out of hand when G. Ray Arnett, Assistant Secretary of the Department of Interior in President Reagan's administration, took me to lunch. Arnett was a devoted hunter and an old-line field trialer who ran a string of Labradors. He too had dropped out of the licensed field trial game, not pleased with the direction they were going. Hunting and fishing in the United States were under his direction in the Department of Interior. Being a devout conservationist, he had an ax to grind. On paper the Labrador could save more game than Ducks Unlimited could produce. But the dog and the hunter were in a sad state. Most hunters never saw a real retriever work, and if they did, they would not know how to train the dog to do his job. Here is an example: A hunter sits in his duck blind with his dog at his feet. He shoots a goose but only wounds it. The bird sails on 100 yards or so before it drops into the reeds across the inlet. The hunter sees where the goose went down. The dog sees none of this action, and has no idea where the bird is. How does the hunter recover the bird?

The "language" the team of man (or woman) and dog uses is called *handling*. The hunter gives the dog a line to follow with his hand in front of the dog's face. The dog goes in that direction, swimming if necessary. He stays on that path until the hunter blows his whistle to make a correction in the dog's line to the bird. The dog stops, turns to receive a new directional command from the hunter, who shows the dog the way to go with hand and arm signals and whistle. Corrections are made a few times, according to the dog's position, to the right or left or farther away, until the dog scents the bird. The dog trails the scent to the game. All hunters know about handling, but only one in a thousand has had this kind of teamwork with his dog.

The law states that a hunter must take only his limit. But if a goose is shot and wounded and not recovered, the hunter has a right, by law, to shoot another and another until he has recovered his bag limit. This Ray Arnett saw as a terrible waste of our natural resources. He suggested that an organization had to be formed that would teach the hunter how to train his dog to accomplish the job the dog was bred to perform, and conserve our game. I agreed with Ray wholeheartedly until he suggested that I had to form such a national organization!

I declined, saying as a writer I had no knowledge of how to start or run anything on a national level. He told me that all I had

The dog is swimming almost 100 yards away.

Handling: Go to your left until you hear the whistle to stop . . .

Take new direction. Go to your right . . .

Go straight back until you hear the whistle to stop . . .

Quarter back and get the scent of the bird.

to do was put a board of directors together and they would do the work. No way; it sounded too easy. I still refused. He argued, pointing out the conservation aspects for both waterfowl and the Lab, who he said was also on the "edge." Thinking to myself that I didn't even have a secretary, let alone a means of starting an organization, I held fast. Then Ray became adamant and proclaimed, "All you writers are alike. You give us good ideas, then you cop out!"

Challenged, I rose from the table, went to the phone, and called long distance to George Spear III. Ned is a small-town Vermont lawyer and voracious hunter—or possibly that should read insatiable duck hunter and small-town lawyer—who accepts no court cases during hunting season. That's when he and his fine Labrador—named, of all things, Penny Rose—hang out the "Gone Hunting" sign. "Ned," I hollered into the phone, "we are going to start a hunting retriever organization in this country and you are going to be the president!" Before I could even say, "Don't you dare cop out on me!" he replied, "Fine. Let's go!"

It took a year to assemble the eight hunters who would make up the board of directors and to get organized: Ned Spear, president; Richard A. Wolters, vice president; Omar Driskill, treasurer; John Krupp, secretary; board members David Maynard, David Follansbee, Jack Jagoda, and Kent Repka. The board were just a bunch of devoted hunters, all of them owning trained Labrador Retrievers, who had no idea of the frustration and heartache that lay ahead. True, they were of one mind as to what kind of dog they wanted ultimately. But reaching that goal, which they did, was a rocky road. In fact, they were so confident that they each personally signed a bank note to borrow $5000 for start-up funds from David Meisner. They put their own money where their mouths were.

The name North American Hunting Retriever Association was chosen so we could include Canada in our operations. Many meetings were called, hundreds of hours of phone conversations took place, and members footed their own bills. It is interesting that from the first brainstorming sessions to getting the final working/running rules on paper, the concept for the dogs never changed. It was David Follansbee who had the foresight to insist that the whole structure of the program should be noncompetitive. The difficult part for the board was to forget what they knew about AKC-licensed field trials, and come up with a working noncompetitive concept that would interest the hunter in training his dog for *his* job. The purpose was three-fold: to train the retrievers for conservation, to train the hunter to accomplish this, and most important, to get enough fine hunting dogs to establish a *working* stud book that would function as a national gene pool for working hunting stock to preserve the retriever's hunting ability.

From the start NAHRA was not interested in becoming a

dog registry. There were two major registries in the country, the AKC and the United Kennel Club. Their stud books were a listing, for a fee, of all dogs that were born and registered. That was supposed to keep a breed pure, but as the media have pointed out, on several occasions dogs have been registered with false papers and other greedy breeders' techniques. The press reported dogs as registered that had never even existed, or sires were misstated in applying for registration. NAHRA was interested in a pure dog, but did not want the responsibility of that business. A NAHRA dog may enter an event just as long as it is registered with any recognized regulatory body of any country in the world. The dog then becomes part of the NAHRA registry, at no fee, only when it has demonstrated in the field that it has passed the work set down in a written standard by the NAHRA board of directors. This then becomes a *working* stud book, the only one of its kind. Breeding dogs from this free registry can almost guarantee working pups.

The working stud book for the hunter was the real purpose behind NAHRA. Giving out ribbons and awarding titles are incidental. The heart of the whole matter for the Labrador Retreiver, who was headed for trouble in the field, was to take action through a working stud book to produce quality working offspring, and proliferate that concept from coast to coast. First you had to find and test the dogs to start the hunter's stud book. Then you would get the desired offspring. It was time to go back to the drawing board and do some redesigning.

Interestingly, if the Labrador Retriever had not been in trouble or had not even existed, NAHRA would never had been born. The Chessie, the Flat Coat, the Curly Coat, American Water Spaniel, and other breeds still being used, in smaller numbers, as working retrievers, were in no trouble from the show ring or the pet market. They never did get into the Labrador's situation and have to be saved from the plight of popularity. The Golden Retriever is another story. It is popular and is in the same trouble as the Lab, but in the Golden's case it's of the Golden club's own making. Relatively few Golden owners recognize the problem. The Golden breed club is show-oriented. The Golden owners hunt only about five percent of their population. The same low percentage of the Goldens are run in field tests, be they AKC-licensed events or NAHRA-hunting tests. For those few dogs there would have been no reason to have an organization such as NAHRA.

Golden owners did not lend much support, in numbers, when NAHRA started, and they give relatively little support now. But NAHRA and the working stud listings are now available for all the retrieving breeds, no matter how small their numbers, and a testing program makes the breeds that much stronger. The point of this is that the *NAHRA story is a crucial part of the Labrador Retriever's history.* NAHRA was born for the Labradors and all the other

The Labrador Is the Reason for NAHRA

Many of the good dog trainers are women.

The Mechanics of NAHRA

George (Ned) Spear III and Penny Rose. "The beginning of NAHRA? It began on a windy day on Lake Champlain," Ned says, "with a cold seven-year-old wishing he had warmer socks. Duke, a great-grandson of the legendary Shed of Arden, made my poor shot look great and soon delivered the heavy duck to hand. Penny Rose came along some three decades later and provided the catalyst for me to seek other like-minded hunters interested in bringing recognition and protection to our Labrador. For all of us, the dogs were really the beginning."

retrievers were swept in behind, to the benefit of all these breeds.

Dogs in NAHRA work toward titles in three categories: Started, Intermediate, and Senior. Age has nothing to do with a dog's category. It depends on ability and degree of training. A dog and handler work up through the ranks.

For the first time in retriever trials, a noncompetitive system was established. Dogs do not compete to win a placement. (As we have said, in the licensed game judges had to make the test harder and harder as the dogs got better and better, in order to place the four best. This diverted the game from hunting and made it into an unbelievable obedience test using guns and birds.) A top licensed field trial dog may be one of the smartest animals in the world. Instead of that kind of precision, with the new NAHRA testing system the dogs work against a written hunting standard that will never have to be changed. These dogs learn other kinds of smarts— they are "hunting-wise." In the 1980s the standard was rewritten three times, not to change the original work required, but only to clarify the wording so there would be no ambiguity. Judges score a dog's work and if he passes with an 80 percent average in the test categories, the dog is awarded points toward a title. A NAHRA Senior dog may not be classified as the smartest of animals, but he is no slouch.

The standard makes the job of judging easier, eliminating the "creative" aspect in which the judge takes the attitude, "OK, see if you can do this one!" But there is a more important reason why the NAHRA board wanted competition removed from the game. Dog against dog really means people against people. There is an old saying in the licensed trial game that one competitor says to another as he walks to "line" to run his dog: "Good luck," then under his breath he adds, "I hope the dog breaks his leg." In the NAHRA game that attitude is eliminated. The work is for the dog alone. The judge does not care if one or all the dogs pass the standard. The handlers, spectators, even the judges are rooting for the dog. With competition eliminated, the more experienced handlers help those coming along. Training secrets are eliminated. If one has a training problem, help is easy to get. This is what the board of directors counted on. They were more interested in producing working dogs than awarding ribbons, and it has worked.

Training a dog to the degree the board was asking would be a process of creation. First, they wanted to establish lines of working stock so that the hunter had the best raw material. Then the hunter would take the raw stuff and make it into a finished product. Just as a sculptor takes a piece of marble and chisels it piece by piece into a statue, producing a fine hunting dog is a personal creation just as important to its maker. It is *his* product. But the quality of our puppies has to be just as good as that of the sculptor's starting marble block.

Politics, greed, power egos, and money have destroyed much that man has done, and the NAHRA board recognized what all this had done to our Labs. Understanding many of the problems people and dogs have had in the past, the board called an important meeting at the famous Mashomack Hunting Preserve in Pine Plains, New York, to address those obstacles. The organization would be set up with the board of directors at the helm. There would be no national officers voted on by the membership at large. There would be no vote for individuals or clubs. Clubs would be formed throughout the country. Once the individual clubs were set up, there would be no way for national politics ever to get in the way of our dogs. Without the vote, NAHRA was set up so factions could not exist. The best possible running rules for the standard were in place. Hunting was not going to change. Why should the rules change? There would be no need for power politics to get in the way, since there would be no changes needed this year, next year, or in ten years. Infighting has been the AKC's biggest problem and, as we have seen, the hunting Labs have suffered. The board was determined to keep politics, greed, power, and egos out of the hunting Lab's future.

Someone once said to Ned Spear, "NAHRA sounds like a dictatorship." Actually it's not. The board is truly open to all suggestions. And it has worked because a good suggestion can be acted upon overnight. Through board meetings held by telephone conference, a decision can be made quickly. This has another advantage: changes such as the wording in a rule book or field procedures can be made without the usual organizational delay. NAHRA learned lessons from the mistakes the AKC had made— too many hands in the pie leads to infighting. The first purpose was to get the Labrador back for the hunter as a working tool for conservation. The second was to prevent the public from changing these initial objectives for the Lab at some time in the future.

Money was the only factor that could destroy this dedicated gang of hunters called the board of directors, because they did not have any. As soon as the running rules, scoring system, titles, and organizational matters were settled, NAHRA was announced to the hunting public through *Gun Dog* magazine. The response was overwhelming. The mail man had to use a cart!

Hunting with a trained Labrador is team work. Hand directing dog to fallen game.

Trouble, But Only the First of It

Before the ink was dry, the United Kennel Club, a privately owned dog registry, contacted NAHRA and offered to sponsor the program. Was that the solution to the money problems? We entered negotiations with them and had two meetings. The board of directors voted against their offer for a number of reasons. The retrievers for 60 years had been registered with the American Kennel Club, and the NAHRA board thought it would be a disservice to the Labrador breed to split the registry and start anew. We did not believe the hunter would especially like to go to the trouble of re-registering his retriever for a fee to an organization he did not know. The working plan the UKC offered would pay for a magazine through which they would make a profit from the advertising. They would also receive a $2.00 running fee per dog, leaving the national organization, NAHRA, with little or no working capital for regional, national, or international club growth, and the judges' clinics that were a major feature of the NAHRA program. The money generated would go mostly to the UKC, a privately owned corporation. Few if any in their organization had any experience with either hunting retrievers or retriever trials. Although they were the coon hound field trial experts, they did not seem to understand that the Labrador owner was a different sort of "cat."

NAHRA faced a crisis before it even got off the ground. For the first gala event Louisiana was chosen as the locale because it was the biggest duck hunting state in the nation, with more Labs than any other ten states. Duck hunting is big revenue for the state of Louisiana, and the press jumped onto this story with everything it could move into the duck marshes. Somehow the Louisiana organizers of the event made two mistakes. First, they said this NAHRA event was for the hunter and would be different. In that "difference" they foolishly ran down the AKC-licensed field trials because the shock collar and other potentially cruel methods are sometimes used to train those dogs. The press loved it, not knowing that any method to train can be cruel if used wrongly. A big flap started in the media, and the AKC-licensed trial people took a terrible beating and had no effective way to answer the charges. Bad blood flowed unnecessarily. The second mistake was that the organizers of the state event advertised that this first NAHRA field test would be sponsored by the United Kennel Club. That blew the lid. The NAHRA board threatened to back out unless that sponsorship was eliminated. The phone wires burned between Vermont and Louisiana: NAHRA alone sponsored the event!

After the event, the NAHRA board member from Louisiana quit and was instrumental in starting an organization called the Hunting Retriever Club, which had as its sponsor the United Kennel Club. They used the basic NAHRA rules (which had taken NAHRA a year to write) to run their program, changing the title names and cutting out upland hunting tests. Young NAHRA, with no money, had no way to stop them. The NAHRA board had to ponder this

problem. They reached two conclusions. If the program was run well in Louisiana, the Labs would benefit and that was, after all, what it was all about. The dog couldn't care less whose rules it ran under, or what the title was, or who sponsored the event. The board's second conclusion was to let the affair continue as planned, since the competing Louisiana club would have little growth because of the business arrangement it would have with the United Kennel Club, which NAHRA turned down. Both assumptions on NAHRA's part have been borne out. The dogs in the Gulf area love running in their events, and the United Kennel's Hunting Retriever Club, up until now, has had little growth nationally. With NAHRA clubs moving into UKC territory, they have suggested a merger with NAHRA on two separate occasions. NAHRA has continued on its own way, and the dogs in both clubs are becoming fine working animals.

From the beginning the secret ambition of the NAHRA board of directors was to become associated with the AKC. It was big, was the legitimate registry body for the Labrador, knew the workings of retrievers through their field trial program, and had money. It seemed to the board that NAHRA was a natural for them. We had a lot to offer with our know-how about running a hunting retriever program. Also, by their own estimate, the AKC figured that half the hunters in the country did not spend the money to register their Labs with them. The hunter was not interested in the AKC. What would they get out of it? But NAHRA's joining the AKC would bring in revenue from the hunter for registering his dog

The AKC Marriage . . . and Divorce

All the handlers watch the test-dog work. The judge signals for the action to start.

and all his future litters. And NAHRA sincerely believed that the big wheels in the AKC would be interested in saving the hunting instinct in the Labrador Retriever. (See pages 177, 179 to 182, quoting Nelson Sills of the AKC Board of Directors.)

I was given the task of making the first contact, and a luncheon meeting was arranged with the AKC president, William Stifel. I expected the meeting to be over at one o'clock and had another meeting to attend. At two we were still at it. Three o'clock passed and we left the table at four. The report to the NAHRA board that night was most enthusiastic. AKC's president seemed to grasp the concept of a new area of coverage for the AKC. Those millions of hunters and their dogs were *a big new Labrador market.* My parting suggestion to the president was to contact Nelson Sills on the AKC board of directors for support for the project. A meeting was set for the following month. It never took place.

Four months later, the NAHRA board was finally given an audience with the AKC's president and field trial director. Two questions they asked summed up the tone of the meeting: "Who are you people? Can you show us a list of whom you represent?" Something had gone wrong.

Five months after that, the NAHRA concept was heard by Ted Eldredge, a member of the AKC board of directors. He suggested that the AKC administration, president and all, reopen negotiation with NAHRA. He felt it was an important new program and that the AKC was missing the boat. George Bragaw, a Labrador show judge (see pages 160, 162) who I have always thought was probably the person who told Eldredge about NAHRA, acted as the intermediary. A meeting was called in Virginia between the AKC field trial director and Jack Jagoda, a member of the NAHRA board. The AKC picked Jack because they thought they could deal with him. They already had learned that president Ned Spear, the lawyer, was a tough cookie. The NAHRA board became suspicious and lawyer Ned contacted a Beagle hunting group in Ohio that had been in similar negotiations with the AKC.

What Ned found out from the Beagle group was most helpful for NAHRA. First, he learned that there should be written agreements only. The AKC was so big that one person there could say one thing and another something else. We were warned to ask *not* to be put on the Field Trial Advisory Committee to the AKC Board of Directors (as had happened to the Beagle group), where we would have only one vote, but to demand that we should be a separate Hunting Retriever Advisory Committee to the AKC board. The NAHRA board should name the members of that committee. NAHRA should be responsible for writing the AKC running rule book for the hunting tests, and it must remain under NAHRA copyright. NAHRA was advised to be very cautious.

The meeting with Jack Jagoda took place, and he was still

stunned when he reported that night that the AKC had agreed to every demand. A joint meeting was called. The NAHRA board, plus Ray Arnett from the Department of Interior, met with the AKC committee. (From then on Ray attended all our meetings with the AKC in order, as he suggested, "to give us hunters some class.") All the demands were spelled out in writing. The AKC signed the agreement without a murmur, and NAHRA/AKC were married!

NAHRA was to organize clubs and run sanctioned events for one year, and the next year conduct licensed tests. The AKC, at their expense, would print the sanction rule book to be distributed through the clubs and to the interested public.

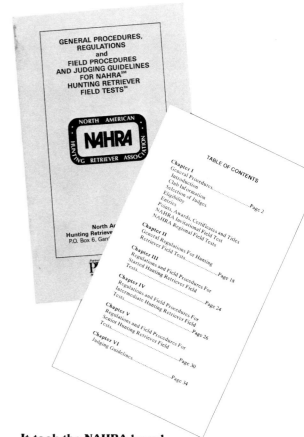

The first thing that went wrong was that the new printed sanction rule book, which NAHRA had worked so hard to write, carried an American Kennel Club copyright notice. Before NAHRA could protest, the AKC field trial director called to say this was a printer's error, and that it would be changed for the licensed rule book that was to be printed in a year. During the year, many field events were successfully run, but nothing was done about NAHRA's request to act as the hunting advisory committee to the AKC board. They stalled, saying it was in the works. Other things started to go wrong. NAHRA was getting double talk from the AKC administration. Things that were clearly agreed upon became unclear. NAHRA asked for a special meeting with Ted Eldredge, its friend on the AKC board of directors. The entire NAHRA group flew to his home in Virginia for a Sunday meeting before that week's AKC board meeting in New York. When Eldredge heard NAHRA's whole story as to what was happening, we could see he was upset. But he calmly assured the NAHRA board that he would straighten the whole matter out at the AKC board meeting that week. It never happened—two days later Ted died. NAHRA and the Labradors lost a good friend.

It took the NAHRA board a year of hard work to write and test the rules. They became the keystone of hunting retriever work.

Affairs were going very well in the field. Hunters started coming out of the woodwork to run their Labs in the new AKC/NAHRA events all over the country. At the next NAHRA meeting with the AKC a new face sat on the AKC's side of the table. He was a member of the AKC board of directors. Here is what he told us: The new rule book would carry the AKC copyright. NAHRA's name would be stricken from the rule book; AKC would be responsible for the rules. Running fees would go to the AKC. There would be no hunting advisory committee to the AKC board of directors. In the middle of the next sentence Ray Arnett stood up to his full six feet, five inches and said to the NAHRA board, "Gentlemen, we can't do business here!" We were divorced.

But the AKC sent a letter the next day to all their clubs and the clubs NAHRA had formed, saying that they were now running the show and to go ahead with each club's plans and continue using the rules in the copyrighted AKC book.

This time NAHRA did not sit by. They brought legal action against the AKC to stop them from using NAHRA rules. Then AKC hired a law firm to fight us. They had the "proof" that the rules were AKC's by the very copyright in the printed book that the AKC had told us was a printer's error. NAHRA lawyers presented the original documents written by the board. This went on for months— why, it is hard to say, except that lawyers love to run up the clock. Just before this case was to go to trial, NAHRA lawyers presented my book *Game Dog*. In the back of the book were the NAHRA running rules. The book was written before the AKC was even involved with NAHRA. I personally owned the copyright, all in print and registered in the Library of Congress. The AKC capitulated and wrote their own program.

Thinking back on the AKC association, never once was there any talk of what this would mean to the future of the Labrador. They never discussed with us what the show ring was doing to the Lab. What was discussed was the dollar volume and the number of new dogs they could register. Most of the people we dealt with in the AKC were corporate types who got a job with a dog registry . . . it could just as well have been a dog food company.

The dog world has a strange fear of the AKC. Get on the inside, however, and you will see that it is not to be feared. They do act much like city hall. Actually the AKC is like any other corporation. There are a lot of nice people caught in a very political game.

Why had there been such a change in the AKC president between that first luncheon meeting, when he was so excited about the new proposal, and the meeting four months later when he didn't even know who we were? The infighting at the top levels of the AKC has been going on for years. NAHRA got caught in just such a palace struggle. The power battle at that time was between a West Coast faction and the Westminster Kennel Club, who have run the AKC for generations. The president NAHRA worked with seemed indecisive at the time, but later we learned his hands were tied. He had a split board of directors. They themselves were in the midst of the power struggle. Those who were against the powers that put the president in place were not going to allow him to accomplish what he believed would be a good move for the organization. Apparently the original four-hour lunch showed what the president really believed. The backing off in the meeting four months later was self-preservation. He saw another battle coming and was trying to avoid it. Ted Eldredge forced the issue. NAHRA was just a pawn that was defeated by the AKC board of directors before it ever appeared on the scene. It is hard to believe that for internal AKC political reasons, and at the expense of the dogs, someone would try to kill the NAHRA movement. It happened! Infighting, self-preservation, ego, and corporate factions can do

The NAHRA board of directors in 1991. Top left: Kent Repka, Jack Jagoda, president. Middle: Tom Rentz, Richard A. Wolters. Bottom: Gary Erickson. Lewis Brothers absent.

strange things to nice people. NAHRA had tried in constructing its program to keep this sort of behavior from endangering the Labrador's future.

Two big corporations, in NAHRA's efforts to save the Labrador, were taken to the wall by the eight little hunters. One, the AKC, capitulated over the use of the NAHRA running rules and procedures, and the other the UKC, left with limited growth despite an expressed desire for a merger with NAHRA. But the battles took their toll. Since no NAHRA board member ever made a dime in compensation, Ned Spear resigned as president, saying that he really had to get back to making a living for his family. Family reasons again caused three other members of the board to resign. Jack Jagoda, an excellent businessman devoted to the cause, became the president. He introduced computers and other office equipment to meet the needs of a growing enterprise. After those setbacks, under Jack's direction NAHRA took off like springing teal. Three new members were put on the board: first Lewis Brothers of Virginia, then Gary Erickson of Washington state, and Tom Rentz of Georgia. Emerging from the AKC disaster with no funds, the new board's first order of business was to sign another note at the bank for more money for the office equipment. Once again the board put their money where their mouths were. The geographical locations of the new board members were very important.

After leaving AKC, NAHRA grew like Topsy from Alaska to Georgia and from coast to coast. In short order the loans were paid back and NAHRA became solvent. The NAHRA magazine is profitable and after the AKC and UKC debacle, NAHRA grew up and rebuilt a strong, loyal club structure. NAHRA events of over 200 dogs entered and run in a weekend are not uncommon. How far will the movement go?

The point system has proven to be a clever device for NAHRA. The dogs couldn't care less. The work is their reward. Winning points depends on ability and training. The dogs in the Started category are only expected to demonstrate interest in birds and the desire to retrieve. This actually comes from the breeding. You can't teach a dog to hunt, only teach him *how* to hunt. Instinct is what is judged in the Started event. There are five simple, single retrieves on land and water. You don't even need judges—the spectators can spot desire in an instant and separate the haves and have-nots.

What about breeding a started dog? Qualifying in this category shows that the dog has the right genes.

Get a young hunter who has just shown the world that he has a hot, driving dog, and the ribbons and points he wins hook him into the program. All the fuss that is made over those ribbons, points, and Started certificate to hang on the hunter's wall is to encourage him to take the dog the next step into the Intermediate class, where the title of Working Retriever (WR) is given.

The Burn-Out, the Rekindle

The Point System Leads to the Invitational

NAHRA testing is as realistic as possible.

Intermediate takes work and is a big step from Started. Here we need a well-mannered, obedient dog who works for his master as a member of the team. If a dog passes in this category, he won't embarrass his master in any hunting situation, on any kinds of birds, in any part of the country. Also, he'll be a major tool for conservation. The Intermediate dog will be able to do double retrieves on land and water. It will be able to do upland hunting and simple blind retrieves. Already it is better than 85 percent of the hunting dogs in the country. For each event in which the dog passes the standard under judgment, it is awarded five points. On accumulating 20 points, the dog is awarded the Working Retriever title. And those points drive the hunter and his dog into Senior work.

The Senior dog is the cream that rises to the top. But its accomplishments are really only an extension of the Intermediate work. A dog receives 20 points each time it passes the Senior standard, and receives its title when it accumulates 100 points. It takes a lot of training to give the dog the necessary experience for this. But you don't have to give up everything else in your life for it. The hunting dog's job is not as precise as AKC field trial work, but it is everything the hunter needs for his pleasure and for conservation. The dog's memory has to be developed so that it remembers three falls and can make that triple retrieve. Blinds are up to 100 yards and require precision teamwork in handling. If the dog has the makings of an upland hunter in its genes, it becomes a master at finding game and trailing wounded birds. This dog is truly a Master Hunting Retriever (MHR).

The title of Grand Master Hunting Retriever (GMHR) is awarded to a dog that wins 300 points in his lifetime—quite an accomplishment.

NAHRA has resurrected an old title that had practically gone out of existence. In the early days, in the 1930s and '40s before the show ring and field people went their separate ways, the coveted title of Dual Champion was awarded to a dog that won both a bench championship and a field trial championship. That was an all-around dog, with good conformation and a fine hunter. Mrs. Marshall Field was one of the first advocates of awarding the Dual Champion title to Labradors.

Today NAHRA awards a Dual title to any dog that has won its show championship with any recognized national registry in the world and has also earned NAHRA titles. Dogs that achieve the Working Retriever title or the Master Hunting Retriever title will receive a NAHRA dual certificate. The board wants to record good conformation along with fine field work.

NAHRA has a unique pedigree policy. All titles are incorporated into a dog's pedigree. Instead of just listing our titles, as all other registries do, NAHRA honors all working titles from any approved registry, be it American, British, Canadian, Australian, or wherever. A NAHRA pedigree is the only complete history of a dog; it considers the dog first rather than the registering body.

A major concern of NAHRA is to ensure that working stock is available to the hunter or field trialer. Puppies are the future of any program. In a short seven years almost 40,000 Labradors have been tested by NAHRA. Where did these dogs who are winning the NAHRA titles come from? In most cases the AKC field trial stock was used. Remember, we have said that as the show ring took the work out of the dog over a period of 60 years, the field trials kept the work in the Labrador bloodlines. These are the dogs that many in the NAHRA program started with. From those few AKC field trial Labs, through NAHRA, many thousands more have sprung. In short order the appropriate field trial titles were replaced by the NAHRA titles. The bloodlines are still from the same source. At this reading, the pedigree of a well-bred Master Hunting Retriever will include many MHR titles representing Labs in the recent past and names of AKC field trial champions in the more distant past. Like the old chain letter trick, now these Labs are dispersed nationally to the hunter.

Thanks to the computer that the NAHRA board members bought, every dog that passes the standard or wins titles at an event is put into the computer. A complete working history is known for each Lab in the program throughout the country. Let's say hunters

Dual Champion

The All-American Team, 1991.

216

Making the American team was an emotional experience.

living in Alaska, Nova Scotia, Georgia, Texas, California, or Iowa want to breed. The NAHRA computer will give them a printout of the records of all the dogs in their local area. The *NAHRA News* carries information about pups and studs all over North America. Now the hunter knows where he can get his breeding stock without depending on the unknowns in the Sunday paper. This is what NAHRA set out to do . . . it's done!

To keep the hunter and his Lab active in NAHRA, which makes the dogs better and better year by year, three programs are run nationally. The Started Brass Band and the Intermediate Brass Band have only recently been initiated. To win a brass band to hang on your whistle lanyard, your dog must pass the standard four times in a given year. That automatically places the dog in a regional event in his area. There are seven such regional events throughout the country. What a proud hunter he is who makes it to a regional with his young dog!

For Senior dogs there is a national Invitational. At this writing, this annual event has been held for five successive years. For the first three years the event was for the 35 dogs with the highest number of points in the country. The Invitational was completely paid for by NAHRA and sponsors. Dogs and hunters were flown from their homes to the event, some from as far away as Alaska. Room, board, dog care, and a four-wheel-drive vehicle for every two hunters were supplied; banquet and the field event itself were all covered. Each Invitational costs about $30,000. It was a gala event. The dogs among the 35 that passed the same regulation NAHRA Senior standard again during the Invitational were awarded the title of member of the All-American Team for that year.

This became such a plum that the hunters were driving and flying, at great expense, from all over the country to gain points in order to win this title for their dogs. Each time a dog passes the standard at the event, he wins 20 points. That became very expensive. Cost was the objection the hunter had to the AKC's licensed field trial game, so NAHRA changed the rules so that the average Joe Hunter could participate. Now the Senior dog has to earn only 100 points in the year to qualify for the Invitational. That means that more dogs will run at the Invitational for this All-American title.

This is another aspect to the saving of our Labradors as working hunters that cannot be ignored. The clubs strung out across the nation each have their social side. People train together and work on the events together. They meet new friends. They have Halloween and New Year's Eve parties and all kinds of social fun because of a common interest in the dogs.

But there is a sad side to the NAHRA story. Though the Labrador is the most popular hunting dog, just behind the Lab is the Golden Retriever, another potentially fine worker. As we have said,

the Labrador Retriever breed club was field- and work-oriented. The Golden Retriever breed club is strongly show-oriented. Only about five percent of the dogs in the NAHRA program are Goldens. If this continues in the future, the Golden will end up, as history predicts, as a beautiful animal in the show ring, a fine pet, but without his working skill. It is already happening.

The story of NAHRA's fight to save the overpopular Lab has been stormy. In the early 19th century, it was the opposite: too few Labradors almost spelled disaster. From the first words that were written about him by Colonel Peter Hawker in 1814, the dog was in trouble. Hawker suggested that the hunter get some of this dog's blood into his hunting stock. There were so few of these black dogs from Newfoundland in England at that time that to do as Hawker suggested would have diluted the dog and cross-bred him out of existence before he ever was established. Fortunately, the earls of Malmesbury "collected" the dogs and kept them pure, thus starting and at the same time preserving the bloodline.

The accompanying photograph, a daguerreotype, of the third Earl of Malmesbury with his Labrador sitting with head on his knee is a rare find. The story is worth telling.

After this book was first published, an art dealer in New York who had some knowledge of Labs contacted me, saying he had something I might be interested in. On seeing this one-of-a-kind photograph, I sure was. I took the silver-coated copper plate and had it examined by the appraiser for the Museum of Modern Art. I was told that the dog and master had sat for their portrait some 12 years after photography was invented. That placed it around 1850. I bought it, realizing it was the oldest known photograph of the Lab. Who the man was was anyone's guess. But it would be fun to know. The man's eyes and shock of black hair haunted me, as if I had seen him somewhere. How old was the sitter? About 40 was my guess. Who would have had a Labrador in 1850 and had the handsome amount of money it would cost to have a half-sized photo plate made, when a quarter- or eighth-size plate was usual? The man's clothing showed his wealth, but it was the eyes and hair that held my attention. Months later it dawned on me. While in England at Lord Malmesbury's home researching the Labrador story, I had seen a painting of the third earl. Born in 1814, he would have been about the same age as the man photographed with his dog. I remembered standing on top of a high, rickety stepladder on a staircase landing and, with flashlight in hand, examining the family portrait collection, which went from floor to ceiling. That's where I had seen those eyes and that hair! A copy of the photo was rushed to England, and indeed from that painting I remembered, and other sketches, the present earl identified his ancestor, the third Earl of Malmesbury.

Another man of importance to the Labrador, as we have told

The Hunting Lab Is Here to Stay

The third Earl of Malmesbury with the first known photograph of a Labrador, c. 1850.

Jack Jagoda, president of NAHRA, with Annie, the country's first MHR. "As we enter the twenty-first century," Jack comments, "we can be confident that the working Labrador will live on. Many have played a role in the fascinating story of this dog. Now he is spared the cruel hand that popularity can deal. The Labrador Retriever was created for the hunt and appropriately the hunter will be his salvation. To know the Lab is to love and admire him. He gives his heart and soul and asks only for a kind word."

you, was Lord George Scott (pages 26, 49–50). Further research has confirmed that it was he who almost singlehandedly was responsible for bringing the Labrador into the 20th century.*

But now the Labrador Retriever is about to enter the 21st century. In the 1980s the North American Hunting Retriever Association started the hunting, field-testing concept and produced the first and only stud book of dogs with working genes. The hunting Labrador will be carried into the next century by the work of those 11 hunters, board members of NAHRA, who were forward-thinking enough to recognize trouble ahead and produced an organization to protect the dog. Happily, against all odds, they stuck to their guns. After the first hunting field test in Louisiana, the UKC's Hunting Retriever Club started their program based on the NAHRA concept and rules. The AKC, after the NAHRA divorce, started their own version of hunting retriever testing. But the real heroes for securing the future of the working Lab are all the hunters who are training and testing their dogs throughout the country. It really makes no difference under which organization's auspices they are doing it; the work of all three organizations has much to be commended. Who really cares who gets the credit? The 1980s was a banner decade for the Labrador. All the other popular hunting dogs have been buried.

In the 21st century, the next hundred years, the future generations of Labrador Retrievers will be *hunting* with our grandchildren and their children.

---

* Lord George Scott's role in developing the Labrador breed is also discussed in R. A. Wolters. *Duck Dogs* (New York: Dutton, 1990), pp. 76–80.

Epilogue

When I left you at the beginning of the book, I'm certain we both shared a common interest in this great dog. Now you, like myself have had the opportunity to share a much deeper and extensive appreciation of our mutual friend, the Labrador Retriever.

If, as one of our philosophers tells us, "history gives man the ability to act with foresight," then the Labrador ought to have a secure future. Some might still feel a bit uneasy about the popularity growth of the breed and others might be resentful that the Labrador is entering its era of being "everyman's dog." The attitude of privilege in possessions dies hard, but die it must. I can't imagine ever being without one or two Labs, nor do I expect to. I need the comfort and companionship they so willingly and amply provide. I have come to absolutely depend on it.

As I write this I have two sitting comfortingly close by. One grey muzzled and cloudy of eye, but ready, however painful it is for her now, to go out to the pond and show you the discipline of a fine retrieve. When her great heart wills it, somehow the body responds — the lines of pride, character and breeding are deep indeed. The other is just a bit more than a puppy; bright-eyed, powerful, and often uncannily intelligent. She will, no doubt, put some bright and shiny ribbons next to the ones on the wall that are fading.

I wish you and your dogs all the pleasures that I have had — and expect to have — with mine. And may there always be a young one full of promise and dedication to take you to those places of wonderment that only admit the person who is introduced by a Labrador.

Gene Hill

BLACK LABRADOR *Ralph McDonald*

Index of Books, Journals and Manuscripts

Index

Designed by Jack E. Stanley with the aid of the author.
Text set in Souvenir Light.
Printed by Holyoke Lithograph Company, Inc.
Bound by Book Press, Inc.